D1382929

*Leo Strauss and the Politics of Exile*

# The Tauber Institute for the Study of European Jewry Series

Jehuda Reinharz, *General Editor*
Sylvia Fuks Fried, *Associate Editor*

The Tauber Institute Series is dedicated to publishing compelling and innovative approaches to the study of modern European Jewish history, thought, culture, and society. The series has a special interest in original works related to the Holocaust and its aftermath, as well as studies of Zionism and the history, society, and culture of the State of Israel. The series is published by the Tauber Institue for the Study of European Jewry—established by a gift to Brandeis University from Dr. Laszlo N. Tauber—and the Jacob and Libby Goodman Institute for the Study of Zionism and Israel, and is supported, in part, by the Tauber Foundation.

For the complete list of books in this series, please see www.upne.com and www.upne.com/series/TAUB.html

# Leo Strauss and the Politics of Exile

THE MAKING OF A POLITICAL PHILOSOPHER

## Eugene R. Sheppard

*Brandeis University Press*

WALTHAM, MASSACHUSETTS

PUBLISHED BY UNIVERSITY PRESS OF NEW ENGLAND

HANOVER AND LONDON

Brandeis University Press

Published by University Press of New England,

One Court Street, Lebanon, NH 03766

www.upne.com

© 2006 by Brandeis University Press

Printed in the United States of America

5   4   3   2   1

This book was published with the generous support of the Lucius N. Littauer Foundation, Inc.

Library of Congress Cataloging-in-Publication Data

Sheppard, Eugene R.

Leo Strauss and the politics of exile : the making of a political philosopher /
Eugene R. Sheppard.—1st ed.

p. cm.—(Tauber Institute for the Study of European Jewry series)

Includes bibliographical references and index.

ISBN–13: 978–1–58465–600–5 (cloth : alk. paper)

ISBN–10: 1–58465–600–X (cloth : alk. paper)

1. Strauss, Leo.   2. Jewish philosophers—Germany—Biography.   3. Jewish philosophers—United States—Biography.   4. Jews—Germany—Biography.   5. Refugees, Jewish—United States—Biography.   6. Jews, German—United States—Biography.
7. Political science—Philosophy.   I. Title.

BM755.S75S54 2006

181'.06—dc22                                                          2006033936

[B]

 University Press of New England is a member of the
Green Press Initiative. The paper used in this book meets
their minimum requirement for recycled paper.

*In memory of my father Albert M. Sheppard*

# Contents

# Acknowledgments

The publication of this book evinces the truly collective enterprise of an otherwise notoriously solitary process of formulating, researching, and writing. I wish to express gratitude to the family, friends, teachers and colleagues who have contributed much to this endeavor. This task is a daunting one for I know that my words will fall short of said goal. And while the book's strengths reflect their creative input, the book's deficiencies I claim as my own.

An earlier incarnation of the book's argument appeared as my doctoral dissertation in the Department of History at University of California at Los Angeles. At UCLA David N. Myers introduced me to the field of Jewish history, and Jewish intellectual history in particular. As my *Doktorvater*, he provided me with many of the tools, encouragement, and criticism required for me to achieve key scholarly goals. As my mentor and friend, he continues to help shape the way in which I approach work and life. I am indebted to Arnold J. Band for teaching me so much about language, texts, scholars, and writers. Perry Anderson's passion to understand the role and legacies of intellectuals inspired me to engage a conservative thinker, who has become more widely influential and controversial than he is understood. The subtle balance of reflection and conscience has been the hallmark of Saul Friedlander's teaching and writing. His unwavering commitment to explore and capture the complexities of writing history about periods of persecution, crisis, and catastrophe is the standard to which I aspire.

Paul Mendes-Flohr has become a mentor to yet another grateful young scholar in German Jewish thought. His generosity of spirit and mind have followed me throughout my career.

Several friends and colleagues have variously read and commented on portions of the book: Kathleen Arnold, Leora Batnitzky, Jonathan Cohen, Steve Dowden, David Engerman, Michah Gottlieb, Moshe Halbertal, Martin Jay, Susan Kahn, Nitzan Lebovicz, Sabine von Mering, Thomas Meyer, Warren Montag, John Plotz, Martin Ritter, David Starr, Stephen Whitfield, Michael Zank, and Steven Zipperstein. Moshe Idel, Alfred Ivry, Michael Brenner, David Biale, William Altmann, and David Ellenson encouraged me in this undertaking. Charlotte Fonrobert always found ways to make me think about legal and textual issues in a new light. Alan Arkush and Bernard Yack have proven to be wonderfully challenging interlocutors on matters Strauss.

Peter Gordon, Ethan Kleinberg, and Samuel Moyn continue to sharpen my thinking on all matters intellectual and philosophical, and their warm friendship has helped to weather New England winters. Courtney Booker's questions and suggestions have informed my thinking about the peregrinations of *Homo viator*. Amnon (Nono) Raz-Krakotzkin's innovative formulations about exile in Jewish history compelled me to reassess the ways in which politics, religion, and history have become intertwined over the last three millennia.

It was fortuitous indeed that I as a student of Jewish refugee scholars in the United States should find an academic home at Brandeis University. I have struggled to hear the voices of my illustrious predecessors, who were themselves contemporaries of the experience, which has captured so much of my scholarly energy. Since coming to Brandeis, I have enjoyed the support of my esteemed colleagues in the department of Near Eastern and Judaic Studies. In particular, Marc Brettler, Sylvia Fishman, ChaeRan Freeze, Antony Polonsky, Benjamin Ravid, Jonathan Sarna, and Ilan Troen continue to take an interest in my work and I have benefited from their collegiality. Countless conversations with Jonathan Decter enabled me to develop an ever more nuanced appreciation for the challenges and allure of multilayered medieval Arabic and Hebrew texts. Brandeis librarians James P. Rosenbloom and Anthony Vaver provided much needed assistance in locating key resources.

I thank Jehuda Reinharz, Richard Koret Professor of Modern Jewish History and President of Brandeis University for inviting me to submit my manuscript to the Tauber Institute Series for which he serves as General Editor. Associate Editor Sylvia Fuks Fried encouraged me through all of the various stages of production. The book has been improved by the incisive comments of Phyllis Deutsch and Ann Brash at the University Press of New England.

Members of the non-existent Center for Exilic Studies must also be acknowledged. Avner Ben-Zaken and Zvi Ben-Dor have become friends and brothers to me. Sandy Sufian has been a dear friend and colleague since we were graduate students conducting research in Jerusalem. Susan Cho remains a cherished friend who conspires with me to embrace the joys of nonsense as well as the splendors of the profound.

My family has encouraged me throughout the writing of this book. Stan Rosen has followed each step of my career with love and support. Hedi and Ronald Sands make me appreciate how special extended family can be. My four older siblings—Barry, Robert, Judith, and Jenene—and their spouses and children have lived far away from me for the last years. The wellspring of their affection and encouragement, however, has kept them near and dear to me. The publication of this book coincides with the beginnings of a new addition to the Sheppard family. Shira Diner came into my life while I was in the final stages of writing and editing this book, and her loving presence has certainly made them the sweetest.

The greatest sources of inspiration in my life have been my parents. Suzanne Sheppard provided her children with a living model of dignity and noble character, especially in the face of adversity.

This book is dedicated to the loving memory of my father, Albert M. Sheppard. My dear father was my greatest teacher. His passionate voice both in and out of the courtroom kindled my earliest appreciation for the true power of words and ideas. His cherished memory continues to guide, enrich, and enlighten me.

Eugene Rosenthal Sheppard
Waltham, Massachusetts.

*Leo Strauss and the Politics of Exile*

# Introduction

The making of Leo Strauss as a Jewish thinker and political philosopher is the subject of this book. Strauss's journey from Germany to the United States involved the struggle of a conservative Weimar Jew with modern liberalism as he toiled to understand the existential and political contours of exile. As a Jewish refugee from Germany, Strauss sought to resolve the conflicts of a Jew unwilling to surrender loyalty to his ancestral community and equally unwilling to adhere to a life of strict observance. Strauss saw truth and wisdom as transcending particular religious and national communities, as well as the enlightened humanism on which he himself had been nurtured. In his own efforts to navigate between the Jewish and the philosophical, the ancient and the modern, Berlin and New York, Strauss developed an intellectual project and distinctive hermeneutic remarkable for its complexity and intrigue.

Much scholarship tends to understand Strauss as an inspirational founder of American neoconservatism.[1] In monodimensional terms, this reputation derives from Strauss's tenure at the University of Chicago, where as a political philosopher he, along with several other conservative figures, combined anti-Communist rhetoric with a valorization of a canon of Great Books written by great minds throughout history. Even though Strauss resigned from the University of Chicago in the mid-1960s, his influence remained strong in the university's Department of Political Science and the Committee on Social Thought. Among the leading students of Strauss who followed his philosophical and interpretive path were Allan Bloom, Joseph Cropsey, Werner Dannhauser, Harry Jaffa, Ralph Lerner, Muhsin Mahdi, Aryeh Motzkin, Harvey J. Mansfield Jr., Stanley Rosen, and Nathan Tarcov. There are deep rifts among these disciples (particularly between East Coast and West Coast Straussians), pertaining to what truths can be openly discussed without violating propriety. All of these students, however, claim to be heirs to Strauss's legacy. Strauss's legacy has also been claimed by the neoconservative political commentators and strategists William Kristol and William Bennett; politicians such as Newt Gingrich; and legal figures such as Robert Bork, Antonin Scalia, and Clarence

1

Thomas. And the administration of George W. Bush has been seen by several leading international newspapers and magazines as a hotbed of Straussian influence: ranging from midlevel foreign policy and defense analysts to high-profile figures such as Paul Wolfowitz and Richard Perle.[2] A number of journalists have drawn attention to the unspoken coherence of a set of ideas and policies that have shaped the Bush administration in the wake of the attacks on the World Trade Center and the Pentagon on September 11, 2001. The domestic and foreign policy agendas of the United States, according to these commentators, have been framed as a miscast Straussian project to defend Western Civilization against its enemies.

Strauss's influence can be more directly seen in the neoconservative periodical *Commentary,* and even more so in the journal *Interpretation,* which still lists him as a member of its editorial board. In addition, several figures associated with the *Weekly Standard* and the think tank Project for a New American Century explicitly invoke Strauss as a seminal influence on their conservative vision. Mark Lilla recently wrote a two-part assessment of Strauss's career and legacy in the *New York Review of Books.* Lilla's division, and the difference in tone between these two parts, mirrors the rift we find elsewhere between Leo Strauss, the European, and the controversial celebrity that emerges in the wake of Straussianism's influence in the academy, government, and think tanks.[3]

It is a curious irony that Strauss's students tend to view his work as Strauss himself viewed canonical philosophical works: that is, as the product of a timeless mind who conveyed concealed truths to the chosen few. Thus, their accounts of him often amount to clever or boring hagiographies written to demonstrate that the authors possess an unsurpassed intellectual intimacy with the revered master. It is also ironic that anti-Straussian defenders of liberalism accept a similar view of Strauss's work as an established orthodoxy, even as they seek to expose and topple it: for instance, Shadia Drury's attempts to examine Strauss's earlier German and even Jewish thought. Because of her rather uncharitable reading of Strauss, combined with limited understanding of Strauss's Jewish context and writings, her pioneering efforts ultimately fail to illuminate the specific dilemmas of politics, religion, and history of a German Jew from Hesse who studied, learned, and published during the crisis-laden interwar period.[4] Indeed, much of the Straussian and anti-Straussian literature fails to grasp the development of Strauss's thought within the context of German-Jewish history and the Jewish refugee experience.

More recently, scholars have begun to attend to the Jewish aspects of Strauss's thought. For example, the work of Kenneth Hart Green has forced scholars to recognize that even though Strauss wrote on a wide variety of non-Jewish thinkers and subjects, a portrait of Strauss that does not account for the Jewish aspects of his thought is necessarily incomplete. Green's book-length study of Strauss, *Jew and Philosopher,* interprets his intellectual development through three interpretive encounters with the medieval philosopher, Moses Maimonides.[5]

Unlike previous scholarship in English, Green's study recognized the significance of Strauss's Weimar writings. The Strauss that emerges from Green's textual analysis is that of a religious thinker who discovers and emulates Maimonides's nuanced response to the dual condition of being a philosopher and Jew. This involves Strauss's "re-discovery" of a putative Maimonidean hermeneutic that turns on the distinction between esoteric and exoteric writing. Green followed up his pioneering book by collecting material in English, most of which had been consigned to esoteric Straussian journals or existed only in transcript form, and published it in *Jewish Philosophy and the Crisis of Modernity*.[6] This volume has the merit of presenting a wide array of Strauss's Jewish writings and lectures to a wide audience and continuing the sustained inquiry into Strauss as a Jewish thinker. My book is therefore indebted to Green's labors for pointing to the specifically Jewish threads that run throughout Strauss's career.

A different tack is followed by Heinrich Meier, who has made a signal contribution to understanding Strauss within the context of German culture and thought. Meier's efforts began with a study of Carl Schmitt and Strauss that included the extant correspondence between the two men. This work paved the way for a reassessment of Strauss's relationship to other European contemporaries, especially during the dramatic period preceding and after Hitler's ascension to power. The first three (of six planned) volumes of Strauss's *Gesammelte Schriften* have provided scholars with an indispensable and reliable repository of Strauss's early published and unpublished writings.[7] The third volume of the *Gesammelte Schriften* also contains some of Strauss's most notable and extended correspondence during the 1930s and 1940s. Present and future scholars owe Wiebke Meier a debt of gratitude for transcribing Strauss's handwritten Latin-based hieroglyphics.

Heinrich Meier's contribution to Strauss studies requires a more political character when looking at his original writings on Strauss and Carl Schmitt. And Meier has played no small part in Schmitt's rehabilitation in Germany over the last two decades, by pointing to an intimate intellectual relationship with Strauss, a German Jew.[8] In his books devoted to Strauss as a "political philosopher," Meier provocatively presents Strauss as a Jewish atheist who tapped into a classical understanding wherein the interest of political order—the irreconcilable conflict between religion and philosophy—must be both preserved and recast so as to introduce a subtle philosophical spin or refounding on existing societal opinions and the moral and political implications issuing from them.[9] Meier's readings are cogently argued; he has mastered Strauss's corpus and the canon of political philosophy as have few others. Ironically, Meier's pioneering efforts in the appreciation of the early Strauss are offset by his gravitation toward the dogmatism of Strauss's mature work. Overdetermined conceptual binary oppositions taken from the mature Strauss, such as Jerusalem and Athens, Revelation and Reason, Ancients and

Moderns, set the interpretive coordinates for understanding Strauss's work and his legacy.

Daniel Tanguay recently published a promising intellectual biography of Strauss in French, offering the most basic biography of Strauss's early years outside of the present book.[10] And Michael Zank has opened Strauss's early German period to an English reading audience in *Leo Strauss: The Early Writings (1921–1932)*.[11] Zank's fastidious editorial notes, illuminating introduction, and literal translation offer the student and scholar alike a sure-footed entrée into a world of names, organizations, and institutions that would leave all but a few specialists in obscure darkness. Zank's interpretation and translation of Strauss has the added strength of someone who is intimately familiar with both the German and German-Jewish currents that shaped Strauss's intellectual and political universe as a young man.

The translation movement of Strauss's writings has entered a Hebrew phrase as well, with the appearance of Ehud Luz's edited collection *Yerushalaim ve-atunah*.[12] Luz presents Strauss as a political philosopher whose political philosophy integrally evolves from his Jewish core, simultaneously approaching universal concerns and achieving general insights into truth and wisdom. Luz follows Green and others in emphasizing Strauss's formative years in Germany as a Jewish thinker; surprisingly, he chose not to select any of Strauss's pre-American writings. Ultimately we are presented with a neat package of Strauss based on Strauss's American persona, qualified only occasionally by his mature reflections on his European career. Straussianism per se offers no illumination on what Luz sees as most significant about Strauss: that he is a Jewish thinker and intellectual model for serious political consideration of the perennial problems relating to the competing interests of the philosopher and the society in which he lives. These competing interests boil down to the legacy of engagement and conflict between Jerusalem and Athens, Judaism (which for Luz is reduced to theology) and philosophy. The rough-and-tumble of Strauss's intellectual development and engaged voice on Zionist politics are relegated to the concerns of the historian.

The aim of this book is to bring together the various dimensions of Strauss's intellectual personality, which currently stand in considerable distance from one another. Thus, I seek to explore the German, Jewish, and American features of Strauss's thought as it developed into an enigmatic orthodoxy. In particular, I shall inquire into the vicissitudes of a conservative Weimar Jew struggling to account for and adjust to his condition as a Jewish refugee in Europe and then as an immigrant to the United States. My study follows the development of Strauss's thought until 1948, focusing on a figure John Gunnell has appropriately referred to as "Strauss before Straussianism."[13] This is the Leo Strauss who had not yet left New York for Chicago, but who nonetheless had set into place all of the pieces that define the intellectual movement known as Straussianism.

 period

*Leo Strauss and the Politics of Exile*

Strauss's move from the New School for Social Research in New York to the University of Chicago marked an important transition from an obscure conservative immigrant amid a sea of liberal- to left-leaning colleagues to a controversial American neoconservative with powerful conservative colleagues such as Mortimer J. Adler, Edward Shils, F. A. Hayek, and Milton Friedman. While an important part of the Strauss story, these later years will be addressed primarily around Strauss's continuous engagement with the complex and unresolved tensions of his own Jewish question, or what he referred to as "the theologico-political predicament."[14]

I seek to understand the relationship between the Jewish and non-Jewish facets of his life, mindful of the creative tension between them. Fittingly enough, this approach to Strauss seems to parallel the approach Strauss undertook in his own philosophical study of Al-Farabi, Halevi, Maimonides, Spinoza, Xenophon, and others. But my reading hardly conforms to Straussian strictures. Indeed, its contextualizing impulse violates a central tenet of Straussian hermeneutics. Rather than seeing Strauss as a timeless mind, it seeks to understand Strauss's thought as it developed and adapted to shifting historical contexts. Illuminating the interplay between text and context, between _method_ Strauss's writings and the environments that shaped and conditioned their changing expression—this is the task I have set myself. While I do not ignore the philosophical and political implications of the ideas that Strauss advanced, my primary task here is to reconnect Strauss's work to his life. While I do offer judgments along the way, this book is intended as neither an indictment of nor apology for him.

Perhaps the major pillar of Strauss's thought was his belief that great authors of the past often wrote texts at multiple levels of meaning. To trace these multiple layers, Strauss deployed the very tactics of dissimulation with which he became so fascinated when writing about these texts. I am fascinated by the various subtleties and larger implications of this hermeneutic strategy. Such a writing and reading strategy is particularly useful not only to conditions of exile, but also to life under tyrannical and totalitarian regimes. This insight echoes the claims of many of Strauss's contemporary writers and thinkers who had published during the dozen years of Nazi rule over Germany. The ethical question of a particular intellectual's complicity with a murderous and/or totalitarian regime is certainly complicated once we account for the complex dynamics of that context. A colleague once related the words of a South African communist who was arrested during the 1950s. When asked about whether he cooperated with the apartheid authorities, the man stated that one would need to share the jail cell with him before judging him. These are the profound moral difficulties facing any historian attempting to assess motive and intent, agency and responsibility, for words spoken or written in dark times. While the historian ought not to evade questions of intellectual integrity and moral reckoning, all too often moralizing replaces the more difficult, challenging, and necessary task of grappling with ambiguous and ambivalent shades of gray.

Strauss never wrote directly under conditions of totalitarianism and persecution and so a very different question arises, one that seems to be the stumbling block to so many thinkers committed to the values of free intellectual expression and intellectual honesty: Why would Strauss adopt tactics of evasive and indirect writing after he came to the United States and settled in the cosmopolitan urban centers of New York and Chicago? For many, Strauss's tactics bespeak a fundamental contempt for liberal democracy. But things are not that simple. Although his multilayered writing style signals a deep ambivalence about his new home, it also paradoxically marks his attempt to accommodate the expression of his ideas to his new surroundings while still retaining his integrity. It is not the truth of Strauss's interpretations or the hidden messages that Strauss may have planted in his commentaries that I seek to capture. Rather, it is to understand Leo Strauss's thought and writings as creative expressions of and responses to the profoundly dramatic challenges he faced during his life. The dynamic tensions and unexpected detours of his thought prior to Straussianism are the focus of this study.

For Strauss, philosophy's recognition of its precarious existence within any existing social order is the first step toward the quest for the premodern sources of wisdom, guidance, and truth. And this goal of individual philosophic enlightenment is the one type of *teshuvah* (redemptive return) available to moderns. In the 1930s, during the course of his European exile, Strauss became convinced that restoration of premodern political orders was not possible. Yet he also became passionately committed to the prospect that a philosophically gifted individual could recover the original intentions and true teachings of premodern philosophy.[15]

Because I take exile as a conceptual linchpin to understanding Strauss's unfolding political thought, I must point to some of the larger problems attending the study of an intellectual history that is ambiguously situated within a particular non-Jewish society and culture. But the problematic features issuing from *galut* (exile) existence situated within Germany, and Strauss's attempt to find an adequate alternative to various forms of exilic Jewish existence in other national and temporal contexts, propel his evolving views of Jewish politics and philosophy. Strauss's ideas about the permeable boundary between Jewish and non-Jewish concerns in Germany reflect cultural dynamics that can be seen operative throughout Jewish history; further, he finds parallels to other diasporic and postcolonial histories. The cultural engagement between a particular Jewish community and its host society rarely entailed a unidirectional process of passive absorption or simple rejection. As David Biale suggests, "the tendency to acculturate into the non-Jewish culture typically produced a distinctive Jewish subculture." But the reverse case creates a parallel paradox: "[T]he effort to maintain a separate identity was often achieved by borrowing and even subverting motifs from the surrounding culture."[16] Much of Strauss's Zionist thinking goes straight to such paradoxes. An "anxiety of influence" emerges from the smuggling and entanglement of ideas taken from different sides of those fuzzy boundary lines demarcating Jewish from non-Jewish culture.[17] Strauss's career is an instructive example of the complex negotiations and necessary interpenetration of specifically Jewish concerns, the concerns of his host state and culture (whether it be Germany or the United States), and transnational universal concerns.

It is not vulgar hindsight to see the connection between Strauss's life and the texts he wrote. Strauss was a German-Jewish refugee vitally concerned with the possibility of Jewish existence in exile. During his own period of exile from his native country, he came to question the wisdom and prudence of any project that called for an overcoming of political imperfection or for any messianic aspiration to overcome exile. Strauss regarded exile as the natural condition of all political societies; he recast the precarious existence of the diasporic Jew, who lives in perpetual fear of persecution, as the normative model of the philosopher. Even upon his entrance into a liberal democratic state that offered him refuge, Strauss still sought to instill the sense of unease or not-being-at-home within a new vision of a conservative political philosophy. This remarkable and compelling dissonance between his appreciation of the dangers and philosophic virtues of exile stands at the center of Leo Strauss's intellectual personality.

Finally, in situating Strauss's thought within the context of his biography, two notable features repeatedly emerge: the conservative, if not radical-conservative, critique of liberalism and the centrality of the problem of *galut*. Both of these elements can be traced back to Strauss's earliest phase of development and both define the unique trajectory of his thought during four subsequent phases: (a) 1921–1932, as a radicalized conservative Weimar Jew active in Zionist politics and Jewish scholarship, while absorbing and reacting to new philosophical currents; (b) 1932–1937, as a bewildered and defiant refugee rediscovering a medieval Islamic Enlightenment while also recasting the foundations of modern political thought; (c) 1938–1948, as an immigrant attempting to accommodate his thought and writing to his new home in the liberal democracy of America; and (d) his career after 1948, when he came to offer mature speculations and reassessments of his intellectual journey and on the Jewish question in particular. What follows is a critical investigation of these phases in Leo Strauss's life. Strauss's ruminations on the problematic of exile are nothing less than profound. While I disagree with many of his political and philosophical prescriptions, his recognition of the intractability of the problem itself deserves to be taken seriously. Strauss neither romanticized powerlessness and alienation nor castigated such conditions to be wholly abject and contemptible. His fascination and appreciation for exile's hardships and virtues, I argue, fueled much of Strauss's labors even where these issues are only implicit and/or a subtext to his works that do not consider Jewish subjects. The acknowledgment of exile ultimately became a marker for caring political reflection. In great part, then, this study attempts to gauge the subject with which Strauss held the deepest and most sustained engagement of his career. In registering the contours of exile in Strauss's work, our understanding of politico-philosophical possibilities is challenged and enriched.

# CHAPTER 1

# Antisemitism and Neo-Kantianism
# From Kirchhain to Marburg (1899–1920)

*L*eo Strauss was born on September 20, 1899. Like so many other German Jews of his generation who participated in the creative intellectual explosion following World War I, Strauss came from a middle-class family. Unlike many of his counterparts, however, Strauss did not come from an urban center, but rather from the town of Kirchhain, situated amid the rural lands surrounding the university city of Marburg within the state of Kurhessen. While the regional ambience can be described as conservative and traditional (including periodic antisemitic stirrings), the University of Marburg stood as a central symbol of enlightened German humanism. Kirchhain Jewry may have had more of a "quasi-urban" character than its non-Jewish neighbors, but its adherence to traditional religious practices and beliefs suggests a loosely defined "Orthodoxy" that was skeptical of Reform.[1]

*Jews in the Marburg* Landkreis *at the Beginning of the Twentieth Century*

Kurhessen was nestled between the eastern and western provinces of Prussia and extended from Frankfurt to Kassel. Rolling hills and small farming basins shaped the region's topography, while its modern political landscape was shaped by Prussian annexation, Bismarck's Kulturkampf against Catholic institutional power, and the rise of populist antisemitic movements.

Jews had dwelled in the larger region of Hessen as far back as the thirteenth century, and as early as the sixteenth century in Kirchhain; Strauss traced his own family roots back to the middle of the nineteenth century.[2] Civic emancipation of Kurhessen Jewry occurred in 1869, three years after Prussia incorporated the medium-sized state. Prior to this point, Jewish rights had been subject to sporadic periods of reform, reaction, and restriction. While other German states introduced legal reforms by the middle of the nineteenth century, Kurhessen electors resisted such reforms as part of a general resistance to forces of modernization and Prussian hegemony. Emancipation acts for Hessen Jewry in 1816, 1823, and 1833 removed legal barriers that barred Jews from entering occupations deemed to be more socially honorable and productive than traditional fields of Jewish activity: for example, peddling, trade, and credit. Structural forces impinging upon the rural economy remained unchanged by such reforms. And yet, struggling small landholders and a fledgling peasantry continued to blame Jewish money lending and the Junkers (country squires or landowning lesser nobility) for their economic woes. Anti-Jewish riots of 1830 and 1848, followed by a series of bills and popular petitions, culminated in 1858 when three edicts curbed Jewish civil rights by means of occupational rather than religious classification.[3]

By 1885 there were more than 140 Jewish households in Kirchhain,[4] establishing it as one of the centers of Jewish communal life within the *Landkreis*—the rural lands surrounding the city of Marburg.[5] Kirchhain Jewry mirrored regional Jewish trends in its basic rural character. Even half a century after emancipation, much of Kurhessen Jewry continued to live in the countryside and concentrate its economic activities in the cattle trade, peddling, and the small-scale credit business. In contrast to the rapid growth of Reform Jewish synagogues and their congregants throughout urban centers, the Reform movement was not able to establish a foothold in the Jewish communities around Marburg. This resistance to liberal Judaism is indicative of a general conservative attitude toward culture, tradition, and authority characteristic of rural Jewry.[6]

The small Jewish communities sprinkled in Kurhessen prior to World War I were characterized by religious observance and patriotism.[7] Religious orthopraxy and political conservatism, taken together, represent a relatively inarticulate but resilient form of resistance to forces of modernization.[8] Here it seems sensible to follow Steven Lowenstein's suggestion that "inertia and tradition," more than any carefully designed conservative "counter-attack," constituted the primary modes of rural German-Jewish resistance to modernization.[9] Lowenstein further suggests that historians have failed to recognize "the traditional and conservative nature of much of German Jewry," in large part because these orthopraxic traditionalists did not have the intellectual leaders and spokesmen able to express their conservative position publicly.[10] The prominent critic of Reform Judaism and champion of Orthodox secessionism, Samson Raphael Hirsch (1808–1888),[11] for example, did not represent the traditionally oriented rural classes, but instead an urban bourgeoisie. Rural orthodoxy's hesitancies regarding the ideology of emancipation and modernization[12] were what Lowenstein described as "a kind of passive resistance, one marked by relatively few 'pitched battles', but a fairly successful passive resistance nonetheless."[13]

In Strauss's last Zionist publication in 1929, he referred to the fate of Jewish life in rural Hessen (*Landjudentums*), which "remained virtually untouched by the liberal Reform movement" in the nineteenth century. While successfully avoid-

*Leo Strauss and the Politics of Exile*

ing the inroads of Reform Judaism, by the late 1920s Strauss could say that Jewish life had more or less completely decayed. "Even today," Strauss wrote, "while some members of the older generation rigorously follow custom, the incorporation of non-Jewish elements of German social life is evidenced by the increasing prominence of Chanukah bushes lit up around Christmas."[14]

Political antisemitism found a receptive regional audience in the 1880s. In fact, Kurhessen was one of the only places in imperial Germany where antisemitism as an organized political movement found electoral and institutional success.[15] The figure of the Jewish moneylender personified the alien forces of secularization, materialism, and liberalism that undermined rural tranquility.[16] The populist antisemitic movement led by the philologist and bibliographer Otto Böckel (1859–1923) scored victories in Kurhessen in the Reichstag elections from 1887 to 1903.[17] Böckel's rhetoric targeted the Junkers and the Jews as the main villains responsible for economic dislocation and sociocultural decline. He pleaded with the peasantry that it was time to overthrow these illegitimate power holders, these "Kings of Our Times." Böckel, dubbed "German king of the peasants," was one of the more prominent figures who attempted to counter the Jewish role within the agrarian economy as middleman and lender. His political success was augmented by other antisemitic forces. For instance, the Kurhessen credit-cooperative movement, founded in 1888, sought to combat a perceived Jewish stranglehold on credit and trade. Moreover, Bismarck's new coalition of conservative and right-wing elements at the end of the 1870s, including the Catholic Center party, exploited popular anti-Jewish prejudices to secure and extend its own electoral bases.[18] During a period in which rural poverty was on the rise, Jewish traders and small businessmen appeared to prosper under conditions of Prussian annexation, civic emancipation, and liberal economic legislation. Thus, antisemitic politics found support in the heart of a region suspicious of—and, in some segments, hostile to—liberalism and capitalism.

These instances of antisemitic agitation unfolded as part of a larger central European phenomenon in the last third of the nineteenth century. A wider constellation of German antisemitic politicians and thinkers included Wilhelm Marr (1818–1904), who founded the Antisemitic League in 1879; Paul de Lagarde (1827–1891), whom Strauss would later see as an important source for understanding the Jewish problem in Germany; and Heinrich von Treitschke (1834–1896), the professor of history at the University of Berlin who brought even greater academic legitimacy to antisemitism. While these individuals achieved various degrees of popularity, the region encompassing Marburg was one of the most successful venues for the antisemitic movement in imperial Germany—all the more remarkable considering that the region housed an institution of higher education in Marburg that stood as a beacon to German humanism. Indeed, Marburg became the site of a legal proceeding that echoed medieval antisemitic phenomena. In 1888 the Talmud and its binding authority on Jewish behavior became the focus of a libel suit. The court proceedings featured the expert testimony of none other than Paul de Lagarde and Hermann Cohen. I shall return to this episode when discussing Strauss's curious and startling views on antisemitism and antisemites.

In a 1962 lecture, "Why We Remain Jews," delivered at the Hillel House at the University of Chicago, Strauss recounted that his father housed a group of Jewish Russian refugees fleeing from pogroms (most likely, the Kishinev pogroms of 1903–1905) on their way to Australia. Hearing the stories of the pogroms made a chilling, permanent impression on Strauss. This "unforgettable moment" shook his previous feeling of security: for the first time he countenanced the possibility of such an event occurring in his native Germany.[19] Böckel's movement was certainly closer to Strauss's region of Hessen than were the pogroms in eastern Europe, but the dramatic experience of sheltering refugees proved to create a much stronger impression. In the midst of a drought in the 1890s, for example, the antisemitic cooperative movement was distressed that the Strauss grain company was the choice of most struggling smallholders in need of fodder.[20] In 1903, at approximately the same time as the refugees from the pogroms in eastern Europe took refuge in Strauss's house, a granary was established in Kirchhain with funds from an offshoot of the regional cooperative movement with the declared purpose of providing an alternative to Jewish grain traders such as Strauss and Sons.[21] And yet, Strauss does not seem to have registered these developments. Perhaps Strauss's family didn't discuss the regional presence of economic and political antisemitism. Strauss once recalled the situation of Kurhessen Jewry as living in "profound peace" with non-Jewish neighbors. While he viewed the government as "perhaps not in every respect admirable," he nevertheless deemed its ability to preserve order "admirable."[22]

### Boyhood, Childhood, and Youth

Strauss's parents, Hugo Strauss (1869–1942) and Jenny David Strauss (1873–1919) were native to the area.[23] Hugo, born in Kirchhain, was a successful merchant.[24] Hugo's father, Meyer Strauss (1835–1920) established a wholesale grain, feed, and wool business with sons Hugo and David. Meyer was a leading representative of the Kirchhain Jewish community for half a century.[25] Meyer and his two sons regularly contributed funds to the synagogue in Kirchhain and served as representatives of the Jewish community's business and social interests.[26] According to Strauss's later reflections, his house was somewhat typical of many observant German-Jewish homes, at least in the following sense: while there was an emphasis on the transmission and preservation of Jewish ritual observance, there seemed to be little substantive knowledge about the origins or even meaning of such practices.[27]

Strauss attended the nearby Gymnasium Philippinum at Marburg and was there introduced to the classical German humanist tradition.[28] The curriculum consisted of the usual diet: mathematics, natural science, Latin, ancient Greek, German language and literature. During the years of Strauss's attendance at the school, the roughly two hundred members of the student body reflected a slightly higher Jewish presence (7 percent) than regional Jewish demographics in Marburg (1–2 percent).[29] The gymnasium offered weekly instruction in religion, separated by confession—enough to impart general impressions, but hardly sufficient to provide a solid grounding in traditional Jewish sources. In 1960, Strauss offered his gratitude to his friend Gershom Scholem for illuminating the sources of many of the Jewish customs such as "the *smirot* [*sic*] of erev Shabbat" (Sabbath-eve songs), which his family followed but of which he had no substantive knowledge. Strauss recalled, "I used to sing [the *zmirot*] as a child in utter ignorance of their 'background.'"[30] Strauss described his early encounters with the classical tradition of German humanism as a gymnasium student in this way:

> Furtively I read Schopenhauer and Nietzsche. When I was sixteen and we read the *Laches* in school, I formed the plan, or the wish, to spend my life reading Plato and breeding rabbits while earning my livelihood as a rural postmaster. Without being aware of it, I had moved rather far away from my Jewish home, without any rebellion. When I was seventeen, I was converted to Zionism—to simple, straightforward political Zionism.[31]

It is easy to see how Strauss's experience at gymnasium—his absorption of the *Bildungsideal,* his exposure to post-Enlightenment critiques of that project, and his idealization of rural contemplative existence—may have pulled him away from his traditional Jewish home in Kirchhain. The abrupt addition of becoming a convert to political Zionism may have reflected an instinctual desire to remain a loyal Jew.

Strauss's affiliation with political Zionism would persist into the late 1920s, and the impact Zionism had upon his thought is one of the main topics of his later reflections. Needless to say, his Zionism did not entail a dramatic break with non-Jewish European influences; he would retain throughout a strongly critical disposition toward the intellectual foundations of the Zionist movement. Strauss recounted the "very honorable" but "merely formal or poor" content of political Zionism; that is, its lack of a cultured sensibility and intellectual depth. Strauss once remembered that when he met with the leader of the militant revisionists, Vladimir Ze'ev Jabotinsky (1880–1940), Jabotinsky was uninterested in the Bible, Jewish history, and even Zionist theory. Instead, Jabotinsky was only interested in whether there was rifle practice.[32] Even though Strauss rebelled against much in the classical tradition of German humanism, he would never relinquish its ideal of the individual's passionate devotion to education in the quest for enlightenment.

Strauss graduated gymnasium in the spring of 1917, just as potential recruits for the war effort were being hurried out of school. As is widely known, the overwhelming majority of German Jews, like their German countrymen, embraced the war's outbreak on August 3, 1914, with enthusiastic displays of patriotism and fraternity. Just two days later, German Jews, without regard to class, denomination, regional, or ethnic differences, flocked to the synagogues in response to the kaiser's call for a national day of prayer.

Eventually this enthusiasm for the war effort waned.[33] Although the young Strauss did not voice public support or opposition to the war, we have anecdotal evidence of Strauss's less than enthusiastic desire to serve on the front. Strauss seems to have resorted to a common tactic in attempting to escape military service: feigned illness. His performance as a man suffering from appendicitis was credible enough to have him brought to the operating room. His scheme was detected, however, once the doctor gauged his temperature as normal. Strauss was then sent to Belgium as an interpreter.[34]

## Marburg and the Legacy of German Idealism

The Philipps-Universität in Marburg was founded in the sixteenth century as the first Protestant university in Germany. Apart from moments of conservative reaction, the university had a long tradition of progressive thinkers, including the Jewish philosopher Hermann Cohen, the founder of the Marburg School of neo-Kantianism. Cohen's philosophical return to Kant rested on the belief in the a priori ordering of the world through human consciousness and the conviction that philosophy could systematically disclose and guide this structuring.

The importance of Hermann Cohen to German Jewry is undeniable. On the simple matter of advancement into the hallowed halls of the German academy, Cohen's position was unique: when he succeeded his mentor Friedrich Lange at the University of Marburg in 1876, he was the only Jew to hold a chair in philosophy in Germany.[35] Cohen's symbolic importance for German Jewry went far beyond his status as one of the leading philosophers of his time. As Strauss later recalled, he was "the greatest representative of German Jewry and spokesman for it," a man who became the greatest philosopher in Germany "by the fire and power of his soul." His reign as the leading philosophical figure in Germany, accordingly, surpassed his own death, coming to an end only in 1925, when the magnetic force of Martin Heidegger assumed Cohen's chair in philosophy at Marburg.[36]

In one of Strauss's last public recollections of his youthful years, we learn that he was drawn to Cohen "because he was a passionate philosopher and a Jew devoted to Judaism."[37] Cohen's unwavering commitment to philosophical investigation and the Jewish religion offered German Jewry the possibility of bridging the worlds of *Deutschtum* and *Judentum*. And Cohen's most widely known Jewish work, *Religion of Reason Out of the Sources in Judaism* (1919), attempted to demonstrate the systematic affinities between the most advanced under-standing of the Kantian philosophical legacy and the Jewish tradition.[38] Although Strauss himself would eventually part from Cohen's legacy, he recognized that other "philosophically minded Jews who were devoted to Judaism" viewed Cohen to be "the master whom they revered."[39] By the time Strauss came to study at the University of Marburg in 1919, Cohen had died; he had not taught there for almost a decade. Yet even though Cohen's legacy would be in dissolution by the time Strauss entered Marburg, Cohen's presence remained. Strauss would think with and through Cohen's interpretations of Plato, Maimonides, and Spinoza during his Weimar writings. While Strauss qualified and rejected several central aspects of Cohen's interpretations, many of Strauss's most important insights were occasioned by his engagements (and even misrenderings) of them.[40]

Strauss's early years were shaped by the bivalent character of his environ-ment. On the one hand, he became steeped in the classical tradition of German humanism as a student in the local gymnasium and university. On the other hand, he was raised in the conservative ambience of German Jewry in Kur-hessen. Thus, even though his adherence to Orthodox observance and belief would wane over time, he nevertheless retained skepticism toward the inroads of modernizing Judaism in the guise of liberal or Reform tendencies. While Strauss's formative environment was marked by the rise of a new form of politi-cal antisemitism—appropriating different elements of racial science, popular myth, and legend while capitalizing on regional socioeconomic dislocations—he claims to have been relatively untouched by such forces. But I suspect that his gravitation toward political Zionism in his youth might be one by-product of this unacknowledged history.[41] Another intriguing consequence of the con-textual backdrop of regional antisemitism was that he was rarely shocked by its occurrences; he claimed to grasp its logic and found such reasoning instructive for Zionists.

## University Studies

Even before his release from the army, Strauss enrolled at the University of Mar-burg in the summer of 1917. He was not able to commence university studies until December 1918, when he finished his seventeen-month army service.[42] As noted, even though Hermann Cohen ceased teaching at Marburg in 1912, his philosophical legacy towered over Marburg when Strauss entered the univer-sity. Following the German tradition of studying at several institutions, Strauss studied not only at the University of Marburg, but also the universities of Frankfurt am Main, Berlin, and Hamburg.

At the University of Marburg, Strauss was introduced to the Western philo-sophical tradition under the neo-Kantians Nicolai Hartmann (1882–1950) and Paul Natorp (1854–1924): among his studies were courses on Plato's theory of ideas, Kantian epistemology and metaphysics, and the history of modern German philosophy.[43] His strong interest in philosophy was complemented by a concentration in classical philology taught by Karl Reinhardt (1886–1958) and Eduard Fraenkel (1888–1970).[44]

Strauss later attributed his decision to go to Marburg as one determined by its proximity to his home in Kirchhain rather than his being drawn to its excellence in philosophy.[45] In fact, Strauss characterized the Marburg school of neo-Kantianism after Cohen's death as being in a state of "disintegration."[46] Consequently, Strauss decided to pursue his doctorate at the University of Hamburg under one of Hermann Cohen's most notable disciples, Ernst Cassirer. Strauss's relationship to Cassirer—and to the entire project of neo-Kantianism—was complicated, to be sure. He was raised on the same ideals and aspirations that the Enlightenment-era philosophy represented. But he quickly began to discern weak links in its execution, even challenging some of the cardinal precepts of his dissertation adviser. The radical force and the conservative character of Strauss's thinking first emerged and then remained in the crucible of the Weimar Republic.

CHAPTER 2

# The Formation of a Weimar Conservative Jew (1921–1932)

The Weimar Republic was born in 1918 in the wake of Germany's defeat in World War I and the abdication of the kaiser. The republic's legitimacy was immediately called into question by conservative and right-wing elements. These elements resented the regime's capitulation to the victors' terms of peace stipulated at Versailles, including military occupation of the Rhineland, limitation of the German army to one hundred thousand soldiers, and—most stinging of all—the onerous Article 231: the war "guilt" clause. Despite the republic's decision in December 1918 to authorize the use of the Freikorps (a paramilitary group composed of decommissioned war veterans) to suppress socialist revolutions, the new regime's liberal promise remained anathema to monarchists, fascists, and other groups on the right. Dramatic bouts of hyperinflation, political assassinations, and social instability marked the tumult of Weimar. Meanwhile, the Weimar Republic held out hope to German Jews that their aspirations for full equality might be realized. In reality, while the path to integration was no longer checked by officially sanctioned legal discrimination, new and virulent waves of antisemitism placed Jews in a defensive position.

Strauss emerged as a Weimar Jewish thinker passionately engaged in the controversies that gripped his generation. And his developing intellectual persona exemplified the crisis thinking that coursed through the interconnected realms of religion, history, art, philosophy, science, and politics. He absorbed and participated in the leading currents and countercurrents of contemporary German philosophy as he grappled with the problematic character of modern German-Jewish existence. Strauss's published writings during Weimar have a definite polemical character directed toward, on the one hand, the uncovering of the shaky foundations and illusory goals of liberalism and, on the other, the Enlightenment faith in reason and historical progress.[1]

But Strauss supplemented this polemical project with the affirmative task of identifying and articulating a Jewish standpoint, or "a Jewish center of gravity"[2] whereby the present situation could be adequately assessed and serve as a strategic basis for future thought and action. In particular, Strauss's writings revolved around the Jewish condition of exile, or *galut,* which he initially understood as a mental disposition (*Gesinnung*) as well as a sociopolitical and existential fact. By the end of his Weimar period, these elements fall under the general and fundamental philosophical question: how should one live?[3]

His intellectual mission from 1921 to 1930 can be understood as emanating from two qualities that he felt were sorely lacking in contemporary German Judaism and liberal German culture: unstinting intellectual probity (*Redlichkeit*) and political realism. Strauss was just one of many young brash thinkers to gravitate toward the intellectual ethos of *Redlichkeit* in the early twentieth century. Indeed, despite his quest to find a political program that would meet the urgent needs of his time, Strauss's aforementioned intellectual qualities made it difficult for him to express an unqualified commitment to an organized political movement or organization. His ambivalent and increasingly tenuous affiliation with Zionism exemplifies his unwillingness to affirm the political solutions available. While he himself would reject categorization as a "free-floating intellectual"—a concept famously explored by Karl Mannheim in *Ideology and Utopia* (1929)—because of its bourgeois liberal (if not specifically social-democratic) and relativistic connotations,[4] Strauss's Weimar Jewish writings consistently attempt to gauge the foundations and claims of various German-Jewish worldviews and ideologies. The severity of the present situation presented a challenge that could not simply be solved by technopolitical wizardry; what was required was an unstinting account of the deep crises facing contemporary philosophy, politics, religion, and bare existence itself.

From 1922 to 1925, while studying theology, philosophy, and history at the universities in Berlin, Freiburg, Giessen, and Marburg, Strauss wrote several articles in Jewish and Zionist publications. Evident in these youthful writings is the rebellious spirit of innovation and sense of purpose that permeated interwar Central European culture. Strauss immersed himself in currents that were simultaneously conservative and radical: combining a conservative appreciation for older structures and traditions with the revolutionary impulse to break completely from the present order of things.[5] Oswald Spengler's best-selling *Decline of the West* (1920–23)[6] expressed the deep-seated cultural pessimism affecting a whole generation of Germans who came to question and reject the liberal view of history as a progressive force while also seeing the premodern world as irretrievably lost.[7]

Of course, the convictions that Germany and the West were immersed in a fundamental crisis and that modern rationalism and bourgeois culture were bereft of meaning did not necessarily entail a political position on the right. There are countless examples of Weimar figures, and specifically Weimar Jewish figures, who held these principles and adopted positions on the left: Gustav Landauer, Walter Benjamin, and the circle of largely assimilated Jewish figures

*Leo Strauss and the Politics of Exile*

associated with the "Frankfurt School" are obvious examples of this phenomenon.[8] The focus of the immediate discussion is to ascertain the forces that conditioned Strauss's trajectory as a conservative German-Jewish intellectual during the Weimar Republic. To sharpen this focus, I shall first examine Strauss's
deep ambivalence regarding liberalism, an orientation that predisposed him to
forces and figures on the right. Second, I shall explore his tenacious commitment
to provide an account of modern Jewish existence, a commitment that drove
him to see the condition of Jewish exile—*galut*—as an enduring and symp-
tomatic feature of a more general state of insecurity and danger offset only by
decisive glimpses of the possibility of justice, clarity, and righteousness restored.
Such a vision, however, is not to be construed either as future-oriented utopianism or mystical messianism.

Initially, Strauss's writings reflect his critical stance toward *galut* consciousness
as something that needs to be overcome because of its servile and unreflective
qualities. Both the Jewish advocates of assimilation as well as Zionists shared
negative views about anything associated with the *galut* as a shameful relic of a
premodern ghetto Jew. By the end of the Weimar period, Strauss came to see the
condition of *galut* as both intractable and essential for any genuine account of
Jewish existence. This change in attitude toward the condition of *galut* reflects
his progressive detachment from Zionist agendas, policies, and much more generally, mass politics, whether democratic or not. Strauss consistently saw Zionism as a vehicle to educate young German Jews about their stateless condition,
but his changing stance required an increasing detachment from the Zionist
movement and its ideology as a whole. Perhaps the most important function
that a politicized understanding of the Jewish diaspora could provide was that
it would guard against an overidentification by Jews with Germany, or any other
modern nation-state (including a state of the Jews) as a redemptive entity. Hermann Cohen's identification of the German state as a vehicle for Jewish redemption is one non-Zionist variant of a Jewish political orientation that attempts to
negate and/or overcome exile as a fixed feature of Jewish existence.

Although German Zionism did develop organizational stability and strength,
no more than twenty thousand German Jews were members of Zionist organizations at any time during the Weimar Republic.[9] And while Strauss contributed
to the Zionist movement as a writer and speaker throughout the Weimar period, his constant oppositional stance within German Zionism overshadows
any earlier and implicit preferences he may have had for particular factions or
policies. In fact, his Zionist writings centered not on any ready-made solution
for nation building, but rather on German Jewry's misguided and dangerous
self-perception of security and triumph.

The problematic nature of German-Jewish existence became for Strauss the
entry point in the larger quest for a standard of truth, a valid "standpoint" that
could transcend the present "anarchy of opinions."[10] While the Enlightenment
intended liberation from the yoke of religious tradition, subsequent attempts to

harmonize Enlightenment and religious tradition resulted in their entanglement. Indeed, Strauss's Weimar writings were increasingly aimed at extricating contemporary self-understanding from the confines of misguided relativism, historicism, and liberalism. By the close of the Weimar period, he forcefully enunciated the goal of breaking free from the fundamental presuppositions of the present. In his 1932 review of Carl Schmitt's *Concept of the Political,* Strauss announced that liberation from the present "horizon of liberalism" was required for the modern resumption of Plato's ancient quest for wisdom and knowledge.[11]

Strauss's fascinating intellectual personality combined the seemingly opposite sensibilities of a Jewish rural conservative and a radicalized Weimar intellectual. At the same time, he embodied the polarized forces that permeated the history of the short-lived Weimar Republic, from its birth in 1918 to its collapse in 1932. Interwar crisis thinking touched Strauss most directly through the powerful intellectual forces he encountered during this period: Franz Rosenzweig, Carl Schmitt, and above all, Martin Heidegger. Central to Strauss's radical-conservative character was fundamental acknowledgment of a deep crisis in which every available response and proposed solution only led to further and deeper entanglement. The urgent situation demanded unremitting honesty and realism; ruthless self-reflexivity and self-criticism would serve as the benchmarks of seriousness. Strauss deployed these demands as a polemical weapon against his opponents, but they also serve as driving forces of his own thinking. When Strauss approached a particular thinker or text, he would consistently begin with what appears to be the most pressing or central claim; he would then go on, however, to expose central conceptual antinomies by splitting apart an argument, allowing a deeper and more radical opposition to emerge from the author's true but often unarticulated motives and intentions. Usually, competing claims would each suffer his critical interrogation, leaving some urgent but ultimately unresolved tension at the end.[12]

One might compare this style to an inverted form of *pilpul,* the conventional mode of Talmudic exegesis: wherein central implicit antinomies unfold by way of hairsplitting fine-spun distinctions associated with *pilpul* and then are deployed to dig down to the hidden roots of the position not only to uncover its inadequacies, but to radically recast the problem as one that requires an urgent reply.[13] And here is the exegetical proclivity that at this stage of his career places him much closer to Heidegger than to traditional modes of interpreting Jewish texts. In "Cohen's Analysis of Spinoza's Bible Science" (1924) Strauss detects a shared stylistic feature between Hermann Cohen's approach to Spinoza and "the way of our intensive and penetrating *traditional* art of interpretation" wherein each word is considered with utmost seriousness and care. Cohen's criticisms of Spinoza's critique of Judaism typifies Cohen's interpretive approach to such works as Spinoza's *Theologico-Political Treatise.* For Strauss, this approach proves Cohen's indebtedness to a traditional Jewish interpretive craft.[14]

Cohen intensively pores over each element of the title so as to reveal the deeper character of Spinoza's project and fundamental ideas.[15] Spinoza's lack of interest in philosophy (which Strauss points out might only be accidentally conveyed) becomes for Cohen a point of departure. And yet Strauss's absorption of diverse intellectual influences exemplifies the dynamic tension characteristic of a constantly transforming tradition of Jewish thought. The position of Strauss as an interpreter of texts can be characterized as an intensified combination of fidelity and alienation. This tendency to unearth and confront irreconcilable positions in order to reveal the standpoint of the interpreter within a larger set of presuppositions and concerns lay at the center of Strauss's early interpretive commitment. Moreover, the mode of analysis remained more or less constant throughout this period. Only in the 1930s would a dramatic change in the mode of presentation occur.

Strauss began his university studies in earnest after his military service had ended in December 1918.[16] Strauss studied at several institutions as a student well into his career as a postgraduate student in the 1920s. The University of Marburg served as a base for Strauss while he also pursued studies at the University of Frankfurt-am-Main, Berlin, and Hamburg. Strauss became grounded in the legacy of neo-Kantianism at the University of Marburg under the instruction of Hartmann and Natorp[17] and decided to pursue a doctorate in philosophy at the University of Hamburg under the direction of Ernst Cassirer, one of the finest products of the Marburg School of neo-Kantianism and the leading Jewish disciple of Hermann Cohen.[18]

## Questioning Faith in Idealism

In 1921 Strauss received a doctorate in philosophy from the University of Hamburg. The following year, he went to Freiburg with the intention of studying under Edmund Husserl, the founder of phenomenology and the most formidable challenger to the Marburg neo-Kantians.[19] Strauss soon found other professors who would exercise a more dramatic influence on his thought at Freiburg; for example, Julius Ebbinghaus, who offered engaged readings of Hobbes. But even more significant to Strauss's development was the young and brilliant philosophical apprentice to Husserl, Martin Heidegger. Strauss would later reflect that Heidegger's thought, which overwhelmed virtually everyone of Strauss's generation "who had ears to hear," had the most profound and lasting influence in determining the direction of his thought.[20] Heidegger's Catholic background and training, according to Strauss, immunized him against the prevalent "danger of trying to modernize Aristotle."[21] Strauss would consciously attempt to resist the impulse to modernize and distort premodern philosophy, but his earliest efforts consisted of an immanent critique of modern philosophy.

We see the sharp difference between Strauss and Cassirer already in Strauss's dissertation, *The Problem of Knowledge in the Teaching of Friedrich Heinrich Jacobi* in 1921.[22] The dissertation explored F. H. Jacobi's (1743–1819)[23] critical response to the epistemological foundations of the German Enlightenment. The title of the dissertation resembles that of Cassirer's four-volume analysis of the problem of knowledge in modern philosophy.[24] Cassirer's work begins by exploring the ways in which modern science has undermined the basis for the certainty of a prescientific picture of reality and truth.[25] While Strauss's study of Jacobi has a similar focus, the student counters his adviser's assertion that modern science renders the prescientific basis of knowledge "naïve" and obsolete by rediscovering Jacobi's critique of scientific rationalism's claims and presuppositions. In some ways, Cassirer's work was an expression of the social democratic promise of Weimar: combining the legacies of the liberal principles of 1789, the highest German cultural traditions, and an embrace of modern science as pillars of the new Republic of Reason.[26] By contrast, Strauss's dissertation recovers an incessant critic of the underpinnings of Enlightenment rationalism and its liberal theological accompaniments. In order to elucidate this, I shall delve into some philosophical issues that will help locate Strauss's attraction to Husserl's and then Heidegger's critique of various reigning scientific models for philosophy such as neo-Kantianism.

Strauss limits his presentation to what he deemed to be those elements of Jacobi's work that integrally relate to the central problems of a theory of knowledge. In an apologetic extract attached to the dissertation, Strauss explained that the dissertation does not present "Jacobi-in-himself" but rather takes a "non-Jacobian approach" to problems that arise from Jacobi's thought. Because Jacobi had no formal "theory of knowledge" (*Erkenntnis-Theorie*) the dissertation had to "resort to many deflections" in order to construct such a model.[27]

Beyond these methodological problems, Strauss casts Jacobi as interested in "the possibility of an immediate experience of God" and determined to think through the ensuing implications that follow from this possibility for positive historical religions. Without such a possibility, the claims on the individual's fidelity to a particular religious tradition lose their epistemological as well as moral grounding. Jacobi therefore prefigures the interwar "reawakening of theology" that for Strauss was "marked by the names of Karl Barth and Franz Rosenzweig."[28] Both of these figures addressed the wedge separating revelation and the modern recipient that had grown deeper and wider during the previous two centuries. The Jacobi dissertation is the first instance wherein Strauss stakes out and elaborates upon a philosophical position that generated from the fusion and collision of the debates of the 1780s and 1790s and the interwar period.[29] In both epochs, the appeal to religious experience centers a critique of the narrow Kantian conception of experience as scientific experience.[30] Both Jacobi and Barth, for instance, argue that the idealist presentation of religion is motivated by the conceit that it can simply evade the decisive moment of experiencing God's separateness from the world. Strauss surely was conscious of Jacobi's paradoxical position in exploring the competing claims of reason and faith. While Jacobi utilized the weapons of rationalism against various Enlightenment philosophies in his critique of secular scientific rationalism, he (as would Barth) nevertheless often expressed militant opposition to the church and to papal authority. And this is why Strauss notes Jacobi's opposition to "literalism" (*Literalismus*) as yielding the dynamic and decisive elements of belief to historical religions as the sole continuation of revelation's authority, truth, and meaning.[31]

But Strauss gives far greater emphasis to Jacobi's *"opposition to idealism and rationalism"* on the basis of maintaining *"the transcendence of and the irrationality of God."*[32] According to this view, the integral role of historical religions—as opposed to abstract enlightened notions of natural religion—is to provide the subject with the necessary form to understand God's truth.[33] Acknowledging God's existence does not emerge as the by-product of theoretical constructions and reductions that are forced upon the world. Rather, the experience gained by belief is derived from the immanent reality of God's existence. Jacobi's doctrine of perception (*Wehrnehmungslehre*) is therefore to be understood as the subject's grasping and coming to the conscious acknowledgment of the transcendent and irrational character of God.[34] The implications for ethics in Jacobi are profound: God's call to obedience is unqualified and therefore trumps any considerations or standards that rest on the natural use of reason.

And thus Jacobi determined a fatal chink in the Kantian understanding of ethics and morality. According to the doctrines of rationalist idealism and materialism, the possibility for ethical and moral judgment and action issues strictly from the subject's dignity as an autonomous individual. And yet the content of this dignity is desiccated by the hubristic desire of the human subject to be completely autonomous from the absolute demands of a transcendent God.[35] For Jacobi, the "I" is conditioned by the "thou."[36] Strauss therefore looks to Jacobi as someone determined to elaborate the ways in which a perceiving subject grasps reality without lapsing into the trappings of subjective knowledge. The directional movement of Jacobian perception (*Wahrnehmung*) from something out there in the world back to the subject provides the orientation and intention to thought that is not accounted for in the scientific models of idealism.

In opposition to the liberal understanding advanced by Descartes, Spinoza, Kant, and especially Mendelssohn, Jacobi's critique therefore tries to recover dignity of the subject based upon the radical limitations of ethical systems once the prospect of an immediate experience of God is countenanced. Moreover, we can now appreciate one of Strauss's later anecdotes about why he was drawn to Husserl away from the Marburg neo-Kantian school of Cohen, Natorp, and Cassirer. Husserl, who was himself trained in that Marburg tradition, once told Strauss that while this tradition was clearly "superior to all other German philosophical schools," it nevertheless made the fatal structural mistake of "beginning with the roof."[37] Strauss recounts Husserl's comments in February 1956 at a lecture at the University of Chicago sponsored by the campus Hillel Foundation. Strauss explains that the neo-Kantian emphasis on "the analysis of science" was shown by Husserl to derive "from our primary knowledge of the world of things." Instead of conceiving modern science as "the perfection of man's understanding of the world," Husserl exposed it as "a specific modification of that pre-scientific understanding." Strauss's presentation of Jacobi's critique of the epistemological foundations of the most visible philosophical constructions of the seventeenth and eighteenth centuries therefore makes him a forgotten precursor of Husserl's preidealistic investigations into the problem of scientific analysis. Strauss further adumbrates how Husserl's approach problematizes the claims of science to be neutral and objective: "The meaningful genesis of science out of pre-scientific understanding is a *problem;* the primary theme is the philosophical understanding of the pre-scientific world and therefore in the first place the analysis of the sensibly perceived thing."[38] The parallels between Husserl and Strauss's presentation of Jacobi are manifold. Strauss identifies Jacobi's method as approximating Husserlian "description" (*Deskription*) while calling his own method of presentation as a *"Problemgeschichte"*—echoing his aforementioned later ascription to Husserl.[39] Strauss writes that the name Jacobi sent shockwaves through all subsequent intellectual history, signaling a singular and "coherent complex of problems" about "timeless problems" of philosophy.[40] But we must remember that Strauss read Husserlian elements into an area that was not of great concern to Husserl. In a 1946 letter to Karl Löwith, Strauss recalled that he had once asked Husserl about theology, and Husserl responded, "If there is a datum, 'God,' we shall describe it." What a philosophical statement that was."[41] In Strauss's recollection, Husserl did not grasp the deeper significance and relevance of the theological reawakening.[42]

Although Strauss seemed not to have placed great weight on the dissertation,[43] it was an undeniably biting assessment of German Enlightenment rationalism and its relationship to nonrationalist traditions and currents. Given its polemical edge against idealist accounts of religion and ethics, the dissertation might be seen as part of the new pantheism debates that developed almost a century and a half after Jacobi.[44] A few remarks about the dissertation will help situate Strauss at this early stage. That Strauss chose to write a measured analysis of a counter-Enlightenment thinker who spent much of his public intellectual life embroiled in controversy directs us toward the young Strauss's proclivity for recovering provocative critics of liberal rationalism.[45] Instead of following Cassirer's neo-Kantian method of philosophical idealism, Strauss experimented with a kind of Husserlian rendering of Jacobi's thought[46] in order to test the possibility of recovering or discovering anew religious "experience" free from modern liberal machinations.

Jacobi's defense of the believer's direct experience of God as a serious possibility could decisively place idealist understandings of religion at bay. At issue is whether philosophical systems are capable of describing and acknowledging the believer's unmediated experience of God or whether they occlude and block such an understanding.[47] Also, Strauss's enthusiastic affirmation of Jacobi's concept of "belief" (*Glaube*) coincides with a parallel appreciation for Jacobi's defiant and perplexing call for a return to orthodoxy in the face of the Enlightenment's desiccated rationalism and ultimate "nihilism."[48] The opposition between *decisive belief* and *weak-willed rationalism* emerges as key in the dissertation. In this light, the otherwise conventional profession of Jewish belief, "Ich bin jüdischen Glaubens," included in the biographical statement (*Lebenslauf*) attached to the dissertation resonates with the defiance so characteristic of his presentation of Jacobi.[49]

Strauss's direct criticism of his former dissertation adviser comes to the fore in "Zur Auseinandersetzung mit der europäischen Wissenschaft," which appeared in *Der Jude* in 1924.[50] Strauss portrayed Cassirer before a Jewish readership as a thinker who had abandoned the Jewish legacy of Hermann Cohen's thought. Strauss criticized Cassirer's understanding of the role of myth in religion as indicative of this abandonment.[51] Cassirer understood the advancement of forms of intellectual expression as a sequence that "leads from myth to language to art, in which the mind attains its highest freedom."[52] For Strauss this idealistic "sublation" (*Aufhebung*)—the dual process of conservation and overcoming—of myth omits the central role of ethics in Cohen's philosophy of religion. Strauss argues that Cassirer's theory of myth and religion is not only incompatible with Cohen's philosophical system, but actually cuts the legs from under it. In Strauss's view of Cohen, the transcendence of God is the crucial element: "the ethical motive of transcendence contains within it, from the outset and in latent form, the power and depth of the religious motive of transcendence."[53] The essence of Cohen's philosophy, as well as the teachings of the biblical prophets, requires the rejection of idol worship (as an intolerable form of mythic religion). The shared commitment of Cohen and the prophets to maintaining the transcendence of God from this world constitutes what Strauss sees as "the inner connection between Cohen's philosophical system and Judaism." Strauss understood Cohen's great achievement to be the realization of a systematic understanding of the Jewish adhesion to God's transcendence and the rejection of mythic religion. By contrast, Cassirer's analysis of the development of myth and religion draws on several ancient and modern religious movements, but conspicuously omits Judaism.[54]

It is telling that Strauss felt more of an affinity with his heretical Catholic contemporary Heidegger than with his Jewish *Doktorvater* Ernst Cassirer. In fact, Strauss and Cassirer held core convictions and predispositions that were irreconcilable. Cassirer exemplified the intense German-Jewish attachment to *Bildung* that imagined a liberal German society in which a German and Jewish synthesis could be realized. This liberal bourgeois model of German-Jewish existence lay at the heart of Strauss's repeated polemics against an assimilationist bourgeois German Jewry that had mistakenly placed its trust in a cosmopolitan faith in humanity and the machinery of a well-functioning German state.

Strauss's criticisms of an established Jewish figure such as Cassirer were launched as he attempted to articulate a Jewish position beyond the bounds of a bourgeois liberal ideology. His criticism of contemporary Jewish biblical criticism is a case in point. In "Biblical History and Science" (1923), Strauss cuts against the norm of modern Jewish biblical exegesis by interpreting its political character as essentially both conservative and radical. The recognition of law as fundamental is Strauss's starting point in discerning how biblical doctrines ought to guide contemporary Jewish politics. Given man's innate tendencies toward domination and violence, law becomes a political necessity in order to protect against man's evil inclination. But this emphasis on law does not entail a celebration of state power as the solution to fundamental political problems. Instead, the biblical emphasis on theocracy promotes the significance of the family and diminishes the importance of the "impersonal state." For Strauss, biblical political theory advanced theocracy as "the only radical defense against the power instinct which rules the state."[55] One of the ironies of Strauss's conservative politics was his atheistic defense of law as fundamental without relying on the state as its only legitimate form of representation or agent of enforcement.

The crucial methodological point in interpreting the legacy of biblical religion was to confront directly the most disconcerting and "uncanny" political elements of early Judaism; they are usually overlooked by an uncritical acceptance of liberalism.[56] While Spinoza advanced a radical method of interpreting biblical Judaism literally, Strauss rejected the modern legacy of Spinozistic metaphysics, which dissolved the absolute biblical distinction between God and nature. Belief in God's absolute transcendence and power over nature was, in Strauss's eyes, essential for any legitimate conception of biblical religion. Barth had advanced a similar idea, and his innovative defamiliarization of Scripture must be seen as providing a fundamental paradigm for resisting the pervasive tendencies to modernize and therefore blunt the full meaning of even the possibility of revelation as understood in Judaism and early Christianity.[57]

Moreover, by taking at face value the realism of biblical violence and miracles, Strauss reveals his indebtedness to Franz Rosenzweig as well as Strauss's own peculiar relationship to orthodoxy. [58] While Strauss held that the most extreme elements of early Judaism could not be legitimately overlooked or swept away, he was not a fundamentalist adherent of Jewish orthodoxy. Although he felt obliged to attack contemporary orthodoxy as a masquerade, he was nevertheless convinced that Judaism's essential elements were to be the same in the eyes of both the believer and unbeliever. The crucial point for him is that any account of Jewish religion and politics must not be infected by disingenuous apologies for belief or unbelief. Only after the most illiberal and untimely biblical doctrines are seen in their raw and extreme character can one seriously engage orthodoxy and appreciate the possibilities for present-day Judaism and Jewish politics. Whether one is an adherent or opponent of orthodoxy is not nearly so important for Strauss as recognizing the integrity of orthodoxy as more serious than what it has become. The young Strauss registers an unqualified need to engage the raw foundations of orthodoxy by quoting Lessing: "Thus, what is so nauseating is not orthodoxy itself, but a certain squinting, limping orthodoxy which is unequal to itself!"[59] Lessing's complex position within and against the German Enlightenment would over the course of the next decade inspire Strauss to deepen his political interpretation and legitimation of orthodoxy. In the 1930s, Lessing's insights become seminal to Strauss's "rediscovery" of "exoteric" writing as a forgotten genre of guarded writing that shaped several key writers in premodern thought, especially in the seventeenth and eighteenth centuries. But this development takes place for Strauss in the 1930s, as we shall see, after he has undergone a "change of orientation."

In the 1920s, Strauss attacked contemporary biblical scholarship as covertly atheistic. That professors of theology are the practitioners of biblical criticism in the land of Germany (which had become "the land of reconciliations [*Versöhnungen*] and sublations [*Aufhebungen*]") has veiled the field's underlying atheism. For Strauss the modern German spirit of harmonizing oppositions is antithetical to the Jewish spirit; "as Jews we are radical and we don't like compromises."[60] This exclamation, which appears as an unsubstantiated ideological assertion, has resonance if we take into account Strauss's understanding of the extreme condition of *galut* as a primary cause of Jewish radicalization. The abnormal condition of a stateless nation facilitates persecution and suffering; paradoxically, however, it also testifies to the perseverance and intransigence of Jewish existence and reinforces the will to resist trends and pressures of the moment.

Strauss's project of articulating the meaning of Judaism and Jewish existence, free of liberal attributes, is evident in his approach to Jewish thinkers. The democratic-socialism of Hermann Cohen and the autonomism of the Jewish historian Simon Dubnow (1860–1941) remained in Strauss's eyes inherently opposed to the biblical insights mentioned above: a pessimistic view of human nature and the theocratic distrust of an impersonal state. When measuring the contribution of Dubnow's ambitious comprehensive history of the Jewish people in a 1924 review essay,[61] Strauss places Dubnow in the group of historians that Nietzsche, Treitschke, and Sybel derided as hopelessly muddleheaded ("dick verbundenen Köpfen").[62] Dubnow, according to Strauss, was not able to liberate Jewish history from the yoke of tradition and fell well short of the challenge he set for himself of presenting a systematically coherent sociological and objective view of Jewish history.

Strauss's reaction to contemporary biblical criticism fit within his broader quest for a Jewish Weltanschauung that could resist liberal currents within European culture. Powerful German (and specifically German-Jewish) countercurrents provided the necessary momentum to push Strauss toward his goal. Cassirer's thought flowed with the older German-Jewish liberal currents, but did not have the same force as the countercurrents of the Weimar Jewish renaissance that swept up Strauss's rebellious generation. Martin Buber and Franz Rosenzweig were at the center of this new movement.

### Franz Rosenzweig, Martin Buber, and the New German-Jewish Return Movement

Strauss's ambivalence toward Martin Buber and attachment to Franz Rosenzweig are certainly an instructive place to begin charting Strauss's place in the "renaissance" of German Jewry. Martin Buber's powerful impact on this movement is undeniable. After all, it was he who introduced the phrase "Jewish renaissance" in 1901.[63] In using this term, Buber aimed at a revitalization of the Jewish people by means of creating modern Jewish culture. This new Jewish culture was to take the form of a Zionism that would consciously incorporate the prevalent cultural forces in Germany, such as nationalism, romanticism, orientalism, the *Wandervogel* youth movement, and modernist aesthetic currents such as *Jugendstil* (art nouveau). The Galician-born Buber sought to combine the experiential wisdom of Eastern European Hasidism with *Lebensphilosophie* as the foundation of his cultural Zionism.

While Buber's Zionism borrowed from the aforementioned elements of non-Jewish culture, he did not wish to perpetuate the condition of *galut*. His negative view of *galut* as a plague to be overcome had its roots in Zionism at least since Leon Pinsker's trained medical eye diagnosed its abject abnormal condition.[64] Buber described *galut* as "a torture screw" (*eine Folterschraube*) that was responsible for the degeneration of the Jewish spirit.[65] Buber set out to purge non-essential and perverse elements of Judaism, such as the suffocating nature of rabbinic legalism, that had accrued during the course of Jewry's two thousand years of exilic suffering.[66] Buber saw this "age of exile" in purely negative terms. The age of exile was an "era of barren intellectuality . . . fed on bookish words, on interpretations of interpretations; poverty-stricken, distorted, and sickly."[67] Buber called for an elite group of creative and decisive Jewish men to confront the passive *galut* Jew in order to activate a buried primal and authentic Judaism—*Urjudentum*—and return to Zion. The task of the renewal (*Erneuerung*) of Judaism and the return was to be implemented by pioneers (*chalutzim*) who were to be drawn from this group of authentic Jews (*Urjuden*) rather than "the motley rabble" of *galut* Jewry.[68]

Although Buber's antipathy for the *galut* resonated with the general Zionist judgment,[69] Strauss's eventual ideas about *galut* were to be demonstrably closer to Buber's future partner in the German-Jewish renaissance, Franz Rosenzweig. Rosenzweig entitled a collection of essays on matters general and Jewish *Zweistromland* (1926), evoking the cross-cultural ferment of Babylon.[70] One might even say that he actually valorized the condition of Jewish homelessness as lifting the Jews out of the corrosive flux of history. "While Christians and

Christianity exist in 'the spiral of world-history,'" Rosenzweig stated in *The Star of Redemption*, "Jews and Judaism occupy a space outside the bellicose temporality [*ausserhalb einer kriegerischen Zeitlichkeit*]."[71] For Rosenzweig the lack of a present-day homeland has compelled "the eternal people" to concentrate on the spiritual rather than the mechanical, on the vital rather than the superficial.[72]

Rosenzweig's entry into the Jewish public eye found its expression in an open letter to Hermann Cohen, "It is Time: Thoughts on the Problem of Jewish Education at This Moment."[73] Rosenzweig called for the formation of an Akademie für Wissenschaft des Judentums, an institution that would facilitate a new generation of trained Jewish laity to bring Jewish education beyond the confines of the synagogue and quench the spiritual thirst of young acculturated German Jews.[74] Rosenzweig's selection for a title and motto was taken from Psalms 119:126: "It is time to work for the Lord, for they have violated Your teaching [*heferu toratekha*]."[75] The motto was employed to convey a sense of urgency regarding the decrepit state of Jewish education and the need to build cultural institutions capable of transmitting the necessary critical tools required for the revitalization of Judaism and its teachings. "The problem of Jewish education on all levels and in all forms is the Jewish task of the moment. The time to work has come."[76]

Strauss would find great inspiration in Rosenzweig's urgent call for an institution of Jewish science to engage the hearts and minds of its surrounding community. Rather than cloister himself in pure scholarship, Strauss made sure to realize Rosenzweig's vision of engaged scholars filling the ranks of the Akademie für die Wissenschaft des Judentums. For while the fellows at the Akademie would prove themselves to be an impressive collection of scholars in matters Jewish, they did not share Rosenzweig's commitment to community outreach. Strauss's lectures and teaching in provincial Jewish communities were certainly atypical of other appointed fellows.[77] Strauss would also find Rosenzweig to be a kindred spirit in launching a rebellion against a stale culture of complacency that both perceived to dominate the German-Jewish establishment and alienate their sons and daughters. Driving this project of Jewish education was Rosenzweig's direct confrontation with the problematic character of Jewish existence: "From Mendelssohn on, our entire people has subjected itself to the torture of this embarrassing questioning; the entire Jewishness of every individual has squirmed on the needle point of this 'why.'"[78] Rosenzweig dedicated himself to break with this tradition by engaging the problematic character of German-Jewish existence directly. Much of the angst and tension in Strauss's early thought emerges from the visceral squirming that Rosenzweig identified and recast in a redemptive quest.

Both Rosenzweig and Strauss represented the dramatic reorientation of Weimar Jewry that overturned normative assumptions. Frustrated by the failure of German universities to formally recognize the legitimacy of Jewish studies,[79] Rosenzweig saw the Akademie as a vehicle to advance Jewish scholarship and to effect the "conquest of historicism."[80]

Rosenzweig announced a program for Jewish adult education in his essay "*Bildung* and No End" (1920).[81] Here he followed Buber's call for a Jewish renaissance insofar as the methods and content of his "new learning" differed from traditional modes of learning that were operative in a seminary or yeshiva. In Rosenzweig's conception of new learning, the tasks of teaching and learning were to be conjoined within an academic atmosphere unencumbered by the limitations of traditional Jewish education. He would infuse his rebellious spirit into the Frankfurt *Lehrhaus* as a cultural space in which highly acculturated German-Jewish intellectuals would seek to avoid the stagnant religious sentiments and knowledge that no longer spoke to the new generation's needs. In this sense, the *Lehrhaus* marked Rosenzweig's departure from the Akademie's ideal of Jewish scholarship conforming to the most rigorous standards of the German academy. At the *Lehrhaus*, he hoped a vital and more durable content of Judaism would come out of engagements with core Jewish texts, that teaching and learning would intersect as passionately relevant.

In the opening address at the Frankfurt *Lehrhaus*, Rosenzweig stated that the method of new learning did not reject, but rather embraced, the alienated condition of German Jewry. The traditional or old method of learning started from the Torah and then attempted to connect it with some aspects of contemporary life. Rosenzweig reversed this order. He wanted to start from the world of acculturated Jews, a "world that knows nothing of the Law, or at least pretends to know nothing of the Law" and bridge this world back to the Torah. In this scheme of learning, "he is the most apt who brings with him the maximum of what is alien."[82] Rosenzweig's commitment to educating German Jews in the throes of dissimilation inspired Strauss to join him in the quest to reground German-Jewish existence.

A point of instructive comparison for the young Strauss and Rosenzweig surrounds their ambivalent attitudes toward Zionism. Rosenzweig's distance and deep-seated criticism of Zionism are exemplified in the image of *Zweistromland*, a land of two rivers.[83] If Jewish nationalism embraces state power in order to achieve normality and become like the other nations, and landedness centers existence, something central and distinctive about Jewish existence will be undercut. Rosenzweig theorized that a dynamic exchange between a Jewish center in Palestine and the diaspora might well bolster both entities.[84] However, a systematic ingathering of the exiles into a Jewish state or state of the Jews would have catastrophic effects for Jews and Judaism.

Despite Rosenzweig's partnership with Martin Buber, Rosenzweig maintained a skeptical attitude toward Zionism. Peter Gordon presents Rosenzweig as a "theorist of Jewish exile" who saw it not as a shameful abject condition to be overcome, but rather as an ontological condition that shapes the possibility of "redemption-in-the-world."[85] As Rosenzweig wrote to Rudolf Hallo, the condition of exile is "Jewish being" (*das Judesein*)": "To be a Jew [*Jude sein*] *means* to be in 'Golus'. Jewish *life* is the form through which we make Jewish-being tolerable."[86] And in *The Star of Redemption*, Rosenzweig explained that Jewish election is constituted in exile. His philosophical understanding of man's urgent wish to "remain" acquires the collective realization in postexilic Jewish survival, Jewish existence as "remnant." The structure and practice of Jewish communal life produce a kind of refined consciousness that places Jewish existence in "defiance of all secular history" because it merely remains in the world as a persecuted remnant.[87]

Strauss's concern with past Jewish thought intersected with his confrontation with various strands of German Zionism and framed his effort to grasp the general "situation of the present."[88] Strauss teased out the inner contradictions of every major Zionist thinker and the movements they represented as he struggled to find an ideological position that did not collapse under the weight of reflection and self-criticism. His writings during the 1920s appear as different interventions in the public space between scholarship and politics.

During the academic year of 1924–25, Strauss joined the ranks of several prominent Jewish intellectuals who lectured at Franz Rosenzweig's Free Jewish House of Study (Freies Jüdisches Lehrhaus) in Frankfurt on Spinoza's *Theologico-Political Treatise* as well as on the theory of political Zionism.[89] Here, Strauss also led a reading of Hermann Cohen's *Religion of Reason Out of the Sources in Judaism*.[90] In response to Strauss's lecture on Zionism, Rosenzweig, who held a skeptical attitude toward political Zionism, beseeched the cultural Zionist Ernst Simon to counter the "really silly" Zionism of the Blau-Weiss[91]—the group Strauss represented.[92] But Strauss would subject a dominant strain of Blau-Weiss to a blistering critique in 1923 once it had come under the leadership of Walter Moses.[93] In "Response to Frankfurt's 'Word of Principle,'" Strauss engaged factional disputes that emerged during and following a 1922 Christmas Zionist convention in Berlin where the K.j.V. (Kartell Verband jüdischer Verbindungen), an umbrella organization of Zionist students, failed to merge with the Blau-Weiss youth movement. Strauss targeted the Frankfurt faction of the K.j.V., which registered a principled protest against the power politics of the dominant Breslau wing of the Blau-Weiss.[94]

Strauss's description and analysis of this all-too-common factionalist dispute register his political points of reference, which would stay relatively fixed for the next decade. Strauss sees an underlying agreement of the warring factions of the Frankfurt K.j.V. and the Blau-Weiss: a belief (*Glaube*) in the collapse of "sovereign science" and "sovereign politics." Strauss demonstrates that both sides espouse countermodern sentiments against the faith in rationalist science and politics, but do so in a thoroughly modern way that renders their positions thoroughly "inner-modern." The more left-leaning Frankfurt faction had principally opposed certain right-wing political demands placed upon them by Walter Moses. Strauss notes that Moses's "pagan-fascist" use of "political" has an ancient connotation. "What is hidden behind this absolute negation of the sphere of the 'private' is not a modern Leviathan, but rather the pagan-fascist counterpart of that, which, in the case of the Frankfurt faction, bears a mystical-humanitarian stamp." The modern Leviathan refers to the Hobbesian idea of a total state. The "mystical-humanitarian" counterpart undoubtedly refers to Martin Buber's influence on the left-leaning Frankfurt faction. Both groups call for the obliteration of the bourgeois private sphere as a necessary feature of the new politics that is to be expected and desired. Strauss raises but then tables the provocative question of whether an intimate relationship exists between "'science' and 'state'—those fruits of the anti-Catholic spirit" and "the innermost Jewish tendency." This connection has often been drawn by such Zionists as Max Nordau and Jacob Klatzkin, whom Strauss indirectly names as "organologists." But unmentioned is another group of thinkers who assert a literal coincidence of Jewish interests or a Jewish spirit with advancement of modern science and the state as sovereign norms—the counterenlightenment thinkers running from F. H. Jacobi to Carl Schmitt, who identified a conspiratorial alliance between Judaism and secularism as the secret forces behind modern liberalism. While setting aside whether the foundations of the "modern spirit can be justified at all," Strauss avers: "it is still self-evident that it is impossible to extricate oneself from modern life without employing modern means." Even in denouncing and attempting to overturn modern norms, Strauss maintains at this point in his career that modern weaponry is the only arsenal available.

But Strauss is less interested in the particular claims of various factions and more interested in arriving at a "genuine standard" that is indigenous to the specific development of German Jewry and can therefore gauge the trajectory of German Zionism. Strauss, speaking in the name of Blau-Weiss, identifies this standard as "Einwirklichung"—a wakeful entrance into reality, marked by the drive "to gain access to normal historical 'reality' (land and soil, power and arms, peasantry and aristocracy)."[95] But Strauss sets up this view of the Zionist return to historical reality only eventually to subvert the bases of this view.

According to Strauss, the Zionist view decisively differs from the conception of reality operative for German Jews who choose the path of assimilation: the former aims at a collective worldview, while the latter limits its understanding of reality to a purely individualist sense. The modern period held forth the prospect of civic emancipation for individual Jews whose religion became reconstructed along the lines of a confession, one based on private belief devoid of coercive clerical authority. But the elusive promise of social inclusion required a transformed worldview wherein the unit of analysis shifted from the premodern corporate collective to the individual. Strauss engages the paradoxes that emerge from the Zionist effort to negate *galut,* leaving the reader and author alike in a state of aporia reminiscent of the early Socratic dialogues. For Strauss, the aforementioned decisive difference of Zionism and assimilation provides the very basis for the formation of "a *single* front against the abnormal existence of the *galut*" that would promise a thorough overcoming of the unreal spectral *galut* existence that horrified Zionists and secular assimilationists alike.

*Leo Strauss and the Politics of Exile*

Until 1925 Strauss's views on different aspects of modern German-Jewish thought and politics had been those of an unemployed academician. In 1925, Strauss became affiliated with the Berlin-based Akademie für die Wissenschaft des Judentums when Julius Guttmann, the institution's director, appointed Strauss as a staff researcher (*Mitarbeiter*). Guttmann was impressed by Strauss's historical criticism of Hermann Cohen's polemical treatment of Spinoza's *Theologico-Political Treatise* (1924).[96] Guttmann was either following Hermann Cohen's example of tolerating and even encouraging difference and dissent or he did not fully grasp Strauss's iconoclastic and antiliberal character. Guttmann was a descendant of a distinguished line of rabbinical scholars, and very much associated with the liberal Jewish establishment in Germany. It would only be a matter of time before he and Strauss would clash.

Strauss held his position at the Akademie until October 1932 when the institution, under financial duress, had to fire several researchers. Strauss's appointment at the Akademie coincided with his study of medieval Jewish philosophy in Guttmann's Berlin seminar at the Hochschule Lehranstalt für die Wissenschaft des Judentums. The 1924–25 seminar focused on Joseph Albo's fifteenth-century *Book of Roots* (*Sefer ha-Ikarim*) and another on Moses Maimonides' twelfth-century *Guide of the Perplexed*. Albo's philosophical indebtedness to the preceding Arab philosophical tradition is most obviously evidenced on an issue that Strauss found useful in his contemporary polemics with liberal Judaism: the definition of religion as a political law.[97] Albo was a late representative of Spanish Maimonidean rationalism, a highly technical philosophical tradition that required literacy in and command of Hebrew, Arabic, and Greek sources.[98] Strauss's developing interest in medieval Jewish rationalism was representative of a broader German-Jewish fascination with Spanish Jewry—itself the object of much attention from Strauss's fellow staff researcher Fritz (Yitzhak) Baer, who focused his energies on Jewish life in medieval Spain. David Baneth was charged with translating Yehudah Halevi's *Kuzari* into German. And Gershom Scholem, who had already emigrated to Palestine in 1923, received the Akademie's subvention for his researches into the possible connections between Moses de Leon and the foundational kabbalistic text, the *Zohar*.

Meanwhile, Strauss's interest in the seventeenth-century Dutch-Jewish heretic, Spinoza, became connected to questions regarding the significance of his crypto-Jewish Marrano heritage and related contextual factors that might account for his overturning of Maimonides' medieval philosophical paradigm. Guttmann initially encouraged Strauss to continue his research and write a book on Spinoza. However, disputes surrounding the final form of Strauss's book, *Die Religionskritik Spinozas als Grundlage seiner Bibelwissenschaft* (1930), hinted at the increasing distance between Strauss's views and the conventional German-Jewish position of Guttmann.[99] Although Strauss had completed the first draft of this book in 1928, because of Guttmann's demands for revisions, the book was not published until 1930. In a letter to Gerhard Krüger, whom Strauss befriended as a fellow student of Heidegger, Strauss apologized for the book's errors and attributed these to the fact that it was written under conditions of censorship.[100]

In conjunction with Strauss's appointment to the Akademie, he took part in Rosenzweig's adult education activities in the provincial Jewish communities as well as in Rosenzweig's home city of Kassel.[101] During this time Strauss contributed several essays on various aspects of modern Judaism and Zionism in leading Jewish venues such as Martin Buber's journal *Der Jude* and the *Jüdische Rundschau*, as well as in lectures at the Hochschule für die Wissenschaft des Judentums in Berlin.[102] Strauss's commitment to Jewish education is particularly evident in his recruitment activities on behalf of the Kartell Verband jüdischer Verbindungen (K.j.V.) as a senior alumnus (*alter Herr*). In 1925 Strauss was a member of K.j.V.'s "Saronia" chapter in Frankfurt and then Altona-Hamburg in 1928.[103] His writings in *Der jüdische Student*,[104] the K.j.V.'s official organ, and his lectures delivered at Zionist youth camps demonstrate that Strauss could hardly be viewed as an unattached or free-floating intellectual.[105] Strauss recruited Jewish students in the university, with apparently mixed results. He failed in his tireless efforts to convince Jacob Klein, another student of Heidegger, to become a Zionist, but their subsequent lifelong friendship was sprinkled with Strauss's playfully sly and rebellious Jewish politics. Strauss also worked behind the scenes to advance his anti-Orthodox vision of Jewish education. In the fall of 1923, for example, Strauss wrote to his fellow Zionist *Bundesbruder*, Joseph Meisl (1883–1958),[106] regarding the establishment of Zionist schools in districts of Hesse such as Kassel. Strauss elaborated a strategy to advance legislation that would facilitate the inculcations of a Jewish national consciousness for Jewish students in Hessen schools. Meisl served as the general secretary of the Jewish Community of Berlin from 1915 to 1934 in addition to holding several other positions of communal leadership. Strauss made his case by sketching the political and legal conditions that produced a peculiarly conservative and "thickheaded" Jewish constituency under the administrative domination of an ineffective Orthodox rabbinate.[107]

Strauss's commitment to politicize Jewish consciousness[108] into a national one may be seen as a Zionist appropriation of Rosenzweig's formulation of a new task of Jewish thought and learning. Rosenzweig declared that God's truth must be approached from the double perspective of philosophy and theology, by the Jewish believer and unbeliever.[109] Indeed, Rosenzweig's commitment to Jewish education was specifically aimed at the passions of the assimilated German Jew, the Jew who found the Jewish tradition and its texts alien and inaccessible. Strauss may have been brought up in a rural orthoprax Jewish home and therefore familiar with the form of Jewish liturgy, but he identified with a generation of German Jews who, in the midst of dissimilation, gravitated toward some concrete and affirmative form of Judaism and Jewishness.

Strauss's early Jewish education was emblematic of the majority of German-Jewish youth of his generation who attended non-Jewish public schools.[110] A

*Leo Strauss and the Politics of Exile*

paltry two hours per week of religious instruction was hardly enough to instill rudimentary tools beyond a superficial familiarity with the Hebrew Bible and Jewish holidays. Strauss's writings presented a strong critique of liberal Judaism, but this certainly did not mean that he believed in and followed the tenets of Orthodoxy. Instead, he was moving toward a radical self-understanding of modern atheism in part by challenging the Enlightenment's disregard for prescientific religion rooted in the possibility and reality of divine revelation as a miraculous rather than natural event. By the mid-1920s, Strauss sought to recapture the intensity of the pitched battles waged between Orthodoxy and atheism in the sixteenth and seventeenth centuries before the latter's claim to ultimate victory. Alienation and distance from tradition rather than simple betrayal (*Vera*) assume a decisive role in Strauss's understanding not only of Spinoza's thought, but also of his own predicament as a modern Jewish thinker.[111]

For Strauss, Spinoza's alienation and distance from the Jewish tradition prefigured the German-Jewish predicament that informed the beginnings and aims of Rosenzweig's intellectual and institutional efforts. In the winter of 1929, while Strauss was revising his first book on Spinoza in order to satisfy Guttmann's concerns, Rosenzweig died. Strauss delivered a eulogy in which he celebrated his former mentor as the true founder of the institution for which Strauss now worked, the Akademie für die Wissenschaft des Judentums.[112] In Strauss's understanding, Rosenzweig's great pedagogic contribution was intended as a Jewish action. Rosenzweig did not intend this new academic institution to practice value-free science. Instead, Rosenzweig "insisted with an unforgettable urgency, that the norm of all science of Judaism be responsibility for existence as Jews." His passionate commitment to the rebirth of a Jewish science, Strauss remarked, "will always remind all those who toil for the sake of this science of their true task."[113] Strauss's portrait of Rosenzweig's vision of the Akademie was undoubtedly intended as a rebuke of the value-free model of detached scientific investigation that the Akademie had assumed. And considering that Strauss adduced the mangled elements of his book to the censorious conditions that Guttmann, the Akademie's director, imposed upon him, Strauss's dedication of the book to Franz Rosenzweig might signal his allegiance to a German-Jewish countertradition that sought to subvert the German-Jewish mainstream. But most powerfully, the dedication to Rosenzweig deepens our appreciation for the deep philosophical and theological allegiances that Strauss felt toward his deceased mentor.

## Reassessing Tradition: Heidegger and Rosenzweig

The philosopher Karl Löwith, who had successfully completed his *Habilitationsschrift* under Heidegger's direction, remarked that if there were anyone who could be called a contemporary of Heidegger's, it would be Franz Rosenzweig.[114] Indeed, in one of the last essays Rosenzweig wrote, he himself acknowledged a striking kinship between his and Heidegger's "New Thinking."[115] Yet Rosenzweig was virtually unknown to the inner circle of Heidegger's students, many of whom came from assimilated Jewish backgrounds. While Strauss may not have been initiated into Heidegger's inner circle of teaching assistants,[116] during the course of his philosophical studies at Freiburg and Marburg, Strauss developed strong intellectual bonds with many of them, and may have been responsible for introducing Löwith himself to Rosenzweig's Jewish thought.[117] One element that distinguishes Strauss as a Weimar Jewish intellectual was that he bridged the sharpest intellectual currents in realms of both German as well as specifically German-Jewish thought. The two most important philosophical figures who exercised inspiration on the young Strauss were Martin Heidegger and Franz Rosenzweig.

Martin Heidegger is not mentioned by name in any of Strauss's early publications. Yet his influence is central if we are to grasp the restless and agitated movement of Strauss's early thought. While Strauss's writings were anything but systematic, one object of his discontent, if not scorn, remained virtually consistent: liberalism. Shades of liberalism were seen in any modern movement or ideology that sought to secure principles of tolerance and social equality. Strauss found liberalism to be dishonest because in the effort to achieve its goals of consensus, decisive tensions and oppositions were overlooked and blunted. The matrix of liberalism in modern Germany was constituted by an embrace of the principles of 1789, cultural Protestantism, Enlightenment rationalism, belief in historical progress, and the ideal of value-free science.

It is instructive to note that two of the most powerful figures to emerge out of Weimar's radical-conservative vortex were Catholics: Martin Heidegger and Carl Schmitt. The Prussian coercion exercised in the Kulturkampf against the Catholic minority in the last third of the nineteenth century certainly conditioned Catholic resentment for the newly emerging liberal nation-state. And even though Heidegger and Schmitt had checkered relations with the church,[118] Strauss's view of alienation and distance regarding German Jewry provides an interesting comparison to the German-Catholic condition. While Heidegger served as a source of intellectual direction, Schmitt emerged as a would-be ally in the radical-conservative attempt to break out of the shackles of liberalism by critically revisiting its sources.

In 1922, having just earned his doctorate, Strauss periodically attended Heidegger's course in Freiburg on Aristotle. According to Strauss's later reflections, he sat in these courses "without understanding a word, but sensed that he [Heidegger] dealt with something of the utmost importance to man as man." Strauss's breakthrough moment in understanding Heidegger occurred during one of Heidegger's early Freiburg courses in which he turned his attention to the beginning of Aristotle's *Metaphysics*. Strauss remarked that he had never before "heard nor seen such a . . . thorough and intensive interpretation of a

*Leo Strauss and the Politics of Exile*

philosophic text." Recounting the same story elsewhere, we learn that Strauss reported to Rosenzweig "that in comparison to Heidegger," the towering figure of Max Weber—the figure whom just prior to this event Strauss claims to have revered as "the incarnation of the spirit of science and scholarship"[119]—now "appeared to me as an orphan child in regard to precision, and probing, and competence." Or, as he states elsewhere, Weber's stature diminished to that of "destitute waif."[120] And Heidegger's impact was deep on the young doctor: "I had never seen before such seriousness, profundity, and concentration in the interpretation of philosophic texts."[121]

Strauss repeats in several places his judgment that Heidegger was indisputably superior to all of his peers. Strauss expounds on the particular dynamics of Heidegger's charisma in a memorial essay in honor of Kurt Riezler.[122] Preceding Strauss's treatment of Riezler's role during the legendary confrontation between Heidegger and Cassirer at Davos in 1929, Strauss tells us that Heidegger's unrivaled philosophical prowess was evident well before Heidegger had become "known to the general public."[123] Drawing on his early exposure to Heidegger in the early 1920s, Strauss offers the following assessment: "As soon as he appeared on the scene, he stood at the center and he began to dominate it. His domination grew almost continuously in extent and in intensity. He gave adequate expression to the prevailing unrest and dissatisfaction because he had clarity and certainty, if not about the whole way, at least about the first and decisive steps. The fermentation or the tempest gradually ceased." The chaotic dissonance of Weimar provided the backdrop for Heidegger's dramatic entrance onto the center of the stage. Heidegger's commanding presence utterly captivated Strauss and his generation. During his presentations, whether in a classroom or at a public disputation at Davos, the audience would eventually become so enraptured that they would find their critical faculties paralyzed.

[P]hilosophizing seems to have been transformed into listening with reverence to the incipient *mythoi* of Heidegger:

> *tum pietate gravem et meritis si forte virum quem*
> *conspexere, silent arrectisque auribus adstant*[124]

The quotation is drawn from the *Aeneid*, where Virgil compares Neptune's calming of the waves to a masterful politician who is able to quell a riotous urban mob. The incited crowd suddenly falls "silent with attentive ears" once they see the great "man dignified by piety and merit."[125] At some points in the above account, Strauss appears to write from the perspective of a listener present during Heidegger's performance at the Davos exchange with Cassirer. But for the present discussion, Strauss's description of the spellbound effect of listening to Heidegger applies, as we have seen, to Heidegger as "soon as he appeared on the scene" as Husserl's assistant at Freiburg.

These anecdotes about philosophic giants hold our interest on several counts. In the interest of determining what Strauss found so compelling in Heidegger's course on Aristotle, and subsequent audited courses, we get an inkling of the powerful effect that Heidegger had upon Strauss and his contemporaries: a model of a new kind of philosophy and the charismatic pedagogy that went with it. Rather than speculate about a direct line of influence, I now take into account some striking affinities with Heidegger in this period as well as the larger backdrop of radical theology and the existentialist turn in philosophy.

In Strauss's first works, the spirit of Heidegger's radical interpretive technique of *Destruktion*—simultaneously clearing and uprooting the unconscious distortions inherited by historical traditions of philosophy and "laying bare" of the authentic and pure roots—informs the criticism of the foundations of the modern liberal state and its culture. Charles Bambach explains that Heidegger's formulation of *Destruktion* by the early 1920s "connotes something other than mere 'destruction'; it also has the positive sense of removing obstacles by de-structuring them and opening up a space wherein what is de-structured can reveal itself." We can get an inkling of the power that Heidegger's *Destruktion* would have on Strauss's account of present German Judaism by going back to one of Heidegger's earliest formulations of its intended purpose. In 1920 Heidegger saw *Destruktion* as a philosophical tool "rendering uncertain one's own existence [*Dasein*]."[126] And by rendering this situatedness a primary focus of questioning, Heidegger transformed philosophical speculation into a matter of urgent relevance where one's place in a tradition became the opening for a radical critique of tradition. Heidegger explains in *Being and Time* that "[t]radition takes what has come down to us and delivers it over to self-evidence; it blocks our access to those primordial 'sources' from which the categories and concepts handed down to us have been in part quite genuinely drawn."[127] Thus, *Destruktion* was deployed in order to make uncanny (or defamiliarize) past thought that had become reduced by tradition into a soporific satisfaction and comfort with the present. This complacency was induced by tradition's forgetfulness of its own origins and a concomitant reification of its present normative status.[128] While Strauss may not have followed Heidegger in exploring "primordial experiences," Strauss saw Heidegger as opening up "the possibility of a genuine return to classical philosophy, to the philosophy of Plato and Aristotle."[129]

These later reflections provide a testament to the unbridled anticipation with which Strauss and other talented brash philosophers received Heidegger's critique of Husserl. Heidegger turned everything against itself and on its head. While Husserl critiqued neo-Kantianism for beginning with the roof, Heidegger saw Husserl as doing the same. The first and most fundamental way in which the world was approached by the Greeks was not to see things as mere object, but rather as "*pragmata*," things that are at hand for use. According to Strauss, Heidegger's critique of Husserl and modern philosophy compelled a questioning of whether the most advanced modern philosophical paradigms fail to envision the basic contours of how ancient philosophers understood the world. At issue are two key concepts that appear as major turn signals in Strauss's development through the 1920s and 1930s: how insight and meaning are conditioned on the *horizon* and *orientation* of the finite existence of the concerned interpreter. "The horizon within which Husserl had analyzed the world of pre-scientific understanding was the pure consciousness as the absolute being. Heidegger questioned that orientation by referring to the fact that the inner time belonging to this time is necessarily finite and even constituted by man's mortality."[130] In these later reflections, Strauss consistently condemns Heidegger for his choice in 1933 to "side with Hitler" and lend philosophical legitimacy to National Socialism.[131] Strauss also dubiously claims that he was so troubled by the amoral aspect of Heidegger's thought in the 1920s that he did not follow his subsequent development.[132] There is evidence from Strauss's correspondence with Hans Georg Gadamer, Jacob Klein, Karl Löwith, Hans Jonas, Martin Buber, and Helmut Kuhn that Strauss kept abreast of many of Heidegger's writings after *Being and Time*.

Second, we find Strauss immersed in an almost desperate milieu of spiritual responses to the crumbling of the old order and a simultaneous corrosion of self-confidence in modern technological solutions. Heidegger, Schmitt, and Rosenzweig were just three figures who articulated critiques and visions by fusing together the ultramodern with the archaic. Rosenzweig, who was also dedicated to new ways of recovering the vitality of premodern truths, eventually called attention to the affinities between his and Heidegger's new thinking in one of his last writings, "Exchanged Fronts" ("Vertauschte Fronten").[133]

Rosenzweig's essay offered a peculiar depiction of the legendary debates that transpired between Cassirer and Heidegger at the second annual Davos congress in March and April 1929.[134] Rosenzweig's reference to the debates is just one indication of the wider significance of the Davos debates, which were attended by some three hundred students and forty faculty, and sent reverberations well beyond the specific field of Kant interpretation, the topic upon which Cassirer and Heidegger delivered presentations.[135] Some reports indicate that Strauss may have himself attended the Davos congress, but Strauss himself never explicitly stated that he attended, and there has yet to appear any concrete record that he did so.[136] Davos 1929 became a highly anticipated philosophical event: Heidegger's *Being and Time* (1927) and the last volume of Cassirer's *Philosophy of Symbolic Forms* (1929) challenged each other as fundamental starting places in contemporary Continental philosophy.

Rosenzweig portrayed the event as a debate between "Cassirer, Cohen's most distinguished disciple" and "Heidegger, the Husserl disciple and Aristotelian scholastic" and holder of Cohen's chair of philosophy at Marburg.[137] Cassirer was the representative of the "old thinking" of the Marburg School whereas Heidegger, not even being aware of it, represented the "new thinking" that Hermann Cohen put forth at the end of his career. Thus Heidegger, in opposing

Cassirer, Cohen's most prominent student, paradoxically became the rightful successor to Cohen's chair in philosophy. And Rosenzweig identified his own understanding of human existence and the process of the individual's self-recognition with that of Heidegger.

Strauss reflected that the confrontation marked the undisputed death of German idealism.[138] Heidegger's devastating critique of Cassirer "revealed the lostness and emptiness of this remarkable representative [Cassirer] of established academic philosophy to everyone who had eyes."[139] Strauss's later analysis follows Rosenzweig's stress on Cassirer's divergence from Cohen's most vital contribution. Whereas Rosenzweig saw the essential difference as the new thinking versus the old thinking, however, Strauss, echoing his aforementioned critique of Cassirer, claimed that the key difference between Cassirer and Cohen related to the question of ethics.[140] While Cohen's philosophic system centered on ethics, "Cassirer had transformed Cohen's system into a new system of philosophy in which ethics had completely disappeared." The problem of ethics in modern philosophy had been "silently dropped" by Cassirer. Heidegger, by contrast, directly faced the problem.[141] Whereas Cassirer abandoned any attempt to present a rational foundation for ethics, Heidegger seized the issue by obliterating it. Strauss therefore saw the debates as setting the stage for a triumph of philosophical nihilism. The greatest area of significance of Davos in Strauss's own development relates to a public intellectual's responsibility not to retreat from the most radical philosophical implications when battling for the best young minds.

Strauss's 1924 essay on Hermann Cohen's analysis of Spinoza's biblical criticism can be seen as Strauss's attempt to "uproot" the inherited views of Spinoza during his dramatic reception in Germany since the close of the eighteenth century. German-Jewish eyes tended to see Spinoza either as the model of the new Jewish citizen-philosopher or as an unfeeling heretic who was disloyal to his people in a time of need. Strauss called for a new basis to form an independent judgment on the matter: a return to Spinoza's classic work, the *Theologico-Political Treatise*, viewed from the perspective of a long tradition of criticism of revealed religion.[142] Strauss's essay on Cohen's approach to Spinoza impressed Julius Guttmann who had become the director of the Akademie für Wissenschaft des Judentums. Guttmann appointed Strauss as a staff researcher (*Mitarbeiter*) assigned to the history of Jewish philosophy. While in Berlin, Strauss struck up friendships with the young Jewish historians Gershom Scholem, Fritz Bamberger, and Fritz (Yitzhak) Baer. Strauss worked on the Akademie's collaborative publication of Moses Mendelssohn's complete writings, but the thrust of his energies were dedicated to the seventeenth-century Dutch philosopher Baruch (Benedictus) Spinoza and the traditions of religion critique that preceded him and that followed in the wake of his revolutionary and decidedly secular method of biblical criticism. According to Strauss, Spinoza's greatest significance lay in his approach to the Bible as an ordinary object of historical literary analysis, a move that aimed at the demotion of clerical authority and intentionally paved the way toward the modern liberal state and society.

This liberal goal required that Spinoza, as well as the Enlightenment as a whole, take aim at the tradition of divine revelation as the most important opponent. Strauss's voice is unambiguous when he called attention to the historical invention of "prejudice" in modern metaphysics.[143] In order for "the struggle of Enlightenment" to have meaning, it needed to define itself in opposition to "prejudice." Thus "the age of freedom" required the historical construction of a fixed opponent to overcome, "the age of prejudice." The invention of "prejudice" as a historical category, Strauss claimed, "constitutes the difference between the struggle of the Enlightenment against prejudices and the struggle against appearance and opinion with which philosophy began its secular journey."[144] If "prejudice" was merely a straw man that the Enlightenment constructed in order to win over Europe to its ideal of freedom, then Strauss found himself critically disposed to find and recover subterranean teachings that might otherwise be dismissed or forgotten.

## Antisemitism and Zionism

From the earliest published writings Strauss sought to smash the coveted idols of Enlightenment rationalism as he questioned the intellectual substrate of the political principles emanating from the French Revolution. Many young Zionists were drawn to the rebellion against the bourgeois assimilationist aspirations of their parents' generation, but rebellion would not be sufficient. A decisive political account, emerging from within and against the historical development of German Jewry, was necessary. In order to survey and assess all of the available standpoints, one needed to break commonly held conventions boldly. Strauss in part puts forward his argument in the spirit of transgressing certain unwritten strictures of diasporic Jewish discourse and consciousness. Strauss saw Herzl's conscious use of antisemitic rhetoric in the pages of *Die Welt* as a model for a new type of Jewish thinking, one unhindered by apologetic concerns.[145] Michael Zank notes that by using the pejorative term "Mauschel" *and* by bringing this internal Jewish fight into the public arena, Herzl broke two major taboos of the exilic mentality.[146] In the eyes of the young, defiant Strauss, Herzl's brazenness signaled a revolutionary change in Jewish consciousness. Are we not secure enough to sling antisemitic charges of hypocrisy in instances where Jews act ignobly? Strauss went fishing in troubled rather than still waters in order to make a further breakthrough.

Franz Rosenzweig had assessed the virtues and limitations of "apologetic thinking."[147] Rosenzweig understands Maimonides' *The Guide of the Perplexed* as exemplifying a mode of thinking that passionately engages perceived threats or potential threats to Judaism. According to Rosenzweig, "this thinking has what systematic thinking cannot have so easily: the fascination—and truthfulness—of thought reacting to the occasion; but therefore a limit is also set for it which only systematic thinking removes: exactly the limit of the occasional; only systematic thinking determines the circle of its objects itself; apologetic thinking remains dependent on the cause, the adversary." Rosenzweig's description of the occasionalist aspect of Jewish apologetic thinking aptly captures the genre of Strauss's Weimar Jewish writings as well as the predicament that Strauss consciously attempted to overcome. In Rosenzweig's understanding, the Jewish thinker defended or reframed Judaism in response to some external stimuli that called into question some element of Judaism. The Jewish thinker, however, had to be mindful of the effects of his thinking on the vulnerable Jewish community in which he lived. The external impetus to Jewish apologetics meant that "[a]nyone who was supposed to reflect on Judaism had somehow, if not psychologically then at least spiritually, to be torn at the border of Judaism. . . . [H]is thinking was then determined by the power which had led him to the border, and the depth horizon of his gaze was determined by the degree to which he had been carried to, on, or across the border."

Strauss dedicated his first book to Rosenzweig's memory and earlier took up the challenge to explore unapologetic approaches to the situation of German Jewry; as part of that endeavor he wondered whether antisemitism might exert a positive influence on Zionism. Strauss notes that his argument will be of no practical use for the all too common practice of Jewish apologetics. The realm of antisemitism has nothing to do "with the simpler and coarser things" such as "figures and charts" preferred by those narrow-minded technicians only interested in apologetics.[148] Strauss clearly is trying to push the boundaries of what may be considered acceptable to think and to publicly state. This mission of overcoming the apologetic *galut* mentality is obvious in his analysis of "Zionism and Antisemitism."[149] He opens the piece with the stark line: "Motto: Joshua 9:7. That passage reads: The men of Israel replied to the Hivites, 'But perhaps you live among us; how then can we make a pact with you?'" For Strauss, these lines held a completely "unambiguous" meaning when applied "to our situation in the *galut*." While Strauss did not explicate the meaning intended here, there is an implicit logic that emerges from shrewd political realism. Modern Jews must consider their contemporary position of powerlessness in the *galut* through the unclouded eyes of those who possess the seat of power. Thucydides, Machiavelli, Hobbes, and the entire realist tradition would agree that claims based upon mercy, justice, or even promises of a mutually advantageous peace do not hold much currency in a world governed by enmity and power. The kernel of political Zionism, once separated from its Enlightenment shell, follows this line of realism. The prognosis for Jewish integration into Europe that emerges from a cold unclouded Zionist analysis is unambiguously negative. And here we find the shared perspectives of a post-Enlightenment political Zionism and antisemitism.

Strauss's realist vision of Zionism is evidenced if we return to the verse from

Joshua, which occurs in the context of the commanded Israelite conquest of Palestine. Just as the ancient Israelites were loath to accept the existence of alien inhabitants, regardless of the latter's expressed intentions to accept Israel's rule, so must modern Jews expect the same intolerance from their host nations. Any clear-sighted view of Jewish politics must then account for exclusion, intolerance, and coercive persecution as an ever-present feature of Jewish life in exile.[150] But such a fundamental distrust of human nature does not mean that an individual, or even a diasporic nation, cannot hold true to a higher vision of justice while immersed in such conditions. As soon as life in the diaspora is seen as holding forth the possibility of total social integration and political redemption, the binding force of *galut* existence has been lost and so too its will to live in defiance of the world's ignominy. Although Strauss's political Zionism militated against any valorization of *galut,* he nevertheless questioned whether the call for a negation of *galut* amounted to a call for the negation of an essential component of Jewish existence.[151]

For Strauss a morally directed calculus of political realism directs us to what are Jewish interests: the reality of force must not be moralized as a negative, but rather taken into account when measuring courses of action or inaction toward Jewish goals. This might also be called "moral radicalism." In his critique of Max Nordau (1923), Strauss recognized the inner contradiction between morality and politics that occurs when a perspective of courageous realism is replaced by some form of naturalized teleology. "The Zionism of Max Nordau" appeared in *Der Jude* in the wake of Nordau's death and provides an early glimpse into Strauss's uncanny tendency to expose a Zionist's vision. Strauss exposes Nordau's vision of Jewish national liberation as not sufficiently radical to effect a true break from *galut* consciousness. Nordau privately criticized Herzl's reliance on deception and shady dealings as a means to achieve national independence. Strauss sees the fundamental weakness of Nordau's thought as emerging from his inability to acknowledge the actual situation and interests that orient his thought toward a spiritual vision of Zionism that rejects the power politics and ethically shameful methods attributed to Herzl's political Zionism. He concludes the essay by comparing Nordau's ambivalence regarding political Zionism to the militaristic rule of Spartans over the enslaved helots: "He [Nordau] has the contemporary sympathy for the helots, and corresponding indignation at the Spartans. But it is self-evident for him that he must replace the helotry of assimilation with the Spartan spirit of Zionism."[152] This unresolved conclusion raises the question: if Jews become rulers who secure the obedience of aliens by force (like Spartans), won't they lose something unique? It is only in persisting in the abject condition of abnormality that the possibility for Jewish existence is most profoundly maximized. Strauss looked at the condition of *galut* as underlying the central paradox of the Jews, but not in entirely negative terms: *galut* affords "the Jewish people a maximum possibility of existence [*Daseinsmöglichkeit*] through a condition of minimum normality [*Normalität*]."[153] The voice here is ambiguous; it would appear that this last line is simply pushing Nordau's argument to its logical end, but as Nordau never explicitly comes up with any such similar formulation, we know that there is something of Strauss in these lines.

The formulation of the paradox seems more akin to Heidegger than Nordau in that Strauss is exploring the greatest potential for human existence in relation to a condition that is radically unstable. Strauss did periodically attend Heidegger's course in Freiburg in 1922 and had been quite eager to inform Rosenzweig of Heidegger's innovative interpretive prowess. And, while never considered one of the true insiders of the Heideggerian circle, he developed various degrees of intellectual intimacy with those at the center of the circle: Karl Löwith, Jacob Klein, and Hans-Georg Gadamer.[154] One might compare Strauss's essay on Nordau with Heidegger's "Introduction to Aristotle" (based on the 1922 course), but the texts are different in both genre and scope. Heidegger was working his way through phenomenology as he approached a pillar of the Western philosophical canon. Strauss, by contrast, demolished a leading Zionist while seeking to determine the position and direction of German-Jewish politics. Both texts nevertheless investigate how the possibilities of existence become formulated and reevaluated in light of the concrete situatedness of the interpreter in the present. Rather than arguing for a fundamental influence, I see some intriguing similarities as a mark of the changing discourse away from earlier romantic trends in *Lebensphilosophie* and toward a new existentialism.

## Schmitt and the Political

If Heidegger is important to this period of Strauss's career, Schmitt also becomes important because Strauss perceived him as not only a senior ally engaged in the critique of liberalism, but as a fellow searcher on the quest to discover an alternative political cosmos. At the same time, Schmitt is important as a thinker outside the German-Jewish subculture who conferred legitimacy on Strauss's abilities and scholarly project.

Schmitt's *Concept of the Political* first appeared in 1927 and reinforced his reputation as a provocative theorist who directly engaged foundational issues of public law and political theory. Schmitt's *Political Theology* (1922) famously begins by defining the sovereign as "he who decides the state of exception [*Ausnahmezustand*]." Sovereignty is not defined by governing conventions and norms, but rather emerges in full clarity at the fateful moment when the suspension of legal and constitutional norms is authorized. Rather than view the imposition of martial law and the suspension of political procedural norms as an exceptional case, applying only to emergency situations, Schmitt conceives this extraordinary moment of an emergency (*Ernstfall*) as defining the fundamental basis of rule. The state of exception in politics is analogous to the miracle in theology. God's majesty over the world used to be clearly determined by his decisive ability to suspend the ordinary laws of nature. But just as liberal theology has difficulty in recognizing the centrality of miracles to religion, so too does liberal political thought have a problem in locating the decisive act that reveals the fundamental godlike character of sovereignty.

We can see how such language may have tapped into the "theological awakening" that affected Strauss following the end of the war and into the early 1920s. Schmitt's political theology cut to the core problems of legitimacy and self-clarity with which Weimar and liberalism more generally struggled. In *Concept of the Political* (1927) Schmitt states that politics fundamentally turns on the distinction between friend and enemy. Liberal political systems have great difficulty in seeing politics so clearly because of their principled embrace of tolerance and pluralism. Enmity, however, for Schmitt characterizes political reality.

In Schmitt's understanding of Hobbes, the fundamental enmity within a commonwealth is neutralized as private acceptable disagreements because of an overarching faith in an unqualified obligation to obey the sovereign's public opinion as truth.[155] While Hobbes aimed at diffusing potential sources of rebellion based on conscience, Schmitt pointed out that the systematic neutralization of views about the most important matters amounted to a type of repression that could not and ought not be sustained. Ultimately, subjects must decide their political loyalties based upon the real possibility of killing and being killed. How could—and why would—a citizen of a state stake everything on the basis of agnosticism?

Strauss revisited Hobbes in his 1932 critique of Schmitt's *Concept of the Political* (second edition), and subsequently marked the appearance of this review as coinciding with a "change of orientation" in his own thought.[156] Through his commentary on Schmitt we can see both important affinities and differences with Schmitt. Furthermore, the various changes in Schmitt's conceptualization of political and legal theory may be a dramatic case study of the German-Jewish dialogue, even if (or precisely if) it was a "hidden dialogue," as Heinrich Meier has attempted to demonstrate.[157]

Strauss's "Comments on Carl Schmitt's *Concept of the Political*" (1932) reveals his overlapping interest in Jewish political thought and general political thought. Strauss turned to Thomas Hobbes, just as he had with Spinoza, as a pillar of the modern world. What should be recalled about Strauss's Jewish thought is the centrality of *galut* in navigating his way through Jewish philosophy and Zionist ideology. Jews in Germany who are not consciously national Jews, in Strauss's view, have simply forgotten the fundamental condition of *galut*. They have placed their hopes in a cultured world and the security of a liberal state that leaves behind the intolerance, persecution, and enmity Jews had suffered in the premodern age of superstition. The complement to this postulate in Strauss's non-Jewish politics is that liberals and socialists have forgotten that human beings are inherently evil and politics must take into account this underlying fact. Strauss views as successful Hobbes's program of extricating man from an unbearably insecure and fearful state of nature and providing for the possibility of commodious life under the construct of a state apparatus. But the program became too successful. People have forgotten the preliberal condition of humanity.

Attuned to the positive and negative views of a condition fraught with insecurity, Strauss was able to decipher Schmitt's inconsistent statements regarding Hobbesian politics. One method Strauss employed in order to crystallize Schmitt's intention was to contrast Schmitt's view of politics with that of Hobbes and liberalism as it developed after Hobbes. Whereas Schmitt embraced the state of nature (on the group level) as a normative guide to authentic politics, Hobbes viewed it only polemically, as an intolerable condition consisting of constant enmity between individuals in which men are anxiously occupied by the fear of suffering an untimely violent death. Strauss vividly presents these differences:

> Hobbes differs from developed liberalism only, but decisively, by his knowing and seeing *against what* the liberal ideal of civilization has to be persistently fought for: not merely against rotten institutions, against the evil will of a ruling class, but against the natural evil of man; in an unliberal world Hobbes forges ahead to lay the foundation of liberalism against the—*sit venia verbo*—unliberal nature of man, whereas later men, ignorant of their premises and goals, trust in the original goodness (based on God's creation and providence) of human nature, or on the basis of natural-scientific neutrality, nurse hopes for an improvement of nature, hopes unjustified by man's experience of himself. Hobbes, in view of the state of nature, attempts to overcome the state of nature within the limits in which it allows of being overcome, whereas later men either dream up a state of nature or, on the basis of a supposed deeper insight into history and therewith into the essence of man, forget the state of nature. But—in all fairness to later men—ultimately that dreaming and that oblivion are merely the consequence of the negation of the state of nature, merely the consequence of the position of civilization introduced by Hobbes.[158]

Strauss explains that liberalism, "sheltered by and engrossed in a world of culture, forgets the foundation of culture, the state of nature, that is, human nature in its dangerousness and its being endangered."[159] Schmitt returned to Hobbes "in order to strike at the root of liberalism" and reverse Hobbes's intention of negating the state of nature. Schmitt confronted "the liberal negation of the political with the position of the political, that is, with the recognition of the reality of the political." Schmitt viewed the state of nature as "totalities engaged in enmity, alliance, and neutrality," a condition that is not only possible, but real and necessary.[160] The difference between Schmitt and Hobbes regarding the state of nature, according to Strauss, is determined by their differing historical contexts. "Whereas Hobbes in an unliberal world accomplishes the founding of liberalism, Schmitt in a liberal world undertakes the critique of liberalism."[161]

Strauss's foray into the waters of Hobbes and Schmitt is a natural extension of Strauss's earlier Jewish writings. For example, the disturbing passage of Joshua 9:7 that Strauss selected as his Zionist motto cuts to the central political problem of Hobbes's political theory: how can fundamental enmity be set aside for a binding covenant? It may be recalled that in Strauss's analysis of Jewish suffering, he posited the national will to survive as something reaffirmed by each generation choosing Jewish existence in the face of inevitable persecution. A way of restating Strauss's 1923 formulation of the *galut*'s paradox, given his concerns with Schmitt, would be that the greatest possibility of political existence is secured only under minimal conditions of normality. For Schmitt, man would cease to be human if he were liberated from the political (defined by a permanent opposition between friend and foe). For Strauss, the Jew would cease to be Jewish if he were redeemed from the *galut*. The *galut* approximates the condition of the dire emergency (*Ernstfall*) in Schmitt's politics or even the confrontation with nothingness in Heidegger's philosophy. Schmitt posits that "[a]ll genuine political theories must presuppose man's dangerousness."[162] This belief in human nature as inherently dangerous fits the fundamental conservative conviction that legitimates the need for dominion.[163]

Strauss stated that the primary intention of his review of Schmitt was to reveal the requisites of the "urgent task" of a "radical critique of liberalism." Strauss concludes his notes by arguing that Schmitt's critique of liberalism is necessarily limited because it takes place within "the horizon of liberalism." Schmitt's "unliberal tendency is restrained by the still unvanquished 'systematics of liberal thought.' The critique introduced by Schmitt against liberalism can therefore be completed only if one succeeds in gaining a horizon beyond liberalism. In such a horizon Hobbes completed the foundation of liberalism. A radical critique of liberalism is thus possible only on the basis of an adequate understanding of Hobbes."[164]

Strauss's own pursuit of the "urgent task" laid out by Schmitt would be enabled by Schmitt's letter of recommendation to the Rockefeller Foundation. Strauss's fellowship sending him abroad coincided with the collapse of the Weimar Republic and the establishment of the Third Reich. We shall see in the next chapter how these events affected the relationship between Strauss and Schmitt.

In one forgotten Zionist essay, Strauss begins with Sigmund Freud's *Future of an Illusion* (1928) in order to set the stage for a dialectical analysis of various forms of Zionism in the present "age of atheism."[165] Strauss goes through various Zionist attempts to forge an identity given the impossibility of a direct return to premodern Judaism. Strauss turns his critical eye toward the political Zionist response to the problem of exile. Jacob Klatzkin (1882–1948),[166] for example, rested his "decisionistic" response to the "crisis" of Judaism on a militant rejection of the *galut*.[167] Strauss argued that Klatzkin's strategy stemmed from the misguided view that the will to normalcy ought to be the driving factor, "the first word," of political Zionism. Strauss connects Freud's demystification of religion to Klatzkin's vitalist construction of Jewish national identity. Because traditional religion has now been demystified and is now considered to be a "lie," the Jewish nation must not ground itself on theological lies, but rather on itself, "on its labor, on its land, and on its state."[168] But these secular political elements are not sufficient for a new basis of a Jewish worldview. Even if supplemented or replaced by cultural criteria, Zionism seems unable to fill the void once occupied by uncompromised premodern Jewish existence as elect enjoying a unique relationship with God. Strauss draws attention to the secular basis of the present; yet he confounds the claims put forth by a seemingly necessary atheist-based vision of Zionism to meet the urgent spiritual problem of Jewish existence.

Strauss's essay provoked a hostile response in *Der jüdische Student*. The exchanges between Max Joseph and Strauss delineate some of the fault lines within student Zionist politics. In all three of Joseph's spirited responses, Strauss is portrayed as a "propagandist of Atheism" who wishes to exclude any type of religious sensibility or attachment to Judaism from the ranks of the Zionist movement.[169] Strauss dismisses out of hand Joseph's portrait. Never willing to make a compromise with an opponent, however, Strauss goes on to argue that the actual conditions of the present—assimilation and secularization—are more effective than any speech or article.[170]

In terms of political theory, political Zionism's will to normality (*Normalität*), security, and peace, assumes the same place of motive that compels men to strike a covenant and exit the Hobbesian state of nature.[171] But Strauss recognizes that this will to normality is operative in both assimilation and Zionism. The messianic hope for a return to Zion as an idea was prevalent in the *galut*. Once coupled with messianism, however, Zionism loses its sense of realism. Assimilation separated messianism from Zionism "in order to facilitate the easy death of the Jewish people in Europe by abandoning Zionism and watering down messianism into missionism." Missionism, the liberal doctrine that Jews are endowed with the *mission* to set an ethical example for the rest of the nations to follow, Strauss argues, is motivated solely by Western "Jewish egoism." He finds it to be a particularly odious and disdainful doctrine because it "secularizes the ideas of the *galut*, which for all their mysticism, had a very sober vital function." Assimilation substitutes the fixed boundaries of ghetto consciousness with the "illusory trust in civilized humanity."[172]

In "Ecclesia militans" (1925),[173] Strauss defended Herzlian Zionism against the counterattack waged by Isaac Breuer (1883–1946), the leader of the Frankfurt separatist Orthodox community and the first president of Poalei Agudat Yisrael.[174] The article was written with the ironic use of military metaphors of offensives and counteroffensives between Orthodoxy and Zionism and reflects deep factions among Orthodoxy, Zionism, and liberal assimilation. But Strauss's critical eye looks to the standards that each movement uses as an authoritative guide. Orthodoxy appeals to tradition, whereas Strauss's vision of Zionism appeals to reason. Strauss urged Orthodoxy to acknowledge the legitimate motives that impel Jews toward Zionism. It is true that Zionism may take a position distant from God and the rule of God's Torah, but this position arises from the Enlightenment critique of religion, not simple rebellion or betrayal based on Epicurean motives. While a nonreflective Zionism may aspire to be like other nations, Strauss argues for a self-critical Zionism that interprets chosenness as reaching beyond the fate of becoming a people of "merchants and lawyers."[175] The will to normalcy posited in Herzlian Zionism is simply not a sufficient motive for a self-critical Zionism.

In "Cohen's Analysis of Spinoza's Bible Science" ("Cohens Analyse der Bibel-Wissenschaft Spinozas") (1924),[176] Strauss's approach to Cohen's criticism of Spinoza's *Theologico-Political Treatise* rests on a conceptual distinction between the motive and intention behind Spinoza's work. Strauss sought to disentangle Spinoza's motive—the various factors impelling Spinoza to write the treatise—and the intended effects he wished for the work to have upon its readers. Cohen posited that Spinoza wrote the political protest pamphlet as an act of vengeance against the Amsterdam Jewish authorities after they had excommunicated him. Strauss did not see such personal and biographical motives here to be compelling or legitimate. Spinoza's critique of the Bible cannot be fully explained merely by pointing to the ban. Rather, Strauss found it necessary to show how the "essential content" of Spinoza's text arose from Spinoza's "own context of thought" (*Denkzusammenhang*). Cohen ultimately judged the Amsterdam Jewish community's excommunication of Spinoza as "necessary and wholly legitimate."[177] Strauss boils down Cohen's view of the treatise as being based on Spinoza's resentment for having been excommunicated. Spinoza, in Cohen's view, thus set out to politicize the Jewish religion sacrilegiously and to destroy the Jewish concept of religion.[178]

Spinoza's primary task, as Strauss would argue in *Spinoza's Critique of Religion* (1930), was to liberate the mind from the prejudices of the theologians so that the freedom to philosophize may ensue.[179] Thus, the questioning of the belief in revelation and the critique of theologians' prejudices (*Vorurteilen*) is therefore a precondition for the starting point of philosophy. The critique of revealed religion does not merely emerge as an achievement of free scientific inquiry. Rather, it constitutes the very basis of the modern secular mode of thought.[180] The political implications required Spinoza to argue for a liberal republic and to reject medieval and absolutist political claims of legitimacy that rested on revelation.

In the center of Hans-Georg Gadamer's magnum opus, *Truth and Method*, Gadamer reassessed the Enlightenment discrediting of prejudice, but most critics have overlooked that this move is explicitly attributed to Strauss's first book.[181] Strauss emphasized that "prejudice" emerged as a historical category in the Enlightenment's polemical treatment of religion. The Enlightenment set for itself the task of freeing itself from the cognitive servitude of clerical authority and the conventional prejudices that underlie it. The modern struggle against "the age of prejudice" stands diametrically opposed to the age of reason and freedom. The construction of "prejudice" as a historical category, and as a central Cartesian metaphysical concept, therefore provides the crucial difference between the modern Enlightenment's war against prejudice and superstition and the classical philosophical attempt to replace conventional opinion with knowledge.[182]

The radical Enlightenment of the seventeenth century seems more instructive to Strauss than the "moderate Enlightenment" of the eighteenth and nineteenth centuries; in the latter period harmonizations, internalizations, and reconciliations were forged between revealed religion and enlightenment. In the earlier period, an uncompromising life-and-death struggle between revealed religion and enlightenment was waged, in which each position attempted to negate the existence of the other. This radical confrontation forced each side to confront a dangerous and worthy opponent.

At the same time that Strauss wrote his comments on Schmitt's *Concept of the Political*, he wrote "The Testament of Spinoza" (1932), in which he explained his interest in the seventeenth century as the foundation for modern politics.[183] If the foundation of the "modern view" is being shaken by doubt, then interest necessarily reverts from its classical exponents to Descartes and Hobbes, the men who laid the foundations of this "world view." If the veneration of Spinoza is to be more than just his genius or character, Spinoza's teaching must be judged on a reassessment of the legitimacy of the foundations of modern philosophy. Strauss explains the need for Jews to reassess Spinoza during a period of marked Jewish dissimilation:

> The convulsion of modern Europe has led to a renewed self-awareness of Judaism. This renewed awareness did not produce a change in the assessment of Spinoza, at least not always and not immediately: Spinoza remained an authority. To be sure, one no longer needed him, or at least one no longer seemed to need him, for one's self-assertion against the Jewish tradition and against Europe. But in the exodus from the new Egypt one saw oneself obliged to take along the bones of the man who had risen to a king-like position in that land and to convey them to the pantheon of the Jewish nation, which venerated him as one of her greatest sons. No doubt this was done in good faith. But was it right not to have asked about the last will of the man thus honored?[184]

According to Strauss, Spinoza's last will was to break with Judaism. He should not be venerated as a Jew, nor as a Jewish heretic, but rather as a member of "the elite group of superior minds" whom Nietzsche called the "good Europeans."[185] Spinoza's lasting testimony is signified by the inscription in his signet ring: "Caute!" In other words, Spinoza will be venerated "as long as there are men who know what it means to utter the word 'independence' [*Unabhängigkeit*]."[186]

Strauss engaged Spinoza and his predecessors precisely from a position of distance from the tradition inherited from them. Strauss contrasted the attitudes of Maimonides and Spinoza in connection to Jewish life (*Lebenzusammenhang*); Spinoza's alienation from the world of Judaism stands in the foreground. Maimonides's approach to philosophy and his interpretation of Judaism emerged organically from a Jewish life, while Spinoza's projects were preconditioned in his alienation from Judaism. The basis of Maimonidean thought, according to Strauss's early understanding, was thoroughly Jewish. Judaism and the concerns of the Jewish community shaped the direction of his thought, already prior to his turn to philosophy:

> As a Jew, born, living and dying with Jews, he pursued philosophy as a Jewish teacher of Jews. His argumentation takes its course, his disputes take place, within the context of Jewish life, and for that context. He defends the context of Jewish life which is threatened by the philosophers in so far as it is threatened by them. He enlightens Judaism by means of philosophy, to the extent that Judaism can be enlightened. He elevates Judaism by means of philosophy once again to the height it originally attained, so far as Judaism had descended from the height as a result of the disfavor of the times; Maimonides' philosophy is based in principle and throughout on Judaism.

This portrait of Maimonides would radically change during the next few years where Maimonides's supposed defenses of the tradition acquire an ever greater creative and subversive quality. But in his first book, Maimonides's philosophy and interpretation of Scripture derive from a tight bond to the lifeworld of Judaism. "Spinoza's scientific approach to Scripture," by contrast, "presupposes total absence of any concern with Scripture, of any need for Scripture; in a word, freedom from prejudice, i.e. alienation from Judaism."[187] Everything relevant in their views toward Judaism ought to be read with an eye to this situational difference.

Maimonides's approach to speculative matters, which takes its bearings from Judaism, would strike Spinoza as "remaining imprisoned in prejudice." Thus, the more one can gain independence from such prejudice, the more one achieves a position of free inquiry. The change in context is noteworthy. Prior to Spinoza's time, the most serious and effective charge against an opponent was "the reproach of innovation." Spinoza flips this fearful sensibility on its head. Now, all prejudices must be thoroughly called into question: "The more radical the doubt, the greater the assurance that one becomes free from prejudices. Innovation, apostasy, arbitrariness as terms of reproach have finally lost their capacity to strike terror to the heart."[188] In Spinoza's brave new world, apostasy marks the birth of intellectual liberty: the freedom to think independently. Spinoza's justifications for his rejection of Mosaic law, whether it be to prove the impossibility of miracles or calling into question the veracity of Mosaic authorship—all emerge from his prior alienation from Judaism.

Spinoza stood at an "intermediate stage" between a medieval religious world and a modern culture and liberal state. While Spinoza "freed himself from the social nexus of Judaism," he entered a netherworld that preexisted the home he sought in the "liberal secular state." Here Spinoza's alienation from positive religion is placed within a continuum of his Marrano predecessors Uriel da Costa and Isaac de la Peyrère who attempted to return to Judaism. They all shared a disposition that rejected Christian doctrines; at the same time, however, they were beyond accepting the yoke of "the concrete and unquestioning Judaism" that predated the experiences of collective alienation from Judaism. These are the sociological factors that explain why this group tended to forms of skepticism that provided the building blocks for modern secular science, culture, and politics: "For the spiritual content of Judaism had—after several generations of un-Jewish living—inevitably faded from the minds of the Marranos. The connection with Judaism was still strong enough to inhibit unquestioning life within the Christian world. On the other hand, the connection was too tenuous to make life possible within the Jewish world."[189]

Given the perception of German Jewry's existential liminality, it is easy to see why such a passionate interest in the Marranos developed during the interwar period. In the preface to the English translation of the book on Spinoza, Strauss offered his perception of the predicament of German Jewry as one of not only political dependence, but spiritual dependence as well. German Jewry's high degree of acculturation, according to Strauss, led to "an influx of German thought, the thought of the particular nation in the midst of which they lived—a thought which was understood to be German essentially."[190] It is this predicament of the modern German Jew, a veritable new Marrano, that captured Strauss's attention during his early career. After Spinoza, the grounds of the debate between religion and science had irrevocably changed. Now religious orthodoxy was put on the defensive, having to adapt its form and content to the changing and alien demands of a particular culture and society. This might not be so problematic for the Jew if he could genuinely gain solid footing in that new place. But once the grounds of German culture and politics became questionable, all the more precarious was the condition of the German Jew who had no other independent ground to secure his existence.

In reassessing Spinoza's decisive rejection of the claims of Orthodoxy, therefore, Strauss was also trying to come to terms with the predicament of German Jewry. If Spinoza's critique of religion was not scientifically sound or simply not compelling, perhaps there was a way to salvage a connection with premodern religious tradition. If Spinoza's critique of religion is truly authoritative, however, then the core of Orthodox dogma constitutes archaic and pernicious irrational tales: a creator God, the possibility of miracles, and the divine origins and character of revelation. Strauss's first book traced a long lineage of an Epicurean critique of religion that takes a decisively new and bold direction with Spinoza and culminates in Nietzsche. Underneath the surface of Strauss's text, one cannot help seeing the rabbinic suspicion regarding *apikorsut*—a pejorative under-standing of Epicurean skepticism—as the motive behind the most dangerous acts of defection from Judaism. Betrayal of a demanding revealed legal tradition was interpreted from the standpoint of rabbinic norms as stemming from man's hubris, a misguided faith in man's autonomous power in securing his own earthly happiness. The Epicurean critique of religion that Strauss traces emerges from concern for securing tranquillity of mind (ataraxia) over and against the anxiety of living in fear of potentially wrathful gods. The critique of religion only becomes necessary according to its premodern incarnation if those gods are fearful and wrathful. The modern version of the Epicurean critique emerges not in the service of gaining felicity, but rather courageous probity. Could Zion-ism be the anthropocentric vehicle that could realize modern Epicurean aims?

Strauss did seriously consider political Zionism to be such an answer. By the end of the decade, Strauss had begun to counter modern intellectual probity with a Socratic concern for the love of truth.[191] This concern marks a shift from his view in 1923 that even if one rejected the modern spirit, it is "impossible to extricate oneself from modern life without employing modern means." By 1930, Strauss will call for a breaking-out of the paradigm of the present. "If we want to know the present as it is," he argues, "free of all prevailing questionable pre-suppositions, then we must be free of the present. This freedom does not fall right into our lap, rather we must conquer it."[192] Invoking Plato's allegory of the cave to explain the natural difficulties of philosophizing, Strauss explains that we find ourselves in a more disadvantageous position than Socrates and his contemporaries were in. We are in a "second cave," one that requires us to rely initially on modern historical tools before we can reach the first cave where-upon Socrates can offer us guidance to the light. The instrumental function of history for us is a "propaedeutic." Whereas Socrates could rely on conversation to ascend with his interlocutors, we can only make progress with the propae-deutic of "learning through reading [*lesendes Lernen*]."[193] Strauss's call for an instrumental use of the history of ideas would animate his next major works (which he wrote as a refugee in Europe) on Maimonides and Hobbes.

# CHAPTER 3

# European Exile and Reorientation (1932–1937)

*I*n the summer of 1932, the thirty-three-year-old German-Jewish scholar Leo Strauss left Germany for France and then England, eventually settling in the United States in 1937. Within a matter of months of his departure, the Nazi regime's legal and extralegal antisemitic actions rendered him, for all practical purposes, an exile. Strauss's struggle, as a Jewish refugee in Europe, to reorient his thought to the condition of exile constitutes the transition between his Weimar and American careers. Zionism and a research post at the Akademie had allowed Strauss to survey the contours of modern Jewish existence in the diaspora as a distilled form of a more general crisis affecting modern thought and politics. It was during Weimar that he commenced his lifelong study of premodern Latin, Hebrew, and Arabic texts, in an attempt to understand and evaluate the emergence of and prospects for modern thought and politics. And his writing evidences a curious and ambivalent fascination with another lifelong concern: the problem of exile.

By the end of the 1920s, Strauss had seemingly exhausted all available Zionist responses to the Jewish question, each of which ultimately failed to prove to him that it could provide a wholly consistent and satisfactory solution. So after having been an active Zionist for more than fifteen years, Strauss remains ambivalent about exile. In the 1930s, however, the relationship between politics and philosophy comes into focus. Strauss arrives at a new interpretive vision by way of a radical reexamination of exile and its forgotten virtues. With the rise of Nazism, the pressing reality of exile became more than just a theoretical matter. In confronting his own émigré status, Strauss enlisted the help of medieval Jewish and Islamic thinkers who had faced crises in reconciling their status as both philosophers and members of a religious community.

After completing the two books of his European exile, *Philosophy and Law* and *The Political Philosophy of Hobbes* in 1935, Strauss's thought acquired a new and specific emphasis. Devoting most of his scholarly energies to exploring the contours of esoteric philosophical hermeneutics, Strauss began to identify key premodern literary devices that had been used to circumvent censors and other potentially hostile or undesirable readers. Given his awareness of contemporary conditions and the suppression of intellectual expression, it is perhaps not surprising that Strauss acquired a fascination with the coded and cryptic prose deployed by past thinkers to avoid persecution. In his particular case, however, this fascination developed into an endorsement of the intellectual creativity involved in such forms of guarded and indirect discourse. Strauss's peculiar attraction to esoteric writing comes to the forefront during the tumultuous years preceding his arrival in the United States.

In 1937, Strauss left England for the United States where he eventually received an appointment at the New School for Social Research. There he continued to explore various philosophic traditions that dealt with conditions of persecution and political imperfection by employing a multilevel style of writing. The innovation during this next period, 1938–1948, involves the transition from a descriptive account of multilevel writing to an adoption of this style of revealing while concealing. By the time war broke out in Europe in the fall of 1939, Strauss had laid the scholarly foundations for a new perspective; he enunciated a project that called for the recovery and rebirth of a philosophical rationalism that would distinguish between the esoteric and exoteric. The articulation of this project appeared in Strauss's 1941 essay "Persecution and the Art of Writing."

Strauss's European exile also witnessed a dramatic political reorientation. Just as his condemnation of modern thought led him to reclaim a medieval tradition of esoteric philosophy, Strauss developed a premodern argument against liberalism. His chastening experiences as a conservative Jewish refugee intellectual compelled him to respond to the pressing reality of living under conditions of imperfection. In response to the condition of exile, he followed the prudential strategy suggested to him by a tradition of philosophic esotericism and its particular form of medieval Platonic politics: namely, that one must accommodate one's speech and actions to the inherent imperfection of all human societies. Secret and contained subversion become a fixed feature of Strauss's post-Weimar thought.

In this chapter I examine the elements that demarcate the form and the content of this transitional phase of Strauss's thought: his post-Weimar critique of liberalism, his rediscovery of multilevel writing strategies, and the continuing centrality of the Jewish concept of exile, *galut,* in his developing political philosophy.

### Departure from Germany: Reassessing Modern Politics

On the eve of Strauss's departure from Germany in the spring of 1932, several dramatic political changes took place in Germany. The Nazi regime's solidification of power, along with the radicalization of its policies against "enemy" groups and individuals, created a situation in which Strauss's older Weimar concerns regarding Jewish existence acquired a new urgency. Throughout the 1920s Strauss criticized philosophical, theological, and political manifestations of German liberalism and within German-Jewish liberalism. He attempted to arrive at a "standpoint" that would rise above the "anarchy of opinions" and offer guidance out of the present crisis.[1] In his essays from 1930 to 1932, Strauss articulated the need to transcend the limitations of the current "horizon," which occluded the possibility of more radical thought that was so urgently needed. Indeed, in the last article published while he was still in Germany, his 1932 commentary on Carl Schmitt's *Concept of the Political,* he articulated the "urgent task" of escaping the imprisoning horizon of liberalism by thoroughly uprooting it.[2] Strauss knew that Schmitt's theoretical critique of the foundations of modern liberalism bespoke the political crisis of the moment. The project of problematizing the whole liberal edifice of modern culture and its corresponding epistemic contours emerged from the knowledge that those foundations had already become questionable in everyday life and politics.

Schmitt's *Concept of the Political* first appeared in 1927 and was immediately recognized as one of the most important and controversial texts in political theory of the time. Schmitt argued that the political is constituted by the fundamental and irreconcilable opposition of friend and enemy. After Schmitt personally saw to the publication of Strauss's commentary on his own *Concept of the Political,* he wrote a strong letter of recommendation on behalf of Strauss, successfully securing a fellowship for him to conduct research abroad on Hobbes.[3] Strauss's tenacious ability to work through Schmitt's own inconsistencies in order to unearth his unarticulated underlying motives and intentions impressed Schmitt. In Strauss's commentary, he identified Schmitt's *true* beliefs as being a radically antiliberal conception of politics. According to Strauss, Schmitt was unable to realize this latent goal because he was operating from a position still entrenched within the conceptual boundaries of liberalism—a position from which Strauss toiled to extricate himself. Heinrich Meier has argued that the most powerful evidence of Schmitt's regard for Strauss's critical acumen is that Schmitt tacitly incorporated and responded to many of Strauss's insights in a revised edition of *Concept of the Political.*[4] Schmitt refrained, however, from acknowledging Strauss in the new edition. Schmitt also ceased responding to Strauss's letters in the early winter of 1933.

Carl Schmitt's decision to break off any public or private dialogue with Strauss was prompted by his association with the new Nazi regime. Schmitt, as well as Martin Heidegger, joined the Nazi party on May 1, 1933.[5] In July, Strauss wrote Schmitt from Paris updating him on his research efforts on Hobbes as well as his general reaction to French scholarship.[6] He concluded the letter by telling Schmitt that he had been "somewhat occupied" with the work of Charles Maurras (1868–1952), the cofounder of the *Action Française* and a leading figure of the French Right.[7] Like Schmitt, Maurras's underlying atheism put him into conflict with the church; nonetheless, for both figures, their rhetorical and symbolic lexicon draw heavily from Catholic traditions and concerns. Strauss noted that he had found some astounding parallels between Maurras and Hobbes, but did not elaborate further. He then requested from Schmitt a letter of introduction to Maurras. At the time he composed the letter, Strauss was apparently unaware that Schmitt had become a member of the Nazi party.[8]

Whatever Strauss's motivations might have been, the timing of his request to Schmitt for an introduction to Maurras merits some comment, as it transpired in the wake of the Enabling Act of March 23. This new legislation sought to purge "non-Aryan" Germans from the German bureaucracy and academic institutions, sending many Jewish scholars to France and England in search of refuge. Given Schmitt's illiberal leanings and occasional use of antisemitic rhetoric, it is not unreasonable to assume that Strauss would have pondered Schmitt's current political leanings in the new environment. Strauss's friends had already informed him that Heidegger had severed his relations with Jewish students, colleagues, and mentors.[9] Strauss's friend and former student of Heidegger, Jacob Klein, implored Strauss to cease writing to Schmitt in the final months of 1933.[10]

When Schmitt shunned Strauss both privately and publicly, the personal disappointment Strauss suffered tapped into the resentment of a German Jew exiled and excluded from the political and cultural life of his native country. The rejection of the liberal bourgeois hope for a German-Jewish symbiosis that was so evident throughout Strauss's Weimar Jewish writings acquired a deepened realization in light of the political and personal events that transpired in 1932 and 1933. There is no doubt that Schmitt's slight and affirmation of the new Nazi regime dealt a heavy blow to Strauss. Strauss had expressed his gratitude to Schmitt for supporting his application for a Rockefeller Fellowship, but Strauss's estimation of Schmitt's personal importance was conveyed in much more dramatic terms.[11] Strauss was still in Berlin in March 1932 when he wrote Schmitt: "the interest that you have shown in my studies of Hobbes represents the most honorable and crucial validation of my scholarly work that has ever been bestowed upon me and that I could ever dream of."[12] Schmitt was a serious thinker on the Right that had privately recognized Strauss's voice; because of the political currents and opportunities in Germany, however, Schmitt had decided to cut short any private dialogue with the struggling young scholar because he was a Jew.[13] Nevertheless, Schmitt would continue to respond to Strauss's work in ways that cut to the decisive similarities and differences in their views of Hobbes and Spinoza, and surrounding the establishment of freedom of conscience and freedom to philosophize—and, as we shall see, the reappearance of the mediating role played by late eighteenth-century figures associated with such public German controversies as the *Spinozastreit:* Jacobi, Lessing, and Mendelssohn.

Strauss began his research on *The Political Philosophy of Hobbes* in Paris in

October 1932. Strauss found himself among other German and Central European intellectuals who came to France as a safe haven from the increasingly discriminatory and hostile measures put into place during the first years of Hitler's assumption of power. By the summer of 1933, more than twenty-five thousand German refugees came to France.[14] While in Paris, Strauss participated in an international community of intellectuals including Jacques Maritain, Alexandre Koyré, Paul Kraus, Shlomo Pines, and Alexandre Kojève (Kojevnikoff). Strauss joined an impressive constellation of intellectuals attending seminars at the École pratique des hautes études taught by Koyré and Kojève on Hegel.[15] Strauss also spent much of this time poring through texts in medieval Islamic and Jewish philosophy at the Bibliothèque nationale.

Strauss's research on Hobbes soon brought him to London and Cambridge with Marie (Miriam) Bernsohn, whom he had married in Paris in June 1933. Strauss's stepson, Thomas Petri, also accompanied them. They arrived in England with no accessible assets. His letters from this time are filled with expressions of financial anxiety. Relying solely upon a temporary extension of his Rockefeller grant, Strauss did not know how or where he would earn a living. The Hobbes manuscript was completed in early 1935 in German, but it was not published until 1936, appearing first in English because of the increasingly difficult publishing climate in Germany.

Strauss began his book by establishing Hobbes as the first to offer a "peculiarly modern attempt to give a coherent and exhaustive answer to the question of man's right life, which is at the same time the question of the right order of society." Hobbes was also the first "who felt the necessity of seeking, and succeeded in finding, a *nuova scienza* of man and State":

> [Hobbes] philosophized in the fertile moment when the classical and theological tradition was already shaken, and a tradition of modern science had not yet formed and established. At this time he and he only posed the fundamental question of man's right life and of the right ordering of society. This moment was decisive for the whole age to come; in it the foundation was laid, on which the modern development of political philosophy is wholly based, and it is the point from which every attempt at a thorough understanding of modern thought must start. This foundation has never again been visible as it was then. The structure which Hobbes, led by the inspiration of the moment, began to raise, hid the foundation as long as the structure stood, i.e. as long as its stability was believed in.[16]

The revolutionary and catastrophic events in interwar Europe, felt particularly at the time Strauss composed this text in the mid-1930s, undermined the common belief in the sturdiness of the modern state. The foundation of modern politics and the modern state had once again become visible because it had once again become a problem. So following Schmitt, Strauss went back to Hobbes as the true originator of modern politics, in order to gain a clear look at the foundation and gauge how the development of his political thinking culminated in the construction of a mortal god, the Leviathan.

Strauss's admiration for the significance of Hobbes's intellectual revolution is nonetheless undercut by what he saw as the deleterious effects of the new paradigm: "The ideal of civilization in its modern form, the ideal both of the bourgeois-capitalist development and of the socialist movement, was found and expounded by Hobbes with a depth, clarity, and sincerity never rivaled before or since."[17] This apparently value-neutral attribution determined Strauss's primary polemical interest in Hobbes. Hobbes initiated the modern West's detachment from the strong roots of ancient political rationalism in favor of a new ideal of civilization ultimately based on the supremacy of *will* over *reason*. As the unacknowledged progenitor of both bourgeois liberalism and socialism, Hobbes marked the beginning of what Strauss saw as the destruction of reason.[18]

Hobbes's political philosophy, according to Strauss, signaled the birth of a new political science: one that not only elevated individual right over law, but also narrowed the scope of politics to techniques of managing and regulating the state. This political science saw its task as restoring or instituting the "right balance" of the state.[19] In so doing, it introduced mechanistic methods that transformed the state into a machine to be assembled, disassembled, and reassembled solely for the purpose of its efficient functioning. For Strauss, this new technical sophistication was bought at a heavy price. The political issue of moral purpose was systematically excluded from the outset. The science of politics would no longer be interested in the questions of what is "good and fitting" and who ought to rule.[20] Political science, recast as the technical regulation of a machine, would have no moral basis to judge instances of moral abdication or deviation.

The ideological underpinnings of liberal individualism, according to Strauss, required the development of a new morality. In this light he read Hobbes's new morality as advancing the market economy. Rather than advancing the greatest good, this new morality was preoccupied with averting the greatest evil. Hobbes insisted that violent death (or, more precisely, the fear of violent death) was the basis of all political understanding. This core understanding of the human situation is precisely what Schmitt had found so compelling in Hobbes. Incidentally, Heidegger found similar insights at the origins of Greek philosophy as well. Strauss glossed over the Hobbesian need to rid humankind of whatever illusions it may have about its status in the natural order:

> For man must be brought to *recognize his position by the violent resistance of the real world, and against his natural inclination, which is to deceive himself as to the horror of his natural situation by weaving a cocoon of vain dreams about himself.* For the man who has once come into contact with this world, joy and laughter are over. Man must be serious and that exclusively. It is the fearfulness of death rather than the sweetness of life which makes man cling to existence. Since man is at the mercy of a fate utterly unconcerned as to his weal or woe, a fate which one may call God's

irresistible power, because man experiences only force, and not kindness from the overwhelming power of the universe, he has no choice but to help himself.[21]

Strauss isolated Hobbes's motive for extricating man from his dependence on divine providence, and emphasized the dangerous implications of a vain forgetfulness that lulls man into an artificial sense of comfort. Strauss explains that this comfortable amnesia is why Hobbes attempted, unsuccessfully, to devise ways in which the reality and horror of man's natural condition, a war of all against all, would not be forgotten. Carl Schmitt and other conservative revolutionaries continually inveighed against the bourgeois ethos of complacency and frivolity that permeated the post-Hobbesian world of liberal civilization.[22] For them, entertainment and a complete lack of seriousness corroded a world that could no longer understand the existential moment of truth: the individual's encounter with violent death.[23]

Until the mid-1930s, Strauss himself found great utility in waking humanity from the "cocoon of vain dreams" that it had woven around itself. True politics, he believed, could never be founded upon bourgeois complacency, but only upon a realistic view of the agonistic relationship man has with the world and other men. Strauss's critique of capitalist egoism paralleled conservative-revolutionary concerns for authentic politics, but stopped short of rooting true values in the pure moment of confronting death. Strauss's critique also shared Marxist concerns that capitalism and the social relationships under its dominance have become reified, mistakenly viewed as natural and/or immutable. As far as the latter political tradition is concerned, Strauss noted that Hobbes viewed man as "the proletarian of creation." Hobbesian man "stands in the same relation to the universe as Marx's proletarian to the bourgeois world: he has nothing to lose by his rebellion, except his chains, and everything to gain."[24] Although Strauss appreciated the radical critique of this Marxist view, he did not agree with it. We recall that Strauss's Weimar writings convey his consistent opposition to socialist views of human nature and their ultimately antipolitical vision of man as consumer and producer. In that period, however, Marxist and conservative criticisms of liberalism shared a radicalized hope for a dramatic rupture with the present state. The fact that Strauss carried this legacy into the 1930s reveals the extent of his intellectual assimilation: he was and remained a critic of Weimar. Even sudden changes in political circumstance did not yield an immediate about-face in Strauss's political leanings.


### Refusing to Crawl to the Cross of Liberalism

In May 1933 Strauss wrote his fellow German refugee, Karl Löwith, offering a remarkable assessment of his current political alignment; he articulates authoritarian principles in defiant opposition to the repulsive monster, Adlof Hitler.

*Leo Strauss and the Politics of Exile*

Just because the right-wing oriented Germany does not tolerate us, it simply does not follow that the principles of the right are therefore to be rejected. To the contrary, only on the basis of principles of the right—fascist, authoritarian, *imperial*—is it possible, in a dignified manner, without the ridiculous and sickening appeal to the "unwritten rights of man," to protest against the repulsive monster."

In the light of recent events Strauss turned to read Caesar's *Commentaries* with a newfound comprehension connecting it with Virgil's judgment that under Roman imperial rule, the subjected are spared and the proud are subdued." Strauss expresses his intransigent defiance of the pressing bleak situation by proclaiming to Löwith: "There is no reason to crawl to the cross [*zu Kreuze zu kriechen*], even to the cross of liberalism, as long as anywhere in the world a spark glimmers of Roman thinking. And even more cherished than any cross is the ghetto." Strauss counsels Löwith that they adopt the disposition of steadfast independence exhibited by "men of science" from the Arab Middle Ages.[25]

This shocking letter, written in a moment of crisis, reveals the fusion of the different elements that anchor Strauss's worldview. Strauss wrote this letter to Löwith, who had expressed skepticism regarding the secularization of Christian Europe. Löwith appealed to the pre-Christian reliance on nature as a model for philosophical speculation into what is by nature true and right. But the force of German antisemitism in the 1930s would also temporarily push Löwith, who had converted to Christianity as a young man, to recover his dual identity as a German Jew.[26]

Löwith feverishly read through all of Rosenzweig's published writings as he left Germany in 1935. Soon after Löwith commenced his exile from Germany, we find a dramatic entry. Löwith invoked a letter wherein Rosenzweig recounts how he had been asked to take a stand on the pervasive and painful question of Jewish and German allegiance during the course of an interview for a position at a Jewish school. "I retorted that I would refuse to answer this question. If life were at one stage to torment me and tear me into two pieces, then I would naturally know with which of the two halves the heart—which is, after all, asymmetrically positioned—would side. I would also know that I would not be able to survive the operation."[27] Although Strauss and Löwith surely had a number of philosophical disagreements, Strauss's letter appeals to a friend who was in a state of panic on how he should realign his politics given the new situation. The pressures of antisemitism will not force Strauss to abandon his dignity by groveling before the cross in a desperate search for refuge and redemption.[28]

Strauss's defiant response to these events finds echoes elsewhere in the German-Jewish press. On April 1, 1933, a national boycott against Jewish businesses in Germany was instituted. A few days later, April 1 was heralded by Robert Weltsch, the editor of *Jüdische Rundschau*, as a day of Jewish reawakening: "It was intended as dishonor. Jews, take it up, the Star of David, and wear it with pride . . . !"[29]

Strauss employs the same phrase in his correspondence with Jacob Klein around the same time. Writing to Strauss in England from Denmark in June 1934, Klein continues a conversation with Strauss regarding the nature of the Nazi regime. Klein, revising his earlier view that National Socialism was one variant of the broader movement of fascism, now delimits the foundations of National Socialism to one principle: antisemitism.[30] Klein's interpretation takes an odd theological spin that echoes later interpretations of National Socialism as a pagan atheistic negation of the Judeo-Christian God and its accompanying morality. For Klein, the advent of Nazism marks "the first *decisive* battle" of the ancient conflict between "God and godlessness [*Gott-losigkeit*]." "The battle is decisive," Klein explains, "because it takes place on a battleground determined by *Judaism:* National Socialism is 'perverted Judaism' [*pervertiertes Judentum*], and nothing else: Judaism without God, i.e., a true *contradictio in adiecto* [insoluble contradiction]."[31]

Klein's expressions of defiance match Strauss's; Klein, however, sees Zionism as a banal nationalist movement that talks about the nation and culture, but ignores its ultimate origins as God's chosen people. In a remarkable and unacknowledged appropriation of Strauss's own criticisms of Zionism, Klein argued that Jewish history and culture could not be adequately understood without accounting for their uniqueness as ultimately dependent on God.[32] For Klein, the question of God had to be addressed directly. "And even if we were to be huddled into the ghetto once again and thus be compelled to go to the synagogue and to observe the law in its entirety, then this too we would have to do as philosophers, i.e., with a *reserve* [*Vorbehalt*] which, if ever so tacit, must for that very reason be all the more determined." Both Klein and Strauss see an essential enmity between philosophy and revelation: while political circumstances may force philosophy to "be brought under one roof with faith, prayer and preaching, [it] can never be brought into agreement with them."[33]

In Strauss's response (June 23, 1934), he counters that given the impossibility of an alliance between philosophy and Orthodoxy against "sophistry," the only option available is political Zionism. "It is not without good reason that I have always been a 'Zionist.'" Given Zionism's noble motivation, it is surely "the most *respectable* Jewish movement"—political Zionism, that is, not cultural Zionism. For Strauss, at this moment, there are only two options available: "political Zionism or orthodoxy."[34] Although Strauss at first agrees with Klein's assessment that Nazism can be understood as a distorted form of de-divinized Judaism, Strauss objects to Klein's "theistic turn."[35] Whatever their political circumstances, they must not "crawl back to the cross" meaning "to speak of God."[36]

Strauss's employment of "zu Kreuze zu kriechen" bitterly plays on the penitential ritual whereby believers enact their complete humility in turning to the symbol of the Cross as the sole source of salvation. The phrase is historically associated with the events in 1077 at Canossa where the Holy Roman Emperor Henry IV begged Pope Gregory VII to lift the ban of his excommunication.[37]

This act of humiliation acquired a central place in Bismarck's Kulturkampf against the Roman Catholic Church when he said in May 1872: "We are not going to Canossa either physically or morally." Nietzsche picks up this biting usage in several of his works. In *Thus Spoke Zarathustra:* "Many of them once lifted their legs like the dancer." Bemoans Zarathustra about his once young joyful apostates: "Just now have I seen them bent down—to crawl before the cross."[38] And in the *Will to Power* Nietzsche employs the phrase "to crawl" in a context that resonates with the antiliberal proclivities resonating in Strauss's letter to Löwith. Nietzsche speculates about the difficulty in finding a philosopher in the present age of egalitarian leveling which expects: "everybody to crawl on his belly in abject submission before the greatest of allies—its name is 'equality of mankind'—and pay homage exclusively to the equalizing, the leveling virtues."[39] Strauss will follow Nietzsche in seeing conditions of liberal-democratic egalitarianism as ultimately occluding the possibility of the philosopher and conversely questioning some of the virtuous effects of persecution.

Strauss tells Löwith that the current crisis will not make him bow before the secularized cross of liberalism either. He sought to protest against the rise of fanaticism on the right in Europe by appealing to the empire of ancient Rome (prior to its Christianization) as the kind of authoritarian imperial rule needed. When Strauss expressed that he would go back to the ghetto rather than disingenuously genuflect to "the cross of liberalism," he certainly could not have envisioned the subsequent radicalization of German antisemitic goals and policies into genocide. However, his stated preference for the ghetto unintentionally resonated with his book on Maimonides, which looked to medieval Jewish models of politics and philosophy at this time.

While these dramatic statements provide us with a unique glimpse into Strauss's underlying political convictions, we still ought to be wary about grafting this position onto his putatively academic works. Nonetheless, his ambivalences with regard to the legacy of secularization and liberal politics also come to the fore in his book on Hobbes. His interpretation of Hobbes is striking for the way in which he countered contemporary scholarship, which read Hobbes as a religious man who defended true Christianity against the distortions introduced by medieval Scholasticism. Strauss, however, saw Hobbes's *Leviathan* as a theological-political treatise, akin to Spinoza's *Theological Polititcal Treatise,* which addressed religion with the same kind of "double-intention" that Spinoza had written: "Exactly as Spinoza did later, Hobbes with double intention becomes an interpreter of the Bible . . . in order to make use of the authority of the Scriptures for his own theory, and then . . . in order to shake the authority of Scriptures themselves."[40] Hobbes concealed his skepticism regarding religion for various political reasons. Rather than directly attacking revealed Scripture itself, he attacks Scholastic and natural theology "in the name of strict belief in the Scriptures." At the same time, however, he "undermines" that belief through his historical and philosophical criticism of the "authority of the Scriptures."[41]

Hobbes's public statements regarding religion are deliberately obscure as the result of his need to accommodate his speech to the legal-religious power of his times. "The fact that Hobbes accommodated not his unbelief, but his utterances of that unbelief to what was permissible in a good, and in addition, prudent subject" explains why Hobbes wrote so cautiously before the Civil War and especially during his early humanist period. Political astuteness required him to conceal his "true opinions" and assiduously appear to follow and support "theological convention." But there is to be no mistake regarding his true and unchanging personal attitude toward positive religion: "religion must serve the State and is to be esteemed or despised according to the services or disservices rendered to the State."[42]

The purely political concern for positive religion is most clearly seen in Hobbes's treatment of the one religious requirement for all subjects in the *Leviathan:* acknowledgment that "Jesus is [the] Christ."[43] Even in this seemingly straightforward confession—which entailed affirmations of such doctrines as the existence of God, providence, and the resurrection of Christ—Strauss sees a great deal of equivocation but an underlying pattern of development that points to Hobbes's decisive secular basis of his mortal God, the liberal state.

Hobbes's interpretation unfolds, according to Strauss, as part of a theologico-political strategy to replace the foundation of positive religion with a natural one. So once the Mosaic revelation is understood in naturalized political terms, Christ is seen as simply restoring God's kingdom as an earthly kingdom, continuing a tradition initiated with Moses.[44] In 1954, Strauss would elaborate his interpretation of "Jesus is the Christ" as meaning "Jesus is the Messiah in the Jewish sense."[45] This later interpretation only draws out more explicitly his reading in 1936.

There are several intellectual somersaults on the way to this conclusion, but all follow from Strauss's argument for a theologico-political usage of a natural explanation for biblical doctrines. Hobbes reconstructs how biblical religion was premised on divine politics, and how this "politics of the kingdom of God" eventually led to a messianic doctrine that set the precedent for Christianity.[46] According to Strauss's reading of Hobbes's interpretation of the Bible, the Jews became bitterly disappointed with the political reality that followed their liberation from Egyptian bondage. Thirsty for maximal liberty in the kingdom of God, the Jews were greeted with the sober realization that "the kingdom of God was in fact a government of priests, i.e., a singularly defective regime." This anticlerical statement, cast as Hobbesian, certainly echoed Strauss's sentiments as well. The discontent with the actually existing regime of a weak king and powerful priests eventually "took on the form of the hope for a Messiah, i.e. a human king who would restore the kingdom of God and administer it: the idea of the Messiah is a correction of the original idea of the kingdom of God, a concession to the political realities which was forced upon the Jews by their bitter experience with the rule of priests."

This conception of the Messiah therefore emphasizes the temporal power of a human king as opposed to a power reserved for the kingdom of heaven. Strauss's Hobbes views Christianity as "an attempt to give an account of the failure of a political movement which was inspired by fantastic political hopes, the account running in terms of belief in miracles and the dualism of substances spiritual and corporeal. Christianity reveals its origin by the fact that the foundation of the Christian faith is 'the belief in this article, *Jesus is the Christ*,' i.e. Jesus is the Messiah in the Jewish sense." With respect to Hobbes's naturalist reading of religion in general and Christianity in particular, Strauss sees him (both in 1936 and 1954) as anticipating the explosive naturalist critiques of Christianity in Germany one century later in a posthumously published work by Hermann Samuel Reimarus (1694–1768) and disclosed by Lessing.[47]

And in briefly noting Lessing's text, Strauss provides a learned cue pointing to the religious controversy that erupted following Reimarus's historical portrait of Jesus as a failed Jewish messiah who was posthumously deified by the opportunistic inventers of Christianity. Lessing defied authorities by publishing Reimarus's heretical views in the form of a supposed refutation, but many of Lessing's contemporaries suspected that some parts of the refutation were disingenuous and intentionally unconvincing. This public controversy was rivaled only by the pantheism debates initiated by Jacobi. Once again we find a twentieth-century engagement of Hobbes mediated through the late eighteenth century.

Schmitt too saw Lessing as an integral culmination of forces set into play by Hobbes—and especially by Spinoza. *Der Leviathan in der Staatslehre des Thomas Hobbes: Sinn und Fehlschlag eines politisches Symbols* appeared in 1938.[48] As the subtitle suggests, Schmitt attempts to uncover the true meaning of the Leviathan as a political symbol and also point out its ultimate failure. In terms of political symbols, the Leviathan and the Behemoth were easily recognizable symbols for England as the great sea power and Germany as the great land power.[49] Schmitt does not write a simple ideological attack upon Hobbes's conception of a mortal God. Rather, his enduring fascination with the Leviathan as a mortal God comes to the fore, even if he ultimately considered the great whale to be vanquished. In the process of wrestling with the problem of the modern state during the previous years, Schmitt identified what he saw as a decisive flaw in Hobbes's Leviathan: "freedom of conscience could ultimately be pitted against the public confession that the King is the Christ." He saw Hobbes's vibrant vision of sovereignty, which had possessed such a decisive power in identifying its enemies, as systematically weakened and eventually killed by a secret alliance between Judaism and liberalism.

Within this work appears what is arguably the most visceral antisemetic and apocalyptic image of Schmitt's corpus. At one point he mentions the "Jewish scholar" Leo Strauss, but refers only to Strauss's earlier treatment of Hobbes in *Spinoza's Critique of Religion* (1930) rather than *The Political Philosophy of Hobbes*

(1936)—which Schmitt undoubtedly read.[50] Schmitt turns his attention to the primordial conflict between the Behemoth and Leviathan wherein each attempts to destroy the other. Drawing on a recently acquired familiarity with midrash through translations of Don Yitzhak Abravanel, Schmitt sees that the Jews stay removed and "watch as the peoples of the world kill one another; for them this mutual 'slaughter and carnage' [*Schlächten und Schlachten*] is lawful and 'kosher.' Thus they eat the flesh of the slaughtered peoples and live upon it."[51]

And we can see how Strauss struggled with the specific political problem that arises from such a reading of religion. At first glance it would seem that Hobbes consistently maintained that "unconditional obedience to the secular power is the bounded duty of every Christian, in so far as that power does not forbid belief in Christ." But this last qualification raises "the crucial question: is the Christian obliged to obey the secular power when that power forbids him the profession of his faith?" In works prior to the *Leviathan,* Hobbes stipulates "the right and duty of the Christian" to resort to "passive resistance and martyrdom" in such an extreme circumstance. In the *Leviathan,* however, Hobbes denies that "the ordinary Christian" has either the right or the duty to follow this course, and restricts martyrdom to only those who have "the special vocation of preaching the Gospel."[52]

Hobbes, according to this reading, limits the scope of resistance to a sovereign power that is either neutral or even hostile to Christianity. Miguel Vatter has demonstrated that Schmitt would explicitly reject this secularized reading of the public confession "Jesus is the Christ" in each of his subsequent books on Hobbes.[53] But Strauss too is worried about the problem that arises from Hobbes's reduction of the laws of God to the laws of nature. In attempting to justify unqualified submission to sovereign authority, Hobbes may have unintentionally provided a potential basis for civil disobedience and the collapse of authority. For Hobbes, "the demands of natural law [are reduced to] to the single demand of keeping one's promises, i.e. of unqualified civil obedience: yet in order to justify that reduction, he is compelled to admit . . . all demands of kindness or charity; the utmost he can maintain is that in case of conflict between two sets of demands, the demand of civil obedience takes precedence." The problem is not serious so long as the competing demands center on narrow practical issues. But when competing claims concern whether the laws are just or unjust and whether the rulers are just or unjust, the secular basis for the precedence of civil obedience can become the basis for dissent and revolt. Strauss explains: "by trying to give reasons for unqualified submission to authority, by appealing from authority to reason, as Socrates did, he is forced to repeat what he regarded as Socrates' fatal mistake, 'anarchism.'"[54]

Strauss followed Schmitt in using his conception of the political to point out the inherent weaknesses and deficiencies of modern liberalism. And he was always concerned that loosening the bonds of obedience could lead to anarchy. Strauss's mode of thought was thoroughly pluralistic in that he made sure to take seriously the truth claims of opposing views and positions—especially those that had been unjustifiably silenced or dismissed. Indeed, we have seen how Strauss made sure always to undermine his own position as well as his opponent's. His stylistic stridency, however, stressed unresolved tensions between extreme positions, signaling his skepticism (if not contempt) for the effects of unguided public exchange of opinions.

Nevertheless, we see a change in Strauss's politics during the 1930s. After he came to be regarded as part of a group that was the enemy of the new German government, he explicitly questioned the political wisdom of basing politics on a hypostasized act of decision. Instead, Strauss emphasized the rational basis of politics; in opposition to Schmitt and other radical conservatives, he de-emphasized bellicose heroism as a necessary or even desirable attribute of authentic politics. Thus, although Schmitt's opinion of Hobbes as a truly systematic political thinker strengthened his interest in the English philosopher, Strauss's interpretation of Hobbes eventually indicted all theories that grounded politics on the subjective will rather than reason. Hobbes, like Spinoza, held Strauss's interest because they were architects of modernity who still stood at its cusp. Strauss's interest in replaying the battle between the ancients and moderns received great impetus from his instinct to disturb and overturn modern complacency.

Strauss's strategy for recovering a classical approach to politics required that the crusted layers of modern thought be cleared away so as to better understand the preliberal world of classical political rationalism. Strauss found the necessary tools to excavate premodern philosophy in the philosophy of Moses Maimonides.

### Returning to Maimonides: Philosophy and Law

When Strauss was appointed to a research position at the Akademie für die Wissenschaft des Judentum in 1925, Julius Guttmann, the director of the institution, embodied an older generation's commitment to a value-free scientific research agenda. He hired Strauss as a researcher in 1925, without realizing the kind of rebellious and iconoclastic scholar he was getting. In addition to pursuing research for a book on Spinoza's critique of religion, Strauss was assigned two further tasks while associated with the Akademie.

Strauss's first collaborative assignment involved the Akademie's endeavor to edit and translate into German Moses Mendelssohn's complete writings (other editors included Alexander Altmann, Simon Rawidowicz, and Fritz Bamberger). Moses Mendelssohn was virtually beatified by German Jewry as the modern incarnation of the biblical Moses and "the Great Eagle," Moses Maimonides.[55] Strauss's contribution to the Mendelssohn project displayed not only his acumen as a comparative philologist but, even more so, his critical exegetical disposition toward Mendelssohn. Strauss saw Mendelssohn as the model figure of the "moderate Enlightenment": a man who sought to "harmonize" Enlightenment rationalism with religion, and with Judaism in particular.[56] The second task followed Guttmann's appreciation for medieval Jewish philosophy. It entailed research on Gersonides's (Rabbi Levi ben Gershon, RaLBaG, 1288–1344) philosophical magnum opus, *Milhamoth Adonai* (Wars of the Lord).[57] The Gersonides project tapped into Strauss's deepening interest in medieval rationalism; contrary to Guttmann's wishes, however, it led Strauss to concentrate more on Maimonides's Arab Muslim predecessors than on his French-Jewish successors. This interest in medieval Islamic and Jewish philosophy and its relationship to Aristotle's and especially Plato's political thought did not follow Guttmann's designs.

In 1924–25, it will be remembered, Strauss first stepped into the field of medieval Jewish philosophy by taking a seminar taught by Guttmann. Some ten years later, after having immersed himself in medieval Jewish and Muslim philosophical texts and commentaries, Strauss offered an innovative reassessment of Maimonides's political philosophy and the Islamic school from which it had emerged.

Strauss's shift in perspective from his Weimar writings is apparent in his work on Mendelssohn and the late eighteenth-century debates of the German Enlightenment; it comes into full focus in the 1930s. The question that propelled Strauss's post-Weimar thought, as he wrote in a letter of 1935, was whether or not "a return to pre-modern philosophy is impossible."[58] Strauss's unexpected response to the political crises of 1933–35, therefore, was to enlist guidance from the medieval Enlightenment, whose greatest exponent was Maimonides, the leading light of medieval Jewish thought.

In England, Strauss found an ideal environment for his research on Maimonides, as well as Hobbes. Toward the end of 1933 Strauss expressed his desire to stay in England.[59] By way of contrast to the Bibliothèque nationale, the British Library at the British National Museum impressed Strauss as an enjoyable place to visit. In a letter to Kojève, Strauss characterized Britain as both "dry (the pubs close at 10 p.m. . . . .)" and "austere"; nonetheless, writing at a time in which France was reacting to the beginning of a Jewish refugee crisis, Strauss preferred English manners to the way in which the French treated foreigners.[60] As far as culinary matters are concerned, Strauss joked that the breakfast "hams taste too good as to consist of pork" and therefore must be allowed by Jewish law according to an "atheistic interpretation" of *halakhic* dietary restrictions.[61] These words of jest point to the different personae of Strauss and Guttmann. Both may have been studying the same canonical Jewish texts, but while Strauss pursued an atheistic interpretive reclamation of premodern Orthodoxy, Guttmann sought to advance a modern scientific understanding of the philosophy of religion.

1935 marked the octocentarian celebration of Moses Maimonides's birth.

Leo Strauss partook in the scholarly celebrations of that year by publishing *Philosophie und Gesetz*,[62] a book that called for a serious reengagement with Maimonides as a genuine guide to the perplexed condition of the philosopher and Jew.

The first chapter in the volume, "The Quarrel of the Ancients and the Moderns in the Philosophy of Judaism: Notes on Julius Guttmann, *The Philosophy of Judaism*," is nothing short of an assault upon Strauss's former research director's magisterial and comprehensive account of the history of the philosophy of Judaism, *Die Philosophie des Judentums* (1933). Strauss subjected Guttmann's interpretation of medieval and modern Jewish philosophy to a devastating critique. Strauss takes note that nearly two-thirds of Guttmann's work was devoted to medieval Jewish philosophy, and yet he argues that Guttmann does not approach this subject seriously. As suggested by the chapter title, Strauss wished to reopen the quarrel of the ancients and moderns, in part because Guttmann's treatment presupposes the superiority of the moderns. Strauss believes Guttmann's treatment of medieval Jewish philosophy never engages its subject on its own terms. Instead, Guttmann selectively filters aspects of medieval thought through the modern historical prism of an ever-advancing scientific understanding of religious consciousness. Guttmann's entire narrative then rests on a naïve faith in the self-evident superiority of the modern philosophy of culture, which disfigures, evaluates, and dismisses past thought.

The polemic against Guttmann, his former teacher and research director, was not, however, the ultimate objective of *Philosophy and Law*. Rather, Strauss took aim at the entire edifice of modern philosophy in order to find a way out of the contemporary crises of religion, politics, and philosophy. Strauss found a tentative answer to these critical problems in Maimonides, who offered a rationalism that was "the true natural model, [and] the standard to be carefully protected from any distortion." Strauss held that Maimonidean rationalism was "the stumbling block on which modern rationalism falls" and announced that the double aim of his work was to "awaken a prejudice in favor of this view of Maimonides, and even more, to arouse suspicion against the powerful opposing prejudice."[63] Guttmann's narrative was one instance of the failure to approach Maimonides with requisite seriousness and humility.

Strauss came to see the thought of Moses Maimonides as a promising alternative to the liberal configurations of Judaism precisely at the time that he was searching for an alternative paradigm to the modern sophistry of relativizing historicism and liberal politics.[64] His Maimonides contemplated Jewish exilic existence and ultimately arrived at a compelling, sophisticated, and prudent understanding of the relationship between the ideal political regime and existing ones.

Strauss argued that a major obstacle to the recovery of a premodern philosophical perspective was the Enlightenment's successful battle against Orthodoxy. To overcome this dilemma, he sought to reset the battle between Orthodoxy and the modern Enlightenment in his own post-Enlightenment era. Accordingly, the conflict boiled down to a matter of deciding between two principled positions: faith or atheism.[65] This was the choice confronting a modern Jew who, no matter how much he deemed it to be "the one thing needful," was nevertheless incapable of accepting the foundation of Judaism: the unqualified belief in divine revelation at Sinai.[66] Here, Strauss referred to the position that he himself occupied: that of a "convert" to philosophy. Sheer intellectual honesty would not permit him to pursue the path that could offer the greatest solace: an unqualified return to Jewish Orthodoxy.

Instead of merely accepting his lot as an atheist who openly betrayed his ancestral religion and community, Strauss attempted to find an alternative response that would neither abandon nor dull his competing loyalties as a philosopher and a Jew. He questioned whether the Enlightenment's supposed victory over religious orthodoxy had been a hollow one. Perhaps unaided human reason needed to be supplemented by religious orthodoxy, or at least called for a rhetorical affirmation thereof.[67] But one could not begin to address the primary sources of the crises of modern rationalism and Judaism so long as she or he relied upon modern presuppositions.

For Strauss, the Enlightenment remained deficient in terms of man's understanding of himself as part of nature and in providing moral and political guidance. The successful use of unaided human reason in the natural sciences encouraged Enlightenment thinkers to believe that it had the power to solve existential problems as well. This confidence, Strauss claimed, amounted to arrogant egotism, rather than a careful assessment of human problems that may not be resolved by means of technical wizardry and rational efficiency. Eventually, the modern critique of religious illusion and prejudice became an end in itself and displaced the original ataraxic goal of making human existence impervious to the fear of wrathful gods and the possibility of eternal damnation. The premodern rebellion against religion was transformed into a challenge to bear any truth rather than attain a happiness whose source was mired in religious delusion.[68]

Strauss cautioned that the post-Enlightenment commitment to destroy all comforting and felicitous illusions inevitably resulted in a romanticized model of courageous nihilism. What began as a revolt against the biblical God ultimately entailed a rejection of biblical morality. The new inverted ethics that emerged in the wake of the destruction of reason extolled courage as the highest virtue and demanded that one should embrace the world in its meanest and most sordid reality.

Strauss's remedy was to revitalize philosophy by employing an instrumental history of philosophy, one that would counter the Enlightenment narrative based on historical progress. The first requirement of his counterhistory was to strip the reified conditions of philosophical reflection of their natural appearance. The belief in inexorable development, according to Strauss, induced modern rationalism to forget the obstacles confronting the individual as he embarked upon the philosophical quest for wisdom and knowledge. Strauss's new history of philosophy countered the belief in historical progress and historicism's dismissal of absolute values and truths. He returned to the original position of philosophy as depicted in Plato's allegory of the cave:

> Only the history of philosophy makes possible the ascent out of the second, "unnatural" cave . . . into the first, "natural" cave that Plato's image depicts, and the ascent from which, to the light, is the original meaning of philosophizing. For we have fallen [into the second cave], less through the tradition than through the tradition of the polemic against the tradition.[69]

Thus, according to Strauss, it was first necessary to "climb back down" from the unnatural second cave and return to the natural Platonic cave where opinion and belief constituted the natural conditions of thought. Strauss understood original Torah Judaism as commensurate with Plato's first cave while contemporary Judaism lapsed into the condition of the second cave. "The Torah speaks according to the language of man," but the bonds of Law and belief had become unraveled in modern Judaism. Although Judaism's foundational constitution, the Torah, could never be corrupted, the remainder of contemporary Judaism had been "determined by the Enlightenment."[70]

In *Philosophie und Gesetz*, Strauss approached the recovery of Platonic philosophy as a modern diasporic Jew. He turned his attention to the specific problem of "a Jew who cannot be orthodox and must hold unconditional political Zionism (the only possible 'solution to the Jewish problem' on the basis of atheism) to be a highly honorable but in the long and serious run unsatisfactory answer."[71] While Strauss did not explicitly identify this predicament as his own, such a position crystallizes the movement of his thought during the previous dozen years. According to Strauss, medieval philosophy saw revelation as a self-evident proposition. It also saw the justification for recognizing this proposition as an "essential desideratum."[72] The defining characteristic of the *political* worlds in which Maimonides and his Islamic teachers lived was belief in revelation. They therefore adapted their own understanding of revelation to that context. They concealed their loyalty to philosophic reason by cloaking themselves in a rationalist interpretation of revelation not just as law, but as the one true perfect Law. The medieval philosophers explicitly declared that the founder of the ideal political order was a prophetic lawgiver invested with divine authority. In this theory, Moses and Mohammed become incarnations of Plato's philosopher-kings.

While the contents of that revelation could be debated, the reality of the revelation and the obligation to obey it were already established before argument. So long as any Jewish or Islamic scholar wished to remain a Jew or Muslim, he had to offer at least a formal recognition of revelation as a reality. "Since the recognition of the authority of the revelation is *prior* to philosophizing and since the revelation makes claim to man *totally*," Strauss explained that philosophizing is made possible "only as *commanded* [*geboten*] by the revealed law."[73] The commandment to philosophize marked a political innovation upon Plato's portrayal of the life devoted to philosophy. Plato attributed the choice to philosophize to such varying factors as the individual's own discretion or as the result of an obscure divine summons. By contrast, these medieval thinkers, even a radical such as Averroës, asserted that the obligation to philosophize came from God. The divine call to philosophize was directed to all those who were appropriately suited to do so, and this direction was clearly and unequivocally established in His revealed law.

The medieval concern to ground philosophy in divine revelation provided Strauss with a powerful alternative to the modern rejection of traditional belief and custom. The connection between politics and revelation brought Strauss to interpret one of the most intricate and elusive aspects of medieval Islamic and Jewish philosophy: prophecy. Maimonides portrayed the prophet as both philosopher and legislator who founds a community aimed at the perfection of man. This figure is not the founder of an ordinary state, but of the ideal state, whose classic model is the Platonic one. Plato suggested that his just regime had never become actualized and that it was a hypothetical model deduced by philosophical conversation. The medieval Islamic and Jewish doctrines of prophecy, by contrast, postulated the formation of the state as a past fact. Mohammed and Moses each acquire the status of philosopher-legislator, the great prophet who has already founded historical communities based on divine authorization and excellence. Platonic politics was therefore reconstituted around the figure of a prophet-legislator who transmitted divine law. Because the philosopher is uniquely qualified and, as such, obligated to interpret its content, both philosophy and the philosopher are secured in the political world where belief in divine revelation establishes rule. Thus, Plato's political doctrine became a philosophic foundation of the revealed law, offering a solution to the ancient question about the ideal state and its possibility of becoming a reality.

Whereas Plato could only speculate about the unlikely chance of the perfect state ever becoming a reality, medieval Platonic politics posited that the perfect state was founded by the law-giving prophet. What mattered most for Strauss was that there be complete agreement on one point: that "the founder of the ideal state is not a possible philosopher-king to be awaited in the future, but an actual prophet who existed in the past." That is, the medievals modified Plato's answer in light of the revelation that had occurred, or at least was believed to have occurred. Because the ideal law was "given through revelation," the only political requirement left was that it be understood through certain interpretive principles. The given status of the Law's perfection meant that "the law was not truly *open* to question."[74]

Strauss asserted that virtually every limitation that the philosopher imposed upon himself under the authority of the Law was in fact no limit at all: philosophers simply reinterpreted the terms that constrained their thought. Neverthe-

*Leo Strauss and the Politics of Exile*

less, it was still necessary for them to keep up the appearance of being subservient to the Law. Strauss wrote: "The freedom of philosophy depends upon its bondage. On this assumption, philosophy as authorized by the law is nothing other than the understanding or the demonstration of the truth already imparted by the law, nothing other than the *appropriation of the law.*"[75] The philosopher could then be innovative under the cover of legal traditionalism.

This characterization of a medieval Islamic and Jewish Enlightenment was clearly set in opposition to the public and egalitarian ideals of its better-known French successor. Strauss nevertheless insisted that Maimonides be seen as a figure of an enlightenment movement, albeit medieval. Maimonides rightfully belongs to the Enlightenment, Strauss argued, because he was passionately concerned with the freedom of philosophizing. Unlike the modern movement, however, Maimonides and his Muslim predecessors never countenanced the spread of unadulterated philosophical knowledge to the multitude. These medieval thinkers repeatedly "enjoin upon the philosophers the duty of keeping secret from the unqualified multitude the rationally known truth."

Further, they held the esoteric character of philosophy to be "unconditionally established." Strauss saw the medieval Enlightenment as "essentially esoteric" and the modern Enlightenment as "essentially exoteric."[76] Medieval esoteric philosophy rested on "the ideal of the *theoretical* life" while the modern Enlightenment was staunchly committed to the conviction of "the primacy of *practical* reason."[77] Esoteric hermeneutics preserved and reinforced the contemplative ideal within the confines of an existing order. Future hopes of establishing the ideal state were traded for an affirmation of a past establishment of the perfect state. In this scheme, the philosopher resigns himself to living within an imperfect society, to communicate his true beliefs privately or "strictly between the lines," and to innovate publicly only in the name of tradition.

Gershom Scholem wrote Walter Benjamin about *Philosophie und Gesetz,* shortly before its publication.[78] Scholem sharply quipped that Strauss's new book opened "with an unfeigned and copiously argued (if completely ludicrous) affirmation of atheism as the most important Jewish watchword." Scholem appreciated creative and original interpretations, but was equally skeptical of all such radical reassessments unless they were accompanied by incontrovertible textual evidence, or unless they were his own. Scholem had encouraged Strauss to publish work in medieval Jewish philosophy since 1933, in an effort to obtain an appointment for him at the Hebrew University in Jerusalem. Thus, Scholem wrote to Benjamin that he anticipated the wide reception of such a bold book from a Hebrew University candidate.[79] But Scholem's enthusiasm was dampened by the opinion that such maverick scholarship ruined the prospects for Strauss's appointment. Scholem wrote: "I admire this ethical stance and regret—the obviously conscious and deliberately provoked—the suicide of such a capable mind." He explained that few members of the humanities faculty would "vote for the appointment of an atheist to a teaching position that serves to endorse the philosophy of religion."[80] Scholem made no reference to Strauss's other statement that might hamper his chances for a position in Jerusalem: Strauss's criticism of political Zionism as an ultimately inadequate solution to the Jewish question. The appointment eventually went to the target of the book's polemic: Strauss's former research director, Julius Guttmann.

It is unclear if Scholem actually advocated the hiring of Strauss.[81] But Scholem's reaction alerts us to Strauss's intellectual independence even at a moment when he was desperate to secure an academic appointment. *Philosophie und Gesetz* remains all the more striking from this biographical perspective. It would be one thing for Strauss to refrain from certain actions even though they might have benefited his career; here, however, we find an instance where Strauss's subversive impulses actually undercut his own position and interests.

### Philosophical Accommodation to Religion and Politics

Though Strauss never developed a doctrine identified as "accommodation," his understanding of the need for accommodation stood as the central element in his reading of medieval Jewish and Islamic political teaching. Philosophy, according to this elitist understanding, must accommodate itself to people's natural capacities and abilities. And because the multitude of humankind is only capable of understanding figurative approximations of truth, the prophet must possess the ability to present revealed truths figuratively through the perfected faculty of the imagination.

For Strauss, accommodation was more than a medieval hermeneutical principle that generated various forms of historical outlooks.[82] It was the strategy by which philosophers lived within the perimeters of political imperfection. His affirmation of Platonic politics caused him to abandon the more open-ended elements of his Weimar critique of liberalism. He would now moderate his former radical inclinations by redirecting them to a more cautious view, at least for regarding attempts to replace flawed current regimes with perfected ones.

The Maimonides book was in part pursued in order to solidify Strauss's credentials in Jewish philosophy as a candidate for a position at the Hebrew University.[83] But with the Jerusalem appointment lost, Strauss continued his research, not knowing which academic discipline would recruit his services. In the summer of 1936 Strauss's financial fears were temporarily alleviated when Cambridge awarded him a grant for that coming academic year. He used this time to bury himself in close but extensive readings of medieval Jewish and Islamic philosophy while he continued in his attempt to secure a teaching position in England or the United States. Even with the enthusiastic sponsorship of the political theorist Ernest Barker and the London School of Economics historian R. H. Tawney, Strauss was unable to obtain an academic post in the United States or England immediately.[84] Like Strauss himself, many universities were uncertain as to which discipline he belonged: his work crossed the fields of Judaic studies, oriental studies, philosophy, history of ideas, and political science. Moreover, he had no previous teaching experience, his English was heavily accented, and his social demeanor appeared as exaggeratedly timid.[85] In the fall of 1936, at the University of Chicago, Strauss delivered a guest lecture in a graduate course on English history, but his teaching abilities were hardly recognized. The professor of the course, Conyers Read, offered the following estimation of Strauss's teaching abilities:

> The substance of his lecture was excellent, but my students told me afterwards that they had great difficulty in understanding his English. . . . He is a little mouse kind of a man without much in the way of a stimulating personality. I think with more experience he will develop into a fair teacher. It seems to me that Strauss would only be fitted for seminar work or advanced graduate work in America until he develops much greater facility as a teacher and lecturer than he is at present. He ought to have a kind of research lectureship which would give him a chance to write much and lecture little.[86]

With uncertain career prospects this émigré scholar continued to bring the medieval Islamic and Jewish philosophical tradition to the center of political philosophy. In 1936, Strauss published an article on the political science of Maimonides and Farabi.[87] Strauss argued that the axis of politics in the Islamic tradition becomes apparent once one realizes that religion, or more specifically revealed Law (Torah or Shari'a), serves a political function within medieval thought. Political science was deemed to be the only philosophic discipline charged with treating this law qua law. Medieval philosophers discussed the basis for their thought only under the rubric of their political science. Because the medieval version of Platonic politics relied on revelation as its source of legitimation, belief in revelation was therefore "the most profound presupposition" that distinguished medieval from both ancient and modern philosophy.[88]

Strauss looked to the "reconstitution" of medieval Islamic and Jewish Platonic philosophy as a corrective to modern trends. Strauss explained the repressive context of Farabian Neoplatonists and their ability to secure philosophical freedom:

> Farabi had discovered in the politics of Plato the golden mean equally removed from a naturalism which aims only at sanctioning the savage and destructive instincts of "natural" man, the instincts of the master and conqueror; and from a supernaturalism which tends to become the basis of slave morality—a golden mean which is neither a compromise nor a synthesis, which is hence not based on the two opposed positions, but which suppresses them both, uproots them by a prior, more profound question, by raising a fundamental problem, the work of a truly critical philosophy.[89]

Although Strauss had treated the subject of prophecy in *Philosophie und Gesetz*, he now offered a fuller and more focused description of prophecy as a fulfillment of Plato's hypothetical lawgiver whose laws are endowed with divine legitimation. His reading of prophecy was influenced by his concern for the tension between the philosopher and the needs of the society in which he lived. It is in this context that Strauss identified the faculty of courage required by prophecy in the thought of Al-Farabi and Maimonides.

The faculty of courage acquires a political function because it relates to the danger the prophet/philosopher must incur upon his descent back into the cave of opinion in order to instruct men. Maimonides wrote that this social function "necessarily displeases unjust men" and therefore subjects the philosopher to "perpetual danger."[90] "Although this danger is inevitable even if the prophet restricts himself to instructing men, it is much more menacing when the prophet *opposes, as a guide of just men, the injustices of tyrants or the multitude.*"[91]

Strauss summarized Maimonides's view of the raison d'être of prophecy as the founding of a perfect nation and the consequent proclamation of a perfect law which served as its constitution.[92] The proof is to be found in the very distinction between the prophecy of Moses and that of the other prophets.[93] Maimonides reserves the unique role of founder of the perfect community for Moses.[94] The repeated statements regarding the superiority of Mosaic prophecy to all others (including the patriarchs) is not the repetition of "something commonplace" but rather "betrays a specific tendency": that Mosaic prophecy is legislative.[95] Thus Maimonides implicitly holds Moses to be the sole Platonic philosopher-legislator and Farabian "first Chief."

According to Strauss, Maimonides resisted the impulse to offer a clear description of this doctrine. Strauss argued that "Maimonides neither wished nor was able, nor had any need, to lift the veil which conceals the origins of the Torah, the foundation of the perfect nation."[96] Maimonides offered "signs" indicating his teaching to "the one who will understand," for the rare "attentive and duly instructed reader." In this philosophical-political reading, it is the *aim*, and not the *origins*, of the Law that distinguishes esoteric philosophy from mysticism.[97] Strauss therefore emphasized the "given" character of Torah in Maimonides' thought. To go beyond this fact risks swallowing what the human intellect is incapable of digesting and therefore will vomit out.[98] The unwise and impertinent attempt to speculate about the origins of the Torah ignores the political nature of the human condition: that man must live in a community with others.[99] As a result, one must accept, at least outwardly, certain obligatory beliefs that secure order in the community.[100]

In order to preserve the ideal character of the Law, the medievals proposed that the law has two decidedly different meanings: "an exterior, literal meaning, addressed to the vulgar, which expresses both the philosophical and the necessary beliefs, and a secret meaning of a purely philosophical nature."[101] Moreover, Maimonides himself "imitated" this bivalence in his own philosophic interpretation of the law. "For if he had distinguished explicitly between true and necessary beliefs," Strauss argues, Maimonides "would have endangered the acceptance of the necessary beliefs on which the authority of the law with the vulgar, i.e. with the great majority, rests." Thus, Maimonides felt obligated to disguise this distinction by resorting to rhetorical devices recognizable only to philosophers when he defends beliefs that are not true, but necessary. This is why Maimonides's philosophic magnum opus, the *Guide of the Perplexed,* ingeniously combines "a strictly demonstrative discussion of the beliefs which are common to philosophy and law" with a "rhetorical discussion of the unphilosophical beliefs peculiar to the law." The most pressing difficulty posed when reading Maimonides, according to Strauss, is that Maimonides offers a bivalent interpretation of a bivalent text. Strauss claims that Maimonides intended there to be two totally different readings of his philosophic works: "a 'radical' interpretation which did honor to the consistency of his thought, and a 'moderate' interpretation which did honor rather to the fervor of his belief."[102] There is a literal meaning that is addressed to a philosophically unlearned audience that stays close to traditional Jewish beliefs, but also a second meaning that is secret and "addressed to true philosophers." This level is "purely philosophical" and should be taken to be the true position of Maimonides.

The philosopher who is born into a Jewish community can negotiate the competing loyalty to Jerusalem (revealed religion) and Athens (philosophy) by providing a Platonic foundation for Torah, Judaism's perfect constitution, without abandoning the call of philosophy. Indeed, the philosopher effectively reinforces the pillars of the politico-religious regime precisely through his honed speculative teachings.[103]

At this point we have touched upon Strauss's understanding of Maimonidean prophecy as it pertains to the relationship between philosophy and the Jew. The other element of Maimonides's doctrine of prophecy relates to possible responses to the condition of exile. Strauss paid special attention to Maimonides's view of the Jew and the natural condition of exile. Strauss argued that Plato's search for the perfect city, the problem he resolved with a hypothetical divine legislation, "could not be forgotten by the Jew." This intransigent memory relates to the self-perceived unique status of the Jewish nation as the recipient of the Law. The Jewish nation is the perfect nation insofar as it is constituted by the perfect law *and* provided that it obeys that law.[104] In the wake of the Jews' disobedience, the prophets still courageously held Israel to that perfect standard. Upholding the eternal and immutable Mosaic constitution was the prophetic legacy handed down to Jews as they were destined to live in imperfect societies.

In the midst of his own European exile, Strauss drew from Maimonides's commentary on Jeremiah to demonstrate the prophets' response to political injustice. Maimonides argued that "the man who loves perfection and justice" must abandon cities "inhabited exclusively by the wicked" and search for a city of good men.[105] But if this noble individual cannot find or establish such a city, he "must prefer wandering in the desert or in caverns to the association with the evil men."[106] Because, for Strauss, there are no existing perfect societies, a noble soul must be careful with whom he associates. If the prophet is resigned to an aloof and private existence, he will remain untouched by the allures of assimilation, wealth, and power.

According to Maimonides, this way of acting is obligatory for every Jew. Strauss identifies the Maimonidean individual who is devoted to "perfection and justice" with the soul of the philosopher, and more particularly, the Jewish philosopher. If such an individual is unable to live in accord with the demands of the ideal city and articulate that content, he must leave that city if he can. If he cannot, or is unable to find a just city elsewhere, then he must find a way to migrate inwardly so as to avoid association with wicked men. This last option is a way of accommodating exile, and is carried out by way of esoteric and exoteric writing and speech.[107]

Strauss was not alone in identifying the strategy for an inner migration for Jewish thinkers. Gershom Scholem, for instance, explored the subterranean channel of Jewish mysticism as the most vibrant strain of Jewish thought.[108] And we also find a much broader renaissance of coded writing and reading strategies for those figures who wished to express or discover discontent with tyrannical conditions under fascist and Soviet Communist rule. Authors and artists conspired with potentially receptive audiences by veiling their criticisms of the existing regime in ways that would avoid suspicion (or at least prosecution) from established authority. The strategy of inner migration runs through the literature of both German refugees as well as those individuals who remained in Germany and expressed alienation from Nazism and the nazification of German society. Although these two groups experienced incomparable moral pressures, both adopted cognitive and rhetorical modes specifically suited to painful conditions of homelessness and alienation regardless of where they are located. Acknowledging this parallel makes the moral question of complicity all the more difficult; there are no simple and absolute lines separating perpetrators, bystanders, dissidents and victims. The most audible dissident voices in a totalitarian environment will not speak long. Strauss would turn his attention to many of these problems in his 1941 essay "Persecution and the Art of Writing."

While Maimonides offered another response to exile in his philosophic interpretation of messianism, Strauss argued that Maimonides regarded this option as inferior to Mosaic prophecy. For Maimonides, the figure of the Messiah is both king and sage, and will enforce law but is not capable of transcending laws of nature. Moreover, the Maimonidean Messiah does not have the power to extinguish crucial differences between "the vulgar masses" and "the philosophers."[109] The messianic figure in Maimonides, Strauss correctly sees, is both natural and determined by purely political criteria. As we have seen earlier in this chapter, Strauss takes this same understanding into his reading of Hobbes's requirement that all subjects of the peaceful commonwealth affirm that "Jesus is the Christ."

The concern for the aim of the perfect law, rather than its origins, reinforces this motive of keeping potentially destabilizing forces in check. It is for this reason that Strauss views Don Isaac Abravanel's (1437–1508) more messianic doctrines of kingship and priesthood as inferior political teachings to those of Maimonides. As part of the quincentennial anniversary commemorations of Abravanel's birth, Strauss published a lecture in 1937, "On Abravanel's Philosophical Tendency and Political Teaching"; in it, Strauss accentuates the divergent paths in Maimonides and Abravanel.[110] Strauss's title is playful in that he concluded that Abravanel's philosophical tendency was a rather "unphilosophic" strand of rationalism and that his political teaching was in the end an "antipolitical" teaching. Strauss attributed Abravanel's divergence from the Maimonidean teaching of the imperative for esoteric writing to his absorption of and reliance upon medieval Christian Scholasticism. Abravanel represents another Jewish thinker who tried to come to grips with the spiritual and political tumult of exile. Strauss argued that Abravanel's utopian, republican vision of politics was the product of a thorough absorption of Christian Scholasticism and that his understanding of prophecy did not take account of unequal intellects. In contrast, Maimonidean prophecy illustrated to Strauss the need for multilevel truths. Maimonides's prophets must have a perfected imaginative faculty because "imagination makes possible the metaphorical exoteric representation of the truths whose proper, esoteric meaning must be concealed from the vulgar. For one neither can nor ought speak of the principles except in an enigmatic manner; this is what not only 'men of the law' but also the philosophers say. Maimonides names only one of these esoteric philosophers: Plato."[111]

Thus, Strauss sought guidance for the tribulations of exile in a medieval Islamic and Jewish actualization of Platonic political philosophy. Strauss offered descriptions of this esoteric tradition in language that is neither purposefully ambiguous nor deliberately invested with hidden meanings. He had yet to reproduce these dissimulating practices in describing them. Strauss subtly introduced this innovation in "Persecution and the Art of Writing" (1941). The appearance of "Persecution and the Art of Writing" marked the beginnings of a distinctive writing style that replicated his hermeneutic. And while Strauss would refine the contours of his thesis and increasingly depart from scholarly conventions, his unmistakable multilevel writing style substantively begins after he had come to settle in the United States.

After several visits to the United States during the autumn of 1936 and winter of 1937, Strauss obtained a temporary position as a research and editorial assistant to Salo Baron at Columbia University. The following fall, Strauss finally secured a teaching position at the newly established New School for Social Research and supplemented this appointment with several adjunct appointments throughout the northeastern United States. It seems only fitting that

Strauss should make his entrance into the American academy at an institution dubbed "The University in Exile." Even within this refuge for persecuted European scholars, however, the current of Strauss's political thought ran counter to the dominant direction of his new colleagues.[112] Strauss continued his investigations into medieval Islamic and Jewish Platonic political philosophy as well as more modern forms of esoteric hermeneutics as he tried to adjust to his new surroundings. The New School became a symbol for the American commitment to protecting freedom of thought and expression (as against European fascism and Soviet Communism). At the same time, Strauss further explored the ramifications of multilevel writing as the philosophical response of one resigned to live in an imperfect society yet not fully willing to surrender a noble vision of the perfect regime.

# CHAPTER 4

# Persecution and the Art of Writing: The New York Years (1938–1948)

*L*eo Strauss arrived in the United States in 1937 as one of many European scholars seeking refuge. As recounted in the preceding chapter, Strauss had spent the previous five years of his European exile in France and England. As a conservative who witnessed the collapse of the European continent into the polarized extremes of fascism and communism, Strauss warmed to England's conservative intellectual tradition and to what he deemed to be its moderate political sensibilities. Unable to obtain a university post in England, Strauss crossed the Atlantic and arrived in New York to commence a temporary position as a research fellow under the direction of the Jewish historian, Salo Baron, in the Department of History at Columbia University. The next year he joined the Graduate Faculty of Political Science and Social Research of the New School for Social Research, where he would remain until 1948.

Strauss adjusted to his new environment and career as a university professor during a decade of war and catastrophe. He learned of the need to accommodate to political imperfection while safeguarding one's path toward individual philosophical advancement. The new element to be found in this period was his attempt to introduce what he considered the intellectual virtues of illiberal societies into the American academic culture. While the political conditions of totalitarianism or tyranny were intrinsically undesirable, they had, according to Strauss, one positive effect: they generated a sense of prudence and caution—dispositions that modern philosophy at first sought to modify, then rejected, and eventually completely forgot. Thus, Strauss wanted to recapture the philosopher's awareness of his or her precarious existence under a totalitarian regime and instill this need for circumspection within the confines of a liberal democracy.

Strauss suffered personal tragedy as the Nazi terror spread and intensified. While Strauss's wife and stepson would join him in New York in the late 1930s, the other members of his immediate family would not survive the war.[1] According to data drawn from the German census, the number of German Jews had declined under the Nazi regime from an estimated 525,000 in 1933 to 185,000 in the autumn of 1939, to a mere 14,574 by September 1944.[2] Leo Strauss's father, Hugo Strauss, died in the spring of 1942 just before the deportation of Kirchhain's Jewry. His stepmother and the rest of his immediate family that stayed in Germany were soon killed after being deported to death camps in the east.[3]

Strauss's only sibling, Bettina Strauss, wrote her dissertation under the direction of Julius Ruska and Paul Kraus. Bettina Strauss and Paul Kraus were married in Cairo in 1936. Kraus was a Czech-born Jewish scholar of medieval Islamic philosophy, science, and medicine as well as the Bible and archaeology. Leo Strauss and Paul Kraus became acquainted in the late 1920s and early 1930s in Berlin.[4] Bettina and Paul traveled to Palestine, Lebanon, and Egypt for research and possible academic appointments. Bettina died in January 1942 while giving birth to Jenny Ann Kraus in Cairo. Just two years after Bettina's death, Paul Kraus committed suicide.[5] Strauss adopted his four-year-old niece, Jenny, and raised her as his own daughter in the United States.[6]

Strauss learned of the tragic fates of his family members while also under the strain of poor physical health and financial pressures. Strauss's financial, professional, and political anxieties began to take their toll. Even though his handwriting had never been particularly lucid, Strauss's personal correspondence during the mid-1940s is replete with apologies for the poor handwriting. According to him, his penmanship reflected not only his poor health, but also a high-pressure working environment. For example, in a letter to Karl Löwith dated January 10, 1946, Strauss wrote: "As you can see from my handwriting, I am not at all well. One grows older and older, and nothing gets finished. Life here in this country is terribly difficult for people such as me. One must struggle for the most modest working conditions, and one is defeated in every battle."[7] Furthermore, like many other refugee scholars at the time, Strauss became increasingly frustrated with the conformism of American academic publishing. "Here, what does not fit the pattern, is lost," complained Strauss.[8]

The weight of events in Europe, adjustment to the demands of American academia, and the struggle against declining health—these are the conditions in which Strauss developed the main components of what would later be his mature teaching. A veritable *Denkbewegung* or intellectual movement known as Straussianism emerged as his followers diffused ossified forms of his thought.[9] By the end of the 1940s, Strauss and several other European (Jewish and non-Jewish) refugees had reshaped the landscape of the humanities and social sciences in the United States.

At first glance, the New School would appear to be a perfect fit for Strauss. The institution welcomed European refugee scholars and identified its mission as defiance of the persecution and suppression of independent thought on the European continent. But Strauss did not accept the New School's ideal of unbridled intellectual expression. Indeed, Strauss considered his rediscovery of "exoteric teaching" to be a positive product of those very conditions that threatened intellectual expression. As will be explained, Strauss's understanding and use of "exoteric teaching" are idiosyncratic.

The tangible dangers posed by the illiberal faces of fascism and Soviet Communism aroused writers to engage in various expressions of covert dissent. Authors living under tyrannical regimes could publish their subversive ideas by availing themselves of coded forms of writing that could escape the eyes of censors. In order for the secret message to be received, a community of sensitized readers joined these dissident authors in this cryptographic movement under totalitarian societies.

Once outside these conditions, émigré scholars who came to the United States and England in the late 1930s and early 1940s were recruited by various intelligence institutions to monitor propaganda media and by military intelligence to break enemy codes.[10] When the United States entered the war in 1942, even some officially classified "enemy aliens" worked for the American Counter Intelligence Corps (CIC); Army Military Intelligence; Naval Intelligence; Allen Dulles's new entity, the Office of Strategic Services (OSS); and other sensitive positions as the U.S. government mobilized intelligence resources. Leftist scholars of the ISS (Institute for Social Research) such as Franz Neumann, Herbert Marcuse, and Otto Kirchheimer formed a research group under the auspices of the research and analysis division of the OSS and the State Department.[11] In this sense, Strauss's project may be seen as a philosophic analogue to the cryptographic practices that flourished in the years leading up to and during World War II. Indeed, it seems more than a coincidence that Strauss began in earnest to pursue the contours of coded writings while much of the world's intellectual labor force had become mobilized by various intelligence agencies.

In Strauss's New York period, he deepened his understanding of a tradition of philosophical circumspection. Moreover, he developed those rhetorical devices that revolved around the distinction between the esoteric and the exoteric. Considering the open and cosmopolitan character of the New York intellectual context, this development appears to be counterintuitive.[12] He began to engage in different tactics of intellectual dissimulation only after he came to live and work within the institutional (the New School) and national (U.S.) entities that proclaimed freedom of conscience and expression as absolute and unalienable rights. Strauss's insistence on counterbalancing and camouflaging philosophical boldness with habits of reticence and caution, especially within the confines of a progressive university and a liberal democracy, attests to more than his acknowledgment of contemporary forces threatening the free exchange of ideas.

It also symbolizes his internalization of the permanence of political imperfection and the persistence of *galut,* the Jewish condition of exile.

A cynical view would be that Strauss suffered from a persecution complex. From a biographical perspective, however, we must take into account the specific experiences that shaped Strauss's exilic disposition before making such a psychological diagnosis. He was, after all, a German Jew born in the heart of rural political antisemitism. As a young participant in Weimar's vibrant and fractious culture, he would soon witness from abroad the birth of a murderous regime that radicalized its racial discrimination against Jews and other perceived enemies. Given the failure of German liberalism, we should not be surprised that such a person would remain skeptical about the prospect of achieving full inclusion and security within any society. In this light, it would be difficult to argue convincingly that his suspicions were mere delusions of paranoia. But the case of Strauss is striking precisely because he was *not* a liberal assimilationist who later became disillusioned with the ideal of an egalitarian, tolerant, and enlightened society. The argument that has run through this book is that Strauss did not fit into George Mosse's portrait of a Jewish *Bildungsbürgertum* (in *German Jews Beyond Judaism*).[13] Distinct from Mosse's model of a liberal bourgeoisie, Strauss exemplified the countermodel of "German Jews beyond liberalism and Bildung" outlined by Stephen Aschheim, which notes the radical reorientation of Weimar Jewish intellectuals.[14] But the case of Strauss is even more intriguing as his rejection of liberalism involved a movement to the right.[15] Like Scholem's gravitation toward Zionism and Benjamin's toward Marxism, Strauss's early thought reflected his rejection of the *Bildungsbürgertum* that had become the cultural ideal of Jewry under the *Kaiserreich.* As a young man, his heightened awareness of the complex dynamics of the Jewish problem in Europe, and the profound theological and political issues subsumed within it, brought him to confront and reject the Spinozistic solution of liberalism and assimilation. In the world constructed in the wake of the seventeenth-century radical enlightenment, the old values of rank, order, truth, and the sacred, were all overturned and despised in favor of egalitarianism, relativism, commercialism, historicism, mass politics, and liberalism. Strauss's discontent with this latter group of modernity's leveling forces continued to drive his thought after the collapse of Weimar and throughout his American career.

Strauss's projection of the persecuted Jew onto the philosopher reminds us of the man who finds himself accused of paranoia and retorts: "Just because I think people are following me doesn't mean that they aren't." A half-joking Strauss might have added, "It also doesn't mean that they shouldn't follow me. And above all, it doesn't mean that I shouldn't think they are or should be following me." Even if this kind of mental disposition is seen as paranoia, it is a distillation of the estrangement and alienation that so informs the modern Jewish—and, more generally, the modern human—condition. Strauss's American thought represents a transformation of a neurotic condition into a creative intellectual agenda.[16]

Strauss's ideas on exile were first intimated in his Weimar writings, but his later thought on the problematic of exile features important differences. The group of people caught in the grips of the predicament of exile shifts from the Jews to philosophers. We should recall that attention to exile, and its specifically Jewish variant, *galut*, permeate his German and European writings. Recall Strauss's 1923 critique of political Zionism, for example, where he claimed that *galut* underlies the central paradox of the Jews. *Galut* affords "the Jewish people a maximum possibility of existence [*Daseinsmöglichkeit*] through a condition of minimum normality."[17] In the 1930s, he would simply project this permanent condition of alienation from the Jewish people to philosophers. Philosophers must safeguard their devotion to one universal truth—the pursuit of intellectual perfection—within the particular context of a city, nation, or state that demands uncontested loyalty from its people. The inherent tension between the philosopher's competing loyalties to philosophy and to the imperfect political order in which she or he is rooted, renders philosophy and philosophers suspect and alien. The abnormality of being the perpetual outsider, however, optimizes the possible forms of philosophy and philosophic existence. Because the philosopher is cognizant of the perennial incompatibility between these competing loyalties, the cave of social imperfection burdens, but does not altogether blunt, the quest for individual perfection promised by philosophical ascent.

Strauss's New York period brought about related transitions. He entered American academia in a manner befitting his paradigmatic strategies of accommodation. He sought to place a group of medieval Islamic and Jewish thinkers at the center of a philosophical and political tradition that had previously received scant attention by those larger fields in the United States. Al Farabi, Averroës, Maimonides, Halevi, and Spinoza anchored Strauss's project of recovering the wisdom of medieval political philosophy. Strauss argued that these philosophers, who operated outside the authority of Christian Europe, promise to redirect our attention to teachings that disappeared with the ascendance of modern forces. Although the modern Western world was created with the intention to serve man's welfare by alleviating his dependence on nature, the technical means required to achieve this goal ultimately turned against man himself. In the 1930s, Strauss was convinced that the reified amenities of modernity prevented man from taking stock of his true situation. Strauss therefore called for a descent from the artificial "second cave" of thought to the first, and natural, Platonic cave. Modern philosophy has lost sight of the natural conditions of the Platonic cave. Strauss wanted to excavate the medieval and ancient ground from which the philosophical ascent must begin. Strauss tried to establish this new foothold as international rescue efforts sought to assist expelled and endangered scholars to emigrate from Germany and its conquered territories.

When Strauss came to the United States in 1937, the crisis of European refugee scholars had already become acute. Strauss's sojourns following his 1932 departure from Germany exemplify the significance and limitations of international rescue organizations that sought to assist émigré scholars during the 1930s and 1940s. The primary options for refugee scholars fleeing Nazi persecution were the very places Strauss sought refuge: France, England, Palestine, and the United States.[18]

Official institutions such as the League of Nations offered little direct help to endangered European scholars. The League of Nations appointed James McDonald as high commissioner for refugees in October 1933, but the short-lived office did not enjoy much support or recognition from its parent organization.[19] Consigned to an office in Lausanne, instead of the league's home in Geneva, the high commissioner was both geographically and politically marginalized. He was not allowed to present any findings or complaints to the league council; significantly, however, he was empowered to negotiate with various governments on behalf of refugees and assist private relief organizations in coordinating their joint efforts. Nevertheless, McDonald resigned within two years of his appointment.[20]

In the specific case of Jewish refugees, there were already some organizations such as the Joint Distribution Committee (JDC), HICEM, and the Jewish Agency for Palestine that had been established decades earlier in order to facilitate Eastern European Jewish emigration.[21] In Palestine, for example, some one hundred German scholars found temporary positions at the Hebrew University and other institutions. These Jewish organizations were supplemented by newly established American organizations to facilitate emigration of endangered European scholars: the New York Foundation, the Carnegie Foundation, the Oberlander Trust, and the Rockefeller Foundation. This last entity proved to be the largest contributor to the rescue effort. The Rockefeller Foundation had been crucial in providing aid to refugee scholars such as Strauss. It should be recalled that a Rockefeller fellowship facilitated Strauss's initial departure from Germany in 1932. And in the wake of the new situation in Germany the following year, Strauss, like many other German scholars, applied for and received an extension on his research grant. The Rockefeller Foundation provided $1.4 million for the rescue of displaced scholars—half of the funding for all such efforts by subsidizing aid organizations.[22]

Some of the more important of these organizations that had been established in 1933 were the Emergency Committee in Aid of Displaced German Scholars in the United States; the Academic Assistance Council (AAC) in Great Britain;[23] the Association Universelle pour les Exilés Allemands in France; and the Notgemeinschaft deutscher Wissenschaftler im Ausland in Switzerland.[24] The first two organizations assisted Strauss and other scholars in their search for academic employment in England and the United States. The Zurich-based Notgemeinschaft placed two thousand German scholars at colleges and universities in Turkey, South America, and the Soviet Union.[25]

The peregrinations of some of Strauss's notable acquaintances and contemporaries give an idea of the ferment of this period. Ernst Cassirer, Strauss's dissertation adviser at the University of Hamburg, initially moved to England in 1933 as part of the transfer of the entire staff and holdings of the famed Warburg Institute from Germany.[26] Gershom Scholem emigrated to Palestine out of Zionist conviction in 1923, while another colleague from the Akademie, Yitzhak (Fritz) Baer, did so in 1930. Julius Guttmann, the director of the Akademie during Strauss's employment, considered settling in the United States in the early 1930s before accepting a position at the Hebrew University in Jerusalem in 1934.

Karl Löwith, whose correspondence with Strauss during the 1930s and 1940s is especially revealing, befriended Strauss while under the tutelage of Martin Heidegger in Marburg and Freiburg. Because Löwith was a Jew, he left for Italy in the wake of the Aryanization of German universities. From there, he would travel with his wife to the University of Sendai, Japan. After the German pact with Japan, Löwith would once again be forced to escape. With the help of Paul Tillich and Reinhold Niebuhr, Löwith obtained a position at the Hartford Theological Seminary in Connecticut just six months prior to the Japanese invasion of Pearl Harbor.[27] Löwith would later arrive at the New School for Social Research in 1949 and then return to Germany, where he held a chair in philosophy at the University of Heidelberg in 1953.[28]

For those threatened scholars still in France when the French surrendered to Germany, the situation became particularly urgent.[29] The U.S. State Department granted only one-fifth of visa applications filed (238) between August 5 and December 18, 1940. Even those who eventually received U.S. visas were forced to take the taxing and dangerous route that has been referred to as the "refugee gauntlet," the course of which ran from southern France through Spain and Portugal to New York. The tragic plight of Marc Bloch is a well-known example of someone who tried to come to the New School but became ensnared in the labyrinth of cold and ever-changing American immigration policies.[30]

Walter Benjamin, who met Strauss in the late 1920s in Berlin through their mutual friend Scholem, also suffered a cruel fate following France's defeat.[31] By the time Benjamin decided to leave France, the exits were closed. Both Benjamin and Bloch faced the obstacle of American policies that sought to weed out refugees with any connection with socialist and communist organizations.[32] Benjamin was unable to acquire a British visa. And his attempted escape was hampered by a heart condition that forced constant short respites from walking every few minutes. Images of impending suffocation and death permeated his thoughts during this angst-ridden journey. Benjamin was among two thousand other refugees who fled into southern France. In September, a U.S. visa was secured on Benjamin's behalf. In order to set sail for New York, Benjamin first had to cross over the Pyrenees into Spain illegally and take a train to Lisbon. Benjamin and his two companions arrived in the Spanish town of Port Bou whereupon they were told by Spanish authorities that a recent Spanish embargo on stateless refugees rendered their documents meaningless. The following morning they were to be escorted back to the French border by the Spanish police, where they would face the prospect of incarceration and deportation to concentration camps. That morning, September 27, 1940, Benjamin died as result of a self-administered lethal dose of morphine.[33] The rest of his companions successfully continued their journey.

### University in Exile: The New School for Social Research

The New School emerged in the wake of a controversy surrounding Columbia University's decision to fire two faculty members who had spoken against American participation in World War I.[34] In 1918 several left-leaning American academics associated with the *New Republic,* the *Dial,* and the *Nation* formed the New School as an alternative to conventional models of academic communities. This progressive enterprise sought to promote scholarly independence and collaborative efforts of faculty and students. The early orientation of the school as an institution devoted to adult education was clearly inspired by the German *Volkshochschulen* that were established after 1918.

Alvin Johnson, who had taken over the leadership of the New School in 1922, revitalized and redirected this progressive mission in response to the Nazi decree of April 6, 1933, that purged Jewish, socialist, and other "undesirable" academics from the German university system. Johnson perceived the gravity of the situation in Europe and immediately responded by spearheading an active recruitment of refugee social scientists to a reestablished form of the New School. While other American institutions of higher learning selectively appointed a significant number of refugee scholars, the New School's new appendage, "The University in Exile," distinguished itself in that it was staffed entirely of expelled academics from Europe.[35] Johnson sought to lend a German character to the new institution, both in its form as well as content. He had already come to appreciate the German tradition of scholarship during the previous decade when he co-edited the *Encyclopedia of Social Science* with Edwin R.A. Seligman (1861–1939), a project which included leading German social scientists.[36] The New School concentrated much of its resources on the recruitment of expelled social scientists for the newly created University in Exile, and its 1935 successor, the Graduate Faculty of Philosophy and Political Science. It secured positions for thirty of the 157 German social scientists dismissed or forced to resign from 1933 to 1939.[37]

A related institution, the Institute for Social Research (ISR), also settled in Morningside Heights, New York, under the auspices of Columbia University and sharing some obvious characteristics with the New School.[38] Yet relations between these two émigré institutions and their faculties were marked by tensions that arose from the different institutional orientations and characters.[39] The ISR was, in general, composed of thinkers politically committed to various socialist agendas and associated with its previous permutations in Frankfurt, Geneva, and Paris. The University in Exile was composed of an eclectic group insofar as it attracted more expelled university faculty from the German social sciences than any other institution in Europe or America. As the threat to European scholars expanded, so did the recruitment efforts of the Graduate Faculty, the nominal successor to the University in Exile. The Graduate Faculty eventually enlisted refugee scholars from Italy, Austria, Poland, Belgium, and France.

Financial status marked another difference between the two institutions. Whereas the Institute for Social Research was financially independent and provided relatively comfortable salary levels, the University in Exile as well as its successor, the Graduate Faculty, relied on public support at a time of worldwide economic crisis.[40]

The University in Exile was initially underwritten, in great part, by an anonymous donation from Hiram Halle, a wealthy Jewish businessman. The University in Exile was renamed as the Graduate Faculty of the New School in 1935.[41] The name change came in response to fears of xenophobic, anti-Communist, and even antisemitic reaction. The Graduate Faculty, as a name, veiled the immigrant makeup of its faculty and thus did not exacerbate xenophobic currents in America.[42]

Prior to the *Anschluss,* social scientists who joined the Graduate Faculty were largely drawn from German social democratic circles. The German members of the Graduate Faculty were disproportionately drawn from the University of Berlin's Hochschule für Politik, the University of Frankfurt's Institute for Social Research (ISR), and the Kiel Institute of World Economics. As the situation worsened in Europe in the late 1930s, the New School recruited a more ideologically diverse second wave of immigration: Strauss is a prime example. And the international makeup of the Graduate Faculty would undergo another dramatic change following Germany's invasion of France in May 1940.

Within a few months after France capitulated to German forces, the Rockefeller Foundation and the New School successfully intervened to bring fifty French scholars to America, thirty-four of whom acquired positions at the New School.[43] The failed integration of this large group of scholars into the largely German Graduate Faculty culminated in the establishment, in 1942, of the École libre des hautes études, which offered courses in French and received recognition by de Gaulle as a French university in exile. The philosopher and historian of science, Alexander Koyré, was at the center of a Gaullist faction of this group of French refugees. Koyré had befriended Strauss in Paris during the early 1930s.[44] According to one historian of the New School, "the Gaullist core" rejected "the entire intellectual direction of the New School." This group defied Johnson's attempts at integration and "went on cultivating its nationalistic hermetism and making frequent verbal attacks on the Graduate Faculty until its return to France in 1945."[45] By 1946, the remaining strands of the Ecole Libre split off from the New School completely and formed an autonomous institute of French culture situated in New York.

When Strauss came to the New School in 1938, academics were in flight from Czechoslovakia, Austria, and Italy as well. He was part of a second wave of émigré appointments at the New School. The strained financial resources and the resistance of many American universities to assist the rescue efforts resulted in less than ideal conditions for prospective émigré scholars. The Emergency Committee tried to encourage American universities to appoint chosen refugee scholars by financing part of their depressed salaries for one or two years.[46]

Like several of his colleagues, Strauss supplemented his initial appointment to the New School's Graduate Faculty with several adjunct lectureships at colleges and universities throughout the northeastern United States. He acquired U.S. citizenship and within a year, he was able to finance and arrange to have his wife and stepson, Thomas Petri, cross the Atlantic and join him in New York. During Strauss's tenure at the New School's Graduate Faculty of Political Science and Philosophy from 1938 to 1948, he advanced from the rank of lecturer to associate professor and then acquired the title of full professor.

Strauss's presence at the New School can be gauged by taking into account his participation in joint projects, scholarship, and teaching. One of the first duties that Strauss received at the New School was to serve as an associate editor for the New School's journal, *Social Research*. Hans Speier (1905–93), who knew Strauss from Berlin in the late 1920s, was the editor.[47] *Social Research* became, in many respects, an American incarnation of the *Archiv für Sozialwissenschaft und Sozialpolitik*, for which Speier served as an assistant editor under his senior colleague at the Berlin Hochschule für Politik, Emil Lederer. *Social Research* sought to draw from the Graduate Faculty's General Seminar so that the faculty could appear as a coherent group to American academia.[48] The General Seminar aimed at an interdisciplinary fusion of *Forschung* and *Darstellung*, research and presentation, operating as the dialectical ideal of the ISR and the Berlin Hochschule für Politik.[49] Johnson conveyed this cooperative vision of the Graduate Faculty's scholarship in *War in Our Time*, the first wartime collection of the New School and *Social Research*. "What one man cannot do alone," Johnson proudly asserted, "a group of men can do . . . working in honest cooperation."[50]

Strauss contributed scores of articles and reviews but, on the whole, his contributions have a complex relationship with the journal. While several issues were devoted to upholding freedom of expression, Strauss's contributions consistently enunciated his ambivalent attitude toward such liberal principles.[51] For the present discussion, we should note that the one arena of liberal democracy that Strauss sought to influence was education.

Strauss's New York writings in this period were not primarily addressed to established professors of philosophy; rather, they were intended to arouse the passionate interests of his students and other potential philosophers. Like Plato, Strauss affectionately referred to this intended audience as "the young puppies."[52] Thus, Strauss's published writings during this period sought to serve the "exoteric" goal of reaching astute young minds. The popular treatments of philosophical topics matter precisely because the younger generation can be won or lost on this plane. Indeed, as will be seen, Strauss blamed Weimar advocates of rationalism for not speaking to the needs and concerns of the younger generation, thereby paving the road to nihilism and ultimately Nazism.

Strauss wrote an extended review of John Wild's *Plato's Theory of Man* with the aim of teaching his students to be careful about accepting the authority of a piece of scholarship that is well received by the popular press.[53] In a letter to Löwith, Strauss explained that the intention of the review was to expose the book as exemplary of "what sort of dung from idiots [*Mist von Idioten*] is praised by the *New York Times, Tribune*, etc."[54]

Strauss's reviews in *Social Research* also expressed his reluctance to embrace American political ideals without qualification. America did, however, represent one of the best alternatives to the other regimes in the world. In an otherwise dismissive treatment of another book on Plato, Strauss did manage to find one element deserving of approbation. Strauss points to one instance in which the author, R. H. S. Crossman, sets Plato in dialogue with a member of the English Parliament. "I should assume in talking to you that your ideals are sound. Of course they are not, but they are less vicious than those of most other nations which I have visited."[55] Even though Strauss thought Great Britain and its leadership under Winston Churchill to be superior to the United States, he could have easily whispered the words above to a member of the U.S. Senate.[56] America was far from the aristocratic model he deemed to be the best regime, but the tribulations of Europe had tempered his expectations. Strauss would be resigned to living in what he thought was an intrinsically imperfect society.

Meanwhile, much of the New School's émigré faculty devoted themselves to understanding the collapse of the Weimar Republic, as well as the nature and meaning of National Socialism. In fact, many of the members of the newly created faculty in the early 1930s in New York saw their institution and its journal as a means of perpetuating the democratic and pluralistic ideals of the Weimar Republic. The University in Exile would transplant the project of Weimar onto American soil. But in the United States, the spirit of liberalism that infused the republic remained an anathema to Strauss. As argued in chapter 3, his excavation of modes of intellectual expression that thrived under premodern illiberal conditions reflected his continued agitation against the ideals of the liberal regime that had been destroyed by the establishment of the Third Reich.

Strauss consulted the ancient authorities of Plato, Aristotle, and Xenophon in his attempt to understand the dynamics of modern totalitarianism and tyranny. Strauss's first essay in *Social Research* conveyed his peculiar response to the political specters of European fascism and the intellectual crisis of historicism.

## Multilevel Writing on Multilevel Writing

As Strauss became disenchanted with intellectuals and their complicity in the advent of modern tyranny, he turned his attention to the political orientation of premodern thinkers worthy of emulation. In "The Spirit of Sparta; or, A Taste of Xenophon,"[57] Strauss set out to recover the ancients' taste for philosophy by reassessing Xenophon's complex critique of the republic spirit of politics.[58] Key to such an understanding is recognizing that Xenophon, who was Strauss's fellow exile, and an entire class of ancient thinkers protected themselves by intentionally misleading the average reader as to their true opinions on the most important matters of religion and politics. Mere concern for one's safety was not the only motive of Strauss's predecessors to play with audience expectations. Brief yet decisive exhibitions of Strauss's new rhetorical disposition appeared in analyses of the various ways in which a transnational and transpolitical elite group publicized its thought. A careful philosophic writer may write two very different kinds of works. In one work, he may "teach the truth according to the rule of moderation," while in another he may convey his teaching "according to the rule of bashfulness."[59] Strauss describes works like Plato's *Laws* and Xenophon's *Constitution of the Lacedemonians* as "most bashful speeches about the most bashful men." In this 1939 article on Xenophon (born 431 B.C.E. and died before 350 B.C.E.), Strauss suggests that "bashful writing" accommodates philosophic positions to what is publicly or visibly good, as opposed to what is truly good.[60]

Strauss reads Xenophon as undertaking a subtle and ironic critique of Spartan hypocrisy and superficiality.[61] The tyrannical spirit of Sparta subjects everything to the requirements of public virtue. But the form of Xenophon's bashful satire of Athens's enemy seems needlessly circuitous, considering that Xenophon was an Athenian. Strauss argues that Xenophon's acquired philosophic taste determined the satirical form of his text. As a philosopher, he could not simply praise Athens because this would have been too easy, and philosophers know that all things noble are difficult. Strauss explains: "By writing his censure of Sparta in such a way that the superficial and uncritical reader could not help taking it as praise of Sparta, Xenophon certainly prevented the uncritical admirer of Athens from being confirmed in his prejudices."[62] Even though the philosopher ought to accommodate his thought to the political society in which he lives, his noble taste prevents him from pandering to the prevalent prejudices. This elitism, then, distinguishes accommodation from cynical and self-interested opportunism.

*Leo Strauss and the Politics of Exile*

Writers like Xenophon, according to Strauss, hide certain crucial views in "an extremely able manner." The task of interpreting Xenophon's texts requires that one "exert all of his powers of understanding and imagination in order to make some progress toward wisdom by taking Xenophon as his guide."[63] Because the reader relies on Strauss's commentary on Xenophon, might it not be inferred that we take Strauss as our guide in order to make the philosophical ascent? This is the kind of issue that cannot be conclusively resolved—but that is precisely the point. Strauss adopts the attitude that those who are capable of understanding will understand. Given the importance that Maimonides attached to chapter headings and beginnings of chapters (*roshe perakim*), Strauss's title and epigraph become key to decoding his commentary on Xenophon.[64] "The Spirit of Sparta; or, the Taste of Xenophon," presents a choice that opposes public-spiritedness to the precious taste of philosophy. Even though Strauss poses as a historian, his real stand as a philosopher becomes clear as the argument develops and is hinted at in the epigraph from Quintillian that opens the article: "I have not forgotten Xenophon, but he will find his place among the philosophers."[65] The Latin quote is not translated and no source is provided—conventions not uncommon at the time. But because Strauss never returns to Quintillian's words, only those who know Latin and can locate the context of the quote will catch on that Strauss is copying Xenophon in fashioning himself as a historian who is actually a philosopher.[66] Just as Strauss would interpret Farabi and Maimonides, Xenophon avails himself "of the specific immunity of the commentator, or of the historian in order to speak his mind concerning grave matters in his 'historical' works rather than in the works setting forth what he presents as his own doctrine."[67]

But Strauss does at least play the role of a historian. In this capacity, he offers an account of his rediscovery and subsequent redeployment of multilevel writing in philosophy. We might offer certain informed speculations of our own, and supplement these with some of Strauss's later reflections on the subject; for present purposes, however, it is safest to begin with Strauss's own analysis. Strauss tells us that this writing was found in the ancients and medievals, but its decline occurred only under modern conditions of liberalism. These conditions made us lose sight of philosophy's radical insecurity and danger. Just as multilevel philosophic writing and persecution disappeared simultaneously, so too did both reappear in the 1930s and 1940s.[68] The rise of contemporary totalitarian regimes and their illiberal environments of persecution signaled the reappearance of "a forgotten kind of writing."[69]

Keeping in mind that Socrates was suspected of and executed for impiety—that is, for not believing in the traditional gods of the city—Strauss argues that Xenophon and Plato learned from Socrates's tragic fate to hide their own philosophic skepticism or unbelief. Yet even as philosophers needed to conceal their unbelief, they also desired to communicate their views to a select group of people who are both "able and willing to accept" these impious views.[70] Because most of these potentially like-minded people belong to future generations, a philosopher feels the need to risk writing and publishing his views for posterity. Multilevel writing, according to Strauss, emerged as a solution to the problem raised by the contradiction between the secret character of philosophic teaching and the public character of writing. This technique, which reveals the truth to the few while hiding it from the many, was based on a simple insight into human habits: "If a man tells a charming story, most people will enjoy the story . . . but only a minority of readers will recover from the charm, reflect upon the story and discover the teaching which it silently conveys."[71]

Strauss does not think persecution is the sole factor in explaining why the philosopher must conceal his heterodox views. Strauss deemed it a

> matter of duty to hide the truth from the majority of mankind. By making the discovered truth almost as inaccessible as it was before it had been discovered, they [ancient philosophers] prevented . . . the cheap sale of the formulations of the truth: nobody should know even the formulations of the truth who had not rediscovered the truth by his own exertions, if aided by subtle suggestions from a superior teacher. It is in this way that classical authors became the most efficient teachers of independent thinking.[72]

At the same time that Strauss explored the multilevel texts of antiquity, he taught courses with Albert Salomon and Karl Mayer that addressed special problems in social theory as it relates to the study of modern tyranny and totalitarianism. Strauss was surely not convinced by the "half-Marxist" and psychoanalytic explanations for the rise of Nazism that many of his colleagues put forward.[73] More to Strauss's taste, however, were his colleagues' interest in coded messages, speeches, and texts. Indeed, Strauss's exploration of traditions of multilevel writing is the most prominent way in which he responded to the phenomenon of totalitarianism.

The following two sections focus on other ways in which Strauss responded to Nazism in 1941. In that year, Strauss delivered two lectures at the New School. One focused on the crisis of German historicism and the other on the advent of German nihilism. Taken together, these lectures convey his peculiar understanding of the intellectual environment that ultimately paved the way for Nazism. In the latter lecture, Strauss plays the role of historian by embedding his analysis of Weimar liberalism in a historical context that takes into account the importance of generation as a conditioning factor for ideas and movements. But the most well known statement that Strauss would make in that year was "Persecution and the Art of Writing," which appeared in the pages of *Social Research*. "Persecution and the Art of Writing" will be viewed as an extension of the two lectures. Taken together, one can see how his lingering antipathy toward liberalism, and especially Weimar liberalism, became the basis for his response to European totalitarianism.

## The Sociology of Knowledge, German Nihilism, and National Socialism

In the same year that "Persecution and the Art of Writing" appeared in *Social Research*, Strauss delivered two different lectures at the New School reflecting his sense of a present crisis. Both lectures grew out of joint faculty seminars. "Philosophy and Sociology of Knowledge" and "German Nihilism" both focus on the crisis of German thought during the first third of the twentieth century and the inadequate responses that resulted in the destruction of reason and ascendance of political nihilism and tyranny. These lectures pinpoint Strauss's complex intellectual relationship with his émigré colleagues; indeed, these lectures were addressed to the audience that represented the intellectual heart of his attack.

Strauss's sustained concern with the problem of historical relativism as it related to the study of politics and philosophy stretches back to his Weimar writings.[74] In "Philosophy and Sociology of Knowledge," his criticisms of Weber, Dewey, Husserl, Mannheim, Heidegger, and Lenin, and their impact on the methodology of the social sciences might have earned collegial respect, but certainly not acceptance: the objects of his criticisms represented virtually the spectrum of methodologies adopted by his colleagues at the New School. Strauss objected that the aforementioned theorists of social science all conflated opinion, knowledge, and philosophy. He had established these lines of criticism during Weimar. At the New School, however, Strauss's critique would point toward an alternative program of how to study philosophy, and especially how to *begin* to study philosophy. Throughout the 1940s, Strauss would realize the aims of "Philosophy and Sociology of Knowledge" by countering Mannheim's sociology of knowledge with an alternate vision of a future *sociology of philosophy*.[75] The polemical impetus of this project of founding a sociology of philosophy (which first appears in the 1952 introduction to *Persecution and the Art of Writing*) derives from Strauss's Weimar critique of the Mannheimian model of a free-floating intellectual who can arrive at a synoptic view of totality while crystallizing the legitimate interests of competing ideologies and social or socioeconomic groups. This type of democratic "knowledge," which relativizes the most urgent political claims offered by all segments of society, may be valued by contemporary social science. For Strauss, however, the fundamental ancient political questions of "How should one live?" and "What is the best regime?" cannot simply end in tolerant pluralism where everyone agrees to disagree. On what basis can a regime be deemed to be good or bad, if the origins and the character of the laws and/or the legislators have been called into question? These are the concerns that animated Schmitt's critique of liberal politics and Strauss's critique of modernity more generally.

The General Seminar of the New School's Graduate Faculty proved to be the breeding ground for many of Strauss's most well known lectures and essays which would appear in a more polished form over the next three decades.

Studies dealing with Jerusalem and Athens, the question of natural right, and the ancient tradition of Platonic politics each found articulation in a presentation at the General Seminar. The General Seminar also proved to be the setting for Strauss's meditation on the "German problem," which became the forum of a study group in 1941.[76] The Institute for Social Research[77] embarked upon several pathbreaking studies of the political, psychological, and economic roots of Nazism; the Graduate Faculty's General Seminar provided a less systematic forum for exploring the character and causes of European fascism from an interdisciplinary perspective.[78] The study group on the German problem brought together the interdisciplinary backgrounds of Eduard Heinemann (economist), Erich Hula (political scientist), Karl Mayer (sociologist), Albert Salomon (sociologist), Kurt Riezler (philosopher), Horace Kallen (philosopher and psychologist), and Felix Kaufmann (philosopher); the group met regularly through the 1941–42 academic year. Members presented papers dealing with a problem that had been at the center of Strauss's writings for the previous two decades: the crisis of European liberalism.

The paper that Strauss presented to the General Seminar focused on German nihilism.[79] The group read *The Revolution of Nihilism: The Warning to the West* by Hermann Rauschning, which was rapidly translated into English for British and American audiences.[80] Rauschning was a German nationalist from Danzig who joined the Nazi party in 1933, but became disillusioned within a few years and wrote several works condemning the Third Reich from 1938 until its defeat in 1945.[81] Strauss's critique of the book is not what interests us most. Strauss used this occasion to reflect upon his own generation that experienced the First World War: a generation that had become disenchanted with liberalism and European civilization. This generation became enamored with a group of thinkers whom Strauss saw as clearing the intellectual ground for Hitler's rise to power. Early in the lecture Strauss focused on a special group of intellectuals: the young noble Germans who came to nihilism with a non-nihilistic motive. Strauss sympathetically reconstructs the group's powerful *moral* protest against the degenerate and empty culture of consumerism and self-satisfaction. He isolates a Nietzschean understanding of the communist vision as what truly frightened this impressionable group of reactionaries. "The prospect of a pacified planet," Strauss explains, "without rulers and ruled, of a planetary society devoted to production and consumption only, to the production and consumption of spiritual as well as material merchandise, was positively horrifying to quite a few very intelligent and very decent, if very young, Germans."[82] That which was a dream to communists was as a haunting nightmare to "those young Germans." Strauss never explicitly identifies himself as belonging to this select group of young and misguided counterrevolutionary nihilists; however, his apologetic analysis of the motivations behind the revolt and the search for a third way between capitalism and communism, Enlightenment rationalism, and romanticism, does convey a sense of disdain for Weimar liberalism.

One ought to remember that the intellectual world of these radicalizing forces and revolutionary desires shaped Strauss's thought during Weimar. In the commentary on Carl Schmitt's *Concept of the Political* (1932), for example, Strauss pointed to the as yet unnamed paradigm that was to burst from the depths of Weimar politics and constitute a "horizon beyond liberalism."[83] The intellectual influence of Schmitt, and especially Heidegger, along with the concomitant distancing from Ernst Cassirer, neo-Kantianism, and even Husserlian phenomenology—all contributed to Strauss's critique of Weimar. Another side of this formative portrait is the Weimar Jewish subculture in which Strauss participated. Like the wider radicalizing forces of Weimar, it also was infused with a spirit of rupture and rebirth.[84]

The lecture on German nihilism reveals Strauss's intimacy with a group of conservative revolutionaries whom he explicitly identifies: Oswald Spengler, Martin Heidegger, Carl Schmitt, Möller van den Bruck, and Ernst Jünger. It is the only instance where one finds Strauss publicly quoting passages from Jünger's *Der Arbeiter*—extolling the experience-based understanding of the soldier who served on the front in the First World War.[85] Strauss mentions Ernst Jünger in a review of Karl Löwith's *Von Hegel bis Nietzsche* (From Hegel to Nietzsche) in the same year as the "German Nihilism" lecture.[86] But Strauss's later reflections on his Weimar intellectual influences omit both Jünger and van den Bruck.[87] Strauss never advocated the conservative revolutionaries' highly astheticized political vision and militaristic ethos of courage. Nevertheless, Strauss's sympathetic treatment of the moral intention underlying "German nihilism" points to the continuity of his conservatism from his Weimar to American stages.

Lecturing in New York almost a decade after the birth of the Third Reich, Strauss blames the collapse of German culture, society, politics, and philosophy on the conservative revolutionary professors and writers who "knowingly or ignorantly paved the way for Hitler" *and* on their most identifiable opponents, Weimar liberals.[88] The latter group is blameworthy, according to Strauss, for two reasons. First, they failed to cultivate intellectual discipline and let the youth groups take over by instilling "emotional discipline." The resulting lack of emotional maturity was conducive to a decisionist and chauvinist disposition.[89] Second, they never attempted to engage or understand what the younger generation found to be so detestable about Western decadence. By ignoring the legitimacy of the youth's discontent, the older and more moderate voices simply spoke past the younger generation:

> They made the impression of being loaded with the heavy burden of a tradition hoary with age and somewhat dusty, whereas the young nihilists, not hampered by tradition, had complete freedom of movement—and in the wars of the mind no less than in real wars, freedom of action spells victory. The opponents of the young nihilists had all the advantages, but likewise all the disabilities, of the intellectually propertied class confronted by the intellectual proletarian, the skeptic.[90]

Strauss employs military metaphors and appropriates Marxist categories in order to recapture the high stakes of intellectual conflict. Moreover, the concern for the future of young minds is not merely theoretical, but political. According to Strauss, "the children's revolt" skipped over the stage of intellectual maturity, and passed directly from "adolescence to senility." The concern for corrupting noble youths, of course, is the most obvious motif of Plato's dialogues, especially, the "Apology" and "Charmides." The accusations of impiety directed against Socrates occur in the wake of numerous acts of treason and the reign of the infamous "Council of Elders," a group of oligarchs who seized power in Athens in 411, and the "Thirty Tyrants" of 403. More than a few from these groups, such as Critias and the flamboyant aristocrat Alcibiades (451–450 to 404–403 B.C.E), were students of Socrates.[91] In the shadow of National Socialism, Strauss places blame on intellectual icons who became engrossed in National Socialism such as Heidegger and Schmitt. But Strauss also holds responsible the blind and impotent liberal educators who were not able to engage the urgent issues that occupied youthful enthusiasm and passion. They could not sustain serious interest for contemporary Weimar authority and its basis of legitimacy. Consequently, the most promising youth were driven into the arms of nihilism for spiritual sustenance.

Considering the importance Strauss attributes to pedagogy, it is notable that he did not mention one of the clearest expressions of a new pedagogic orientation that arose during the first quarter of the twentieth century: the model of a charismatic leader and his inner circle. Notable circles around Stefan George and Martin Heidegger, as well as the Jewish examples of Alfred Nobel, Martin Buber, and Franz Rosenzweig—all rejected liberal models of education in favor of the pedagogical principle of the charismatic leader. All of these groups devoted themselves to a revolutionary spirit of restoration and/or rebirth. These circles represent the models under which Strauss's conservative elitism developed and that he would reestablish in the United States. Strauss would eventually adopt a philosophic version of the Georgian model of pedagogy as he developed a circle of devoted disciples around him who patterned their own idiosyncratic scholarship upon the insider-outsider approach to scholarly publications and teaching.

The political import of pedagogy was central to Strauss's more exoteric essays—multilevel essays intended to reach a considerable audience—that appeared throughout the war years. If young noble Germans were misled into the abyss of nihilism due to a lack of a sufficiently charismatic leadership, Strauss would seek to draw in young American students by writing a series of essays outlining a history of philosophy that utilized strategies of multilevel writing. The essays appear to conform to the academic conventions of clarity and voice, but tacitly employ some of the very multilevel tactics described. After experimenting with these tactics, Strauss reveals a new point of clarity in his seminal 1941 essay "Persecution and the Art of Writing."

Although Strauss had written descriptive accounts of esoteric and exoteric writing before he came to the New School, he now set forth an agenda centering on this subject that secured his place in scholarly controversy for the rest of his career. Throughout his European writings on the subject, Strauss delineated three different contexts in which esoteric and exoteric traditions flourished: Greece in the fourth and fifth centuries B.C.E.; medieval Islamdom, from the tenth to thirteenth centuries; and Europe from the seventeenth to late eighteenth centuries. In 1939, Strauss devoted a sustained and rather straightforward descriptive account, "Exoteric Teaching," to the phenomenon as it emerged in the third context.[92] The essay, which was only posthumously published, traces a European lineage of published texts that were encoded with sensitive political and moral teachings, intended for only a select group of the works' potential readers. According to Strauss, this manner of writing disappeared at the close of the eighteenth century. The last representative of this forgotten tradition was the German *Aufklärer*, Gotthold Ephraim Lessing. In Strauss's eyes, Lessing "united in himself in a unique way the divergent qualities of the philosopher and of the scholar." In some crucial, but often overlooked writings from the 1770s,[93] Lessing discussed the distinction between esoteric and exoteric writing

> as clearly and as fully as could be done by someone who still accepted exotericism not merely as a strange fact of the past, but rather as an intelligible necessity for all times and, therefore, as a principle guiding his own literary activity. In short, Lessing was the last writer who revealed, while hiding them, the reasons compelling wise men to hide the truth: he wrote between the lines about the art of writing between the lines.[94]

I suggest that just two years after this essay was written, Strauss attempted to pick up where Lessing left off. "Persecution and the Art of Writing" and the essays that would later be collected in the similarly titled volume are Strauss's effort to write "between the lines about the art of writing between the lines." This section explores why and how Strauss would undertake this task in the United States.

The opening sentences of "Persecution and the Art of Writing" draw attention to the contemporary condition of many modern states that "enjoyed practically complete freedom of public discussion," but now find themselves under authoritarian regimes that seek to compel and conform public speech to the official views of the government.[95] Insofar as the essay begins by taking note of the present dangers posed to freedom of thought and expression, it would seem to meet the expectations of a reader of *Social Research*. The first lines establish the case for considering the effect of compulsion or persecution "on thoughts as well as actions."[96] The differences as well as the connections between thought and action introduce the leitmotif of political conspiracies and the legal burden of proof required to prosecute them successfully.

This leading thread runs through all three sources in the first footnote to the essay. A reference to the legal principle that connects writing and action, "Scribere est agere," analyzed by William Blackstone in his *Commentaries on the Laws of England*, begins the note.[97] Blackstone addresses the general subject of "high treason" (*alta proditio*) in this chapter and then focuses on the specific question of what constitutes a treasonous act of speech and the prosecution's onerous burden to prove authorial intent. Within the first footnote, on the heels of Blackstone, Machiavelli's discussion of conspiracies is cited as a comparison.[98] Blackstone, the man of law, is careful to emphasize the heavy burden of proof attached to prosecuting treasonous intent of words uttered, written, or published. Machiavelli, the philosopher of action, looks at the determining factors of whether a conspiracy against a tyrant or a republic fails or succeeds. Machiavelli warns that plots demand the combination of both the most extreme prudence and daring. The primary problem is that confiding one's plot to others may be required to garner co-conspirators, but also increases the risk of being betrayed. The figure invoked for comparison on this issue is Descartes, who offered an account of why he did not publish his treatise on the physical nature of the universe. In the sixth chapter of the *Discourse on Method*, Descartes confesses that the likelihood of persecution made him fearful of the repercussions of publishing a heterodox work even though the work, like those of Galileo and Bruno, would have advanced science and thereby promoted the general good of others. In the preceding chapter Descartes offered a précis of the content of the suppressed work: a heretical text that he claims to have written, but for which the only incriminating evidence against him is his own description and self-accusation. Whether Descartes wrote such a work is not crucial here. Rather, in the context of a discussion of "Scribere est agere," his confession aims to strike at the scandal of censorship and persecution.[99]

Strauss's public disclosure of exoteric and esoteric writing must account for these factors when looking at past texts. But if Strauss's intent is not merely to draw attention to a past conspiracy, but actually to encourage selective participation in a current conspiracy, he must also then exercise caution and daring if he is to succeed.

Strauss already tips his hand with the opening epigram from the Victorian historian of morals, W. E. H. Lecky (1838–1903): "That vice has often proved an emancipator of the mind, is one of the most humiliating, but, at the same time, one of the most unquestionable, facts in history."[100] The emancipatory vice in Strauss's essay is, as its title indicates, persecution. The opposing "virtue" of liberal tolerance, according to Strauss, ironically results in intellectual subjugation, or at least, intellectual stagnation. The animus against liberalism that appears in Strauss's German and European career reappears in this essay with particular force. Strauss explains that what is commonly known as "freedom of thought" usually boils down to "the ability to choose between two or more different views presented by the small minority of people who are public speakers or writers." "If this choice is prevented," continues Strauss, "the only kind of intellectual independence of which many people are capable is destroyed, and that is the only freedom of thought which is of political importance."[101]

Strauss's interest in forms of communication under conditions of persecution does, in a particular way, resonate with the concerns of his colleagues at the New School and contributors to *Social Research*. In April 1941, Strauss's colleagues at the New School formed the Research Project on Totalitarian Communication under the directorship of Hans Speier and Ernst Kris. This research group devoted its labors to the study of German propaganda during the Second World War. Speier temporarily left the New School in order to continue this project in Washington, D.C., as chief German analyst of the foreign broadcast intelligence service of the Federal Communications Commission.[102]

According to Strauss, a government may censor public opposition to the things it wants people to believe, but stifling true intellectual independence is far more difficult, as not all human beings are credulous.[103] While "ordinary human beings" may be credulous enough to believe something to be true simply because it is repeated over and over again, truly independent thinkers do not succumb to this common way of thinking. Illiberal political conditions have the virtue of pushing a special group to explore ways in which one can gain access to, safeguard, and perpetuate truly independent forms of thought that transcend the limitations of their environment. Strauss defiantly states that in illiberal countries, "all those capable of truly independent thinking, cannot be brought to accept the government-sponsored views. Persecution, then, cannot prevent independent thinking."[104] Liberalism, by contrast, can lead to soporific intellectual complacency.

Strauss goes even further in claiming that "even the expression of the heterodox truth" cannot be prevented, "for a man of independent thought can utter his views in public and remain unharmed, provided he moves with circumspection. He can even utter them in print without incurring any danger, provided he is capable of writing between the lines."[105] The progamatic essay addresses the effect of persecution on writing and action. As we shall see, the effect of persecution on action is dealt with only in a circumscribed manner. Persecution has the virtue of compelling "writers who hold heterodox views to develop a peculiar technique of writing, the technique . . . of writing between the lines."

Strauss's understanding of the dynamics of political conditions and the interpretive dispositions they engender represents a genuine sociological interest on his part. He emphasized the hermeneutic sensitivity to various expressions of dissent that arises under settings of suppression and censorship. Modern conditions of relatively little persecution in Western European countries have accordingly led to a collective amnesia regarding the utility and necessity of older forms of multilevel writing. Thus, the central paradox is that the rise of intolerance and persecution in the 1930s induced the rebirth of truly independent modes of thought. This renaissance of what Strauss referred to as "exoteric teaching" or "Socratic writing" allowed one to express his or her subversive views as long as they were not obvious to an average censor, but rather, confined (metaphorically) "between the lines."[106]

But the question arises: as Strauss published the essay in a liberal environment—in New York under the auspices of the official organ of the New School for Social Research—was there any legitimate reason for him to resort to coded prose on the subject of coded writing, especially if, as he claimed, both esoteric and exoteric literature thrive under illiberal political conditions? And there are other considerations that might lead us to believe that "Persecution and the Art of Writing" was not an esoteric or exoteric text. Strauss explicitly prohibits reading between the lines "in all cases where it would be less exact than not doing so." He cautions that the interpreter begin "from an exact consideration of the explicit statements of the author." The next step is to place such explicit statements within the context of the geography of the work.[107] "The context in which a statement occurs, and the literary character of the whole work as well as its plan," Strauss elucidates, "must be perfectly understood before an interpretation of the statement can reasonably claim to be adequate or even correct."[108]

Strauss generally refers to multilevel writing in this essay as a literary phenomenon and speaks in the voice of a historian. But, as we have seen in his interpretation of Xenophon, Farabi, and Maimonides, Strauss elsewhere explicitly cautioned against confusing an author's stated viewpoint as his true opinion.[109] Indeed, Strauss consistently described the role and competence of the historian as inferior to the philosopher. As Strauss pointed out in "Exoteric Teaching," although scholars who approach the history of thought may rightfully "decide whether and where the distinction between exoteric and esoteric teaching occurs in the sources, it is for philosophers to decide whether that distinction is significant in itself."[110] While Strauss's Xenophon and Maimonides, as well as Strauss himself, may employ the voice of a historian for various literary, pedagogical, and political reasons, their ultimate fidelity is to philosophy. They hold themselves accountable to answer the most important and eternal questions of what is right and fitting rather than the more mundane historiographical question of what once was.

Because "Persecution and the Art of Writing" is a carefully constructed essay written by an author explicitly concerned with the strategies and tactics of multilevel writings, it is necessary to address basic issues of form and the intended audience in order to assess the author's intent. The form of the essay is striking in that it is divided into three sections—the same number of sections that Strauss says is commonly used to camouflage the natural order and divisions of a larger work of multilevel writing.[111] Moreover, while Strauss generally assumes the voice of the historian, the central section of the central paragraph oddly solicits the opinion of the philosopher, whose opinion the historian is not competent to judge for himself.

Strauss explicitly mentions the important absence of the philosopher in several studies from this time. He accounts for the absence of the philosopher throughout the bulk of Yehuda Halevi's *Kuzari* by arguing that this omission was intended by Halevi to "compel the reader to think constantly of the absent philosopher." Because the author refrains from spoon-feeding his reader on such a crucial issue, the curious reader must engage the text and "find out, by independent reflection, what the absent philosopher might have to say." "This disturbing and invigorating thought," Strauss explains, "would prevent the reader from falling asleep [and] from relaxing in his critical attention for a single moment."[112] Fitting a larger pattern of dropping brief suggestions, Strauss immediately backpedals from this "disturbing and invigorating" possibility and escorts the reader to "safer ground." But not really.

Strauss claims that Halevi was at one point "converted to philosophy," thereby entering a brief period of "spiritual hell," but then "returned to the Jewish fold." Once again, Strauss's words of biographical speculation of a past thinker apply to Strauss's own experience. "After that moment, a spiritual hell, he returned to the Jewish fold. But after what he had gone through, he could not help interpreting Judaism in a manner in which only a man who had once been a philosopher, could interpret it." This view of Halevi's supposed defense of Judaism casts Halevi as an *apikores* with a conscience: a man who had undergone a reorientation after realizing that philosophy rendered him and his religious community utterly vulnerable to the desiccative powers of philosophical skepticism. Strauss asserts that Halevi "had experienced the enormous danger of philosophy. The manner in which he defends Judaism against philosophy testifies to this experience."[113] While it is beyond the scope of the present discussion to explore the veracity of Strauss's interpretation of Halevi's *Kuzari*, Strauss's comments about Halevi might well apply to Strauss himself. Halevi's philosopher, who disappears earlier in the dialogue, was never truly defeated.[114] Thus Halevi outwardly defends Judaism, but secretly accommodates his philosophical loyalties to the necessary political truths of his ancestral faith and community.

## The Best Regime and the Existing Regime

In general, Strauss refrained from stepping into the public fray of political life and was resigned to a "private" existence as a scholar and teacher at a university. But even in this more or less private capacity, removed from organized party politics, Strauss's thought was decisively political. At the basest level, Strauss recognized that the social order in which he lived conditioned his existence and his activity of philosophy. Therefore, as a matter of self-preservation, the philosopher must necessarily occupy himself with the status of the political order in which he lives. Strauss's original and ultimate interest in philosophy was the political, and politics remained the driving force behind his thought throughout his career.

Throughout his articles in *Social Research,* Strauss sought to neutralize the modern concept of popular enlightenment paved by the radical Enlightenment thinkers of the seventeenth century. He did so by counterposing a classical and premodern aristocratic conception of philosophy and science to that advanced by Bacon, Descartes, and Hobbes.[115] Strauss unveils the politically engaged project of the latter conception by pointing to its rejection of the contemplative life as the philosophic ideal. Instead, modern philosophy sought a "revolutionizing influence . . . on society as a whole."[116] The concept of popular enlightenment rests on the egalitarian belief that all human beings are capable of becoming and ought to become philosophically enlightened.

Moreover, according to Strauss, the diffusion of knowledge to the masses is connected to a political function for science and philosophy; that is, to reshape society on the basis of an assumed natural harmony between philosophy and politics. The future-oriented ambition to establish a society in which philosophy and power coincide took the form of an egalitarian mass society—a prospect that remained odious to Strauss. He was convinced, as was the elitist philosophical tradition of Plato, Maimonides, and Nietzsche that he traced, that only the few were potential philosophers and that there was an insurmountable divide separating the noble souls capable of philosophy and the many who cannot attain philosophical understanding.

Strauss revealed his true political leanings in a letter to Karl Löwith in January 1946. "I *really* believe," he confessed, "that the perfect political order, as Plato and Aristotle have sketched it, *is* the perfect political order."[117] The sincere profession that follows is worth quoting in full. Strauss confides in Löwith his skepticism regarding utopian visions of united humankind in a political or intellectual form:

> If it is true that genuine unity [*echte Einheit*] is only possible through knowledge of the truth or through search for the truth, then there is a genuine unity of men [*eine echte Einheit aller Menschen*] only on the basis of the popularized final teaching of philosophy (and naturally this does not exist) or if all men are philosophers (not Ph.D.'s, etc.), which likewise, is not the case. Therefore, there can only be closed societies [*geschlossene Gesellschaften*], that is, states. But if that is so, then one can show from political considerations that the small city-state is in principle superior to the large state or to the territorial feudal state. I know very well *today*[118] it cannot be restored; but the famous atomic bombs—not to mention at all cities with a million inhabitants, gadgets, funeral homes, "ideologies"—show that the contemporary solution, that is, the completely modern solution, is *contra naturam.* Whoever concedes that Horace did not speak nonsense when he said "Expel nature with a hayfork, but it always returns,"[119] concedes thereby precisely the legitimacy in principle of Platonic-Aristotelian politics. Details can be disputed, although I myself might actually agree with everything that Plato and Aristotle demand (but that I tell only you).[120]

*Leo Strauss and the Politics of Exile*

This densely packed statement cuts to the heart of Strauss's political vision. In a subsequent letter to Löwith, dated August 20, 1946, Strauss elaborates upon the contours of this ideal Platonic-Aristotelian order:

> I assert that the polis—as it has been *interpreted* by Plato and Aristotle, a *surveyable, urban,* morally serious [*übersichtliche staedtische, moralisch-ernste*] society, based on an agricultural economy, in which the gentry *rule*—is morally-politically the most reasonable and most pleasing: which still does not mean that *I* would want to live under such a polis (one must not judge everything according to one's private wishes)—do not forget that Plato and Aristotle preferred democratic Athens as a place to the well-ordered polises: for philosophy's moral-political considerations are necessarily secondary.[121]

Modern philosophy has embraced the principle of mass enlightenment in an attempt to efface the difference between the few and the many and thereby break down all other divisions between human beings, such as class, religion, nation, gender, and so forth. Given the impossibility of mass enlightenment, according to Strauss, such a vision of egalitarian unity is equally impossible. Thus, the tension between the one and the many, both in geopolitical and intellectual terms, is a permanent and natural one. While it may be historical accident that determines whether one is born an Athenian under the rule of Pericles or an Englishman under Cromwell's revolution, the philosopher should accommodate to the particular regime under which he lives, yet always retain a hidden loyalty to the secret kingship of philosophy.

Strauss did, however, raise one legitimate alternative to his view of the best regime: "There is only *one* objection against Plato-Aristotle: and that is the *factum brutum* of revelation, or the 'personal' God." Belief in divine revelation and/or a personal Creator-God cannot be refuted by philosophy. Strauss consistently held, from his earliest writings, that the philosophical critique of religion (for example, proving the impossibility of miracles) only holds so long as one's standard is philosophic. Although Strauss had openly adopted the position of "principled atheism" in the opening pages of *Philosophy and Law* (1935), he nevertheless kept up his guard against misguided philosophical claims to have objectively decided the conflict between faith and reason.

Although Strauss firmly held to notions of a hierarchy of human beings and their place in society, he nevertheless, like Plato and Maimonides, remained an advocate of universal education. Part of the reason may be what Nietzsche referred to as the higher man's "loving contempt" for the many.[122] Indeed, in *Beyond Good and Evil,* Nietzsche explicitly connected the natural rank of human beings to the philosophic art of esoteric and exoteric speech.[123] Universal education could be the tool to return the average citizenry to the moorings of a particular religious/national (theologico-political) tradition and guide them toward the nearest approximation of truth and happiness available to their intellects. Moreover, such an emphasis on education would inculcate respect for the wisdom of the ancient Western philosophic tradition.

Strauss's view of the philosopher was that he was obligated to act as a critic of the bourgeois sense of comfort yet also reinforce the conservative ideals that ought to guide that social order. In refraining from personal political ambitions, Strauss followed the path in accord with his reading of Plato's *Republic*. There, the philosopher descends back into the cave of society and pursues politics only upon compulsion, a compulsion that could be legitimated only if the philosopher lived in "the perfect social order." In imperfect societies, Strauss gleans from Plato, "the philosopher is not likely to engage in political activity of any kind, but will rather lead a life of privacy."[124]

For Strauss, philosophy's recognition of its precarious existence within any existing social order is the first step toward the quest for the premodern sources of wisdom, guidance, and truth. And this goal of individual philosophic enlightenment is the one type of *teshuvah* (redemptive return) available to moderns. In the 1930s, during the course of his European exile, Strauss became convinced that restoration of premodern political orders was not possible; nevertheless, he also became passionately committed to the prospect that a philosophically gifted individual could recover the original intentions and true teachings of premodern philosophy.[125]

It is not vulgar hindsight to see the connection between Strauss's life and the texts he wrote. Strauss was a German-Jewish refugee vitally concerned with the possibility of Jewish existence in exile. During his own period of exile from his native country, he came to question the wisdom and prudence of any project that called for an overcoming of political imperfection or for any messianic aspiration to overcome exile. Strauss regarded exile as the natural condition of all political societies and recast the precarious existence of the diasporic Jew, who lives in perpetual fear of persecution, as the normative model of the philosopher. Even upon his entrance into a liberal democratic state that offered him refuge, Strauss still sought to instill the sense of unease or not-being-at-home within a new vision of a conservative political philosophy. This remarkable and compelling dissonance between his appreciation of the dangers and philosophic virtues of exile stands at the center of Leo Strauss's intellectual personality.

It should be recalled that Strauss rejected all political programs that aimed at some implementation of utopia during his European exile. By universalizing the conditions of *galut* and projecting the status of the persecuted Jew onto the philosopher, Strauss valorized the ways in which an elite group accommodates to its host environment while retaining its nobility and loyalty to an ideal of the true good. Strauss revisits Maimonides's redemptive view of the contemplative life under conditions of political imperfection: esoteric grappling with grand problems and truths offers the philosopher the possibility of redemption from a state of internal exile. According to such a model, the border between the secret society of the initiates and the uninitiated must be fastidiously guarded. The

*Leo Strauss and the Politics of Exile*

chosen ones who have earned entrance into the "secret kingship of philosophers" are in turn expected to transmit this tradition to their own carefully selected intellectual progeny.[126] The dynamics of transmitting a tradition of chosenness, of course, are not unique to either Judaism or Straussianism, but Maimonides was one of the most important models for Strauss. Maimonides's strong influence is especially evident in Strauss's approach to the conflicting demands of being a Jew and a philosopher, or to rephrase this problem in ancient philosophic terms, the conflict between the one and the many.

## Different Philosophical Paths

To avoid a misunderstanding regarding the philosophic esoteric tradition that Strauss sought to recover, I hasten to note that Strauss was not interested in mystical traditions of esoteric thought. Because Strauss modeled his own interpretive practices upon his peculiarly subversive readings of those he considered to be canonical figures, Maimonidean esotericism can serve as an exemplar of Strauss's own brand of philosophic esotericism. Maimonides was not a mystic, according to Strauss, but he made use of mystical esoteric traditions toward philosophic ends.[127] Maimonides tried to demonstrate that the philosophical worldview was integral to Judaism by interpreting traditional texts from a philosophical perspective. Maimonides countered the suspicion that philosophy was alien to Judaism by employing an exegetical strategy that invested philosophic meaning in traditional Jewish texts.[128] According to Strauss, Maimonides reinterpreted central concepts from the Bible, the Midrash, and the Talmud in order to show a lineage of legitimate philosophic concern in Judaism. Embedding philosophic elements within authoritative Jewish sources, however, dramatically transformed the meaning of those concepts. It is the nature of this transformation that was and still is so objectionable to many custodians of normative Judaism.

Strauss, thinking of Aristotle, initially called the method of writing employed by certain "masterful" premodern authors as "exoteric teaching."[129] The basic tenet of exoteric teaching is that a philosophical discussion could only be understood by the listener (Aristotle's *Politics* is a compilation of lecture notes) if he possessed the necessary knowledge of the philosophical discourse within which the particular discussion is rooted. In a 1939 essay, Strauss gave his exclusive attention to the "rediscovery of exotericism."[130] Here Strauss echoes intimations present in *Philosophy and Law* (1935) that Lessing was key in awakening Strauss's attention to esoteric and exoteric writing. Of course, the subtle yet central reference to Nietzsche in *Philosophy and Law* reveals that he was always lurking in the background as well.[131]

Lessing's own application of a circumspect strategy of writing was motivated by certain misgivings he had regarding the Enlightenment's militant skepticism toward religion and religious political authority. Lessing began to wonder, along with Jacobi, whether secular despotism posed a greater danger than did papal despotism. Lessing thus became concerned that the Enlightenment had thrown out the baby with the bathwater. Its public criticism of revealed religion had become too immoderate. "Exoteric Teaching" is a straightforward account of the phenomenon of modern esotericism/exotericism.

Strauss begins to use indirect ways of describing this tradition of esoteric and exoteric speech in 1939. In that year, he reviewed a Hebrew-English edition of Maimonides's *Mishneh Torah*.[132] There, Strauss complicated his previous treatments of Maimonides in which he had thought that Maimonides's philosophic works were the product of authorially intended bivalent readings. By the end of his review article, Strauss pointed to a mysterious quality of Maimonides's *halakhic* work as well. Most of Strauss's reading of the *Mishneh Torah* treated it as a decidedly nonphilosophic exoteric work. This attitude was based on Maimonides's explicit statement that the *Mishneh Torah* was addressed to "all men" rather than just the philosophically inclined individual for which the *Guide* was written. It would thus appear that the *Mishneh Torah* was addressed to a general audience and that it should be considered "less scientific and more exoteric than the *Guide*."[133] But Strauss throws a wrench in this slightly nuanced understanding of Maimonides as a philosopher and a *halakhist*. Strauss offers the following quizzical remark: "Now, an exoteric book, if it is the work of an *unexoteric* or initiated mind, is, by its very nature, more difficult to decipher than is an esoteric book. For in an exoteric book, the author can explain his views only in a rather haphazard way." Strauss suggests the following paradox: when Maimonides, a philosopher and writer of the highest rank, claims to write an exoteric text such as *Sefer hamada* (The book of knowledge) or the *Mishneh Torah* as a whole, the end product is "much more esoteric than are most esoteric works."[134] Strauss cut short this explanation by offering a summary view: "we shall simply say that the *Sefer hamada* is a book full of mystery."[135] This supposed clarification actually confounds. In order to get beyond this aporia, the reader is left to his or her own devices.

This use of a Maimonidean device—that is, to insert a bewildering clarification in the first person plural in order to refrain from further argument and proof—is not new to Strauss, but its new stylistic prominence signals the first traces of Straussianism. He has not only described a lost art of reading and writing; he has begun to experiment with these techniques in his own published writing. Strauss has begun to think about exoteric writing as a strategy for his own approach to commentary, interpretation, and scholarly contributions. From this point forward, Strauss increases the frequency with which he deliberately sets literary ruses and manipulates readerly expectations. The key issues that hint at the employment of such playful habits usually relate to the status of crucial opinions and beliefs. The objective in writing and speaking this way is to obscure the authorial voice so as to let only a select few comprehend the message. It becomes debatable whether a specific view belongs to Strauss, or to the author whom Strauss interprets, or to the prejudices of Strauss's likely readers. Perhaps the beliefs and opinions that are most clearly endorsed are mere accommodations to certain politically necessary and useful beliefs.

A few years after this review of the *Mishneh Torah*, Strauss published *The Literary Character of the Guide of the Perplexed* an interpretation of Maimonides's philosophic magnum opus. While conceiving this study, Strauss wrote to Jacob Klein in 1938 about the firestorm that would surely follow his radical interpretation of Maimonides. Echoing Scholem's reading of *Philosophie und Gesetz*, Strauss acknowledges the seriousness of interpreting Maimonides as a thinker who concealed his atheism precisely at a time when Jewry is in crisis. Strauss writes, "If I let this bomb explode in a few years (should I live that long), an enormous battle will flare up." Strauss relates to Klein that Nahum Glatzer had told him that "for Judaism Maimonides is more important than the Bible— thus if one deprives Judaism of Maimonides, one deprives it of its basis." Strauss parenthetically analogizes the situation to Thomas Aquinas's importance to Catholicism. So what will result of this supposed pitched battle? "That Maimonides was absolutely not a Jew in his belief—is of extremely timely significance: the incompatibility in principle of philosophy and Judaism ('clearly' expressed in the 2nd verse of *Genesis*) will be demonstrated *ad oculos*."[136]

Compared to *Philosophy and Law*, however, Strauss's 1941 essay is written in a style less polemically charged; indeed, Strauss's voice is difficult to discern. The article caused a stir within Maimonidean scholarship, but there was a much greater explosion regarding another Jewish thinker's attempt to deny revered status to another central figure of Judaism: Sigmund Freud's *Moses and Monotheism*. Like Strauss, Freud himself acknowledged the weight of his historical revision of Moses as an Egyptian who was eventually murdered by the Israelites.[137]

While Freud's work did not have a linear narrative, Strauss's essay seems to have taken Maimonides's own allusive writing as a model. At first glance the essay seems to follow scholarly conventions (such as extensive documentation of primary and secondary material in the footnotes), but it is most difficult to pin down the author's viewpoint on a whole host of issues raised. Certainly there appears no straightforward presentation of Maimonides as philosophical loyalist who was unable or unwilling to accept the God of Judaism.

Strauss's essay presented the difficult position in which Maimonides found himself regarding the rabbinic prohibition on public disclosures of the secrets of the Torah.[138] Maimonides, according to Strauss, endeavored to "steer a middle course between oral and confidential teaching, which is permitted, and teaching in writing, which is forbidden." Maimonides therefore garbed the *Guide* in the literary fiction of private letters addressed to a bright and favored pupil named Joseph. "By addressing his book to one man," Strauss explained, "Maimonides made sure that he did not transgress the prohibition against explaining *ma'aseh merkabah* to more than one man." Moreover, Maimonides was sure to mention that Joseph possessed all of the qualities required for oral transmission in such secrets. The justification for written communication, then, hinged on his student's imminent departure. Because Maimonides was about to lose personal contact with his valued student, Maimonides wrote the *Guide* to serve as an extension of his instruction while Joseph wandered into other lands. The exigency of keeping a young and bright Jew loyal to his tradition amid the allures and uncertainties of the Jewish exilic condition, is, according to Strauss, the primary reason offered by Maimonides to legitimate the disclosure of the secret teaching of the Torah. "Joseph's departure," in Strauss's view, "was the consequence of his being a Jew in the Diaspora. Not a private need but only an urgent necessity of nation wide bearing can have driven Maimonides to transgress an explicit prohibition. Only the necessity of saving the law can have caused him to break the law."[139]

Confronted with the possibility that the tradition of communicating the secrets of the Torah orally may die, Maimonides wrote the *Guide*. Thus, according to Strauss, Maimonides acted prudently, even in his apparent transgression of rabbinic prohibitions. Strauss's Maimonides "insisted on taking a middle course between impossible obedience and flagrant transgression." Maimonides dutifully offered a "written explanation of the Biblical secrets" in a manner that would essentially "meet all the conditions required from an oral explanation." In order for this strategy to be employed effectively, Maimonides needed to become "a master of the art of revealing by not revealing and not revealing by revealing."[140]

Strauss's ultimate judgment in "The Literary Character of the *Guide of the Perplexed*" is that "[t]he *Guide* is devoted to the explanation of an esoteric doctrine. But this explanation is itself of an esoteric character. The *Guide* is, then, devoted to the esoteric explanation of an esoteric doctrine. Consequently it is a book with seven seals. How can we unseal it?"[141] This last question is not answered in a purely scholarly way. Strauss finds it necessary to account for the moral duties of a conscientious interpreter of Maimonides. The fourth section of the essay, "A Moral Dilemma," follows in the wake of the question regarding the unsealing of the *Guide*.

Strauss here initially appeals to moral standards that bind the historian:

> No historian who has a sense of decency and therefore a sense of respect for a superior man such as Maimonides will disregard light-heartedly the latter's emphatic entreaty not to explain the secret teaching of the *Guide*. It may fairly be said that an interpreter who does not feel pangs of conscience when attempting to explain that secret teaching and perhaps when perceiving for the first time its existence and bearing lacks that closeness to the subject which is indispensable for the true understanding of any book. Thus the question of adequate interpretation of the *Guide* is primarily a moral one.

The fundamental difference between the historical situation of Maimonides and the present is clear to Strauss. The dominant opinion in the twelfth century was rooted in the "belief in the revealed character of the Torah or the existence of an eternal and unchangeable law, whereas public opinion today is ruled by historic consciousness." Just as Maimonides legitimated his violation of the talmudic injunction against publicly revealing secrets by appealing to the necessity of saving the law, Strauss instrumentally appealed to the "requirements of historic research" in order to legitimate the violation of Maimonides's own injunction.[142] As stated in the previous chapter, Strauss had called for the instrumental use of history in the 1930s in order to clear the artificial ground that obstructs even the basic understanding of medieval Jewish and Islamic philosophy.[143] In this period, he sometimes omits the merely instrumental role of history in his hermeneutic project. In accommodating to the ruling force of historical consciousness, Strauss goes about his counterhistoricist aim by redefining history to meet philosophical ends. Just as Maimonides redefined central terms in the Torah toward philosophical ends, Strauss redefined central terms of historical consciousness toward philosophical ends. Strauss viewed the "progressive" and "historicist" conceptions of the history of philosophy as relativist opponents that could only be successfully resisted by first appearing to operate within the framework of historical consciousness.[144] "The task of the historian of thought," as Strauss redefined it in one 1944 lecture, "is to understand the thinkers of the past *exactly* as they understood themselves, or to revitalize their thought according to their *own* interpretation of it."[145]

The second part of this clause is what strikes us as unusual. Here, Strauss molds the historian of thought into a figure whose independent creative action is emphasized. Because understanding past thinkers exactly as they understood themselves (especially when they wrote with reticence and by way of indirect suggestion) is so difficult, Strauss appears to be making room for the Nietzschean understanding of an instrumental use of history, one that can utilize certain advantageous elements of history without succumbing to the relativism and nihilism that Strauss saw at the core of modern German historicism. I shall explore this understanding further when discussing Strauss's response to Gershom Scholem's criticisms of medieval Jewish philosophy. I shall then show that Strauss aimed for nothing less than a philosophical "conversion" of the historian.

Strauss refers loosely to one's conversion to philosophy in several of his writings after "Persecution and the Art of Writing." We find in his correspondence concrete references to the implications that such a changing of fundamental loyalties has for the person who has distanced himself from traditional notions of divine providence, resurrection of the dead, and the like. For example, Strauss and Scholem often play cat-and-mouse games where each one playfully pokes at a perceived vulnerability of the other, but then retreats. When Scholem sent Strauss a copy of *On the Kabbalah and its Symbolism*, Strauss told Scholem that he found the book to be his most impressive work yet. The book awakened in Strauss a first-time understanding of "the infinite attraction exercised by this deep and rich world, your home, which enigmatically and dissolubly unites the universal and the particular, the human and the Jewish—which transcends all moralism and punitiveness without disintegrating into aestheticism or the like."[146] After praising Scholem as "a blessing to every Jew now living" for achieving "a harmony of mind and heart on such a high level," Strauss explains why he has never and could never produce such a work. Given Scholem's dispositional "home" in Judaism and his intellectual abilities to illuminate that home for others, he has "the right and the duty" to make his voice heard. But Strauss no longer shares that "home" and because of his sworn allegiances, he is neither privileged nor obligated to speak up in such a manner. "Unfortunately," Strauss writes Scholem, "I am constitutionally unable to follow you—or if you wish, I too have sworn to a flag, the oath to the flag being (in the beautiful Arabic Latin created by some of our ancestors, which to Cicero would appear to be *in ultimitate turpitudinis*): *moriatur anima mea mortem philosophorum* [my soul dies the death of philosophers]."[147]

As Leo Strauss's American career unfolds, many of the most confounding aspects of his writing become deliberate. If one accepts this view, then the idiosyncratic character of Strauss's thought is seen as an intentional tactic to leave behind enough clues to arouse the suspicions of the sharp and careful reader while eluding the attention of an average and careless reader. It is not surprising that Strauss steadfastly attempted to erase or obscure any incontrovertible evidence of his real position on what he considered to be the crucial issues of his times. This obfuscation is one reason why certain articles and lectures that I examine in this chapter did not get reprinted in later collections, and may even be considered as suppressed works: they may have revealed too much of Strauss's genuine views.

Strauss saw himself as following Maimonides in exercising necessary restraint in divulging truthful opinions. However, whereas Strauss's Maimonides stands as a medieval Islamic-Jewish representative of an older Platonic tradition of dissimulation, Strauss saw himself as a modern who sought to challenge modern philosophy's dismissal of older philosophy.

### Medieval Jewish Philosophy versus Jewish Mysticism

Strauss's forays into medieval Jewish philosophy unfolded as his friends and former German colleagues in Jewish studies published innovative reassessments of medieval Jewish thought. Yitzhak Baer, for example, completed decades of research on a two-volume history of the Jews in Christian Spain (1936–45) that reassessed the romantic view of medieval Sephardic rationalism and mysticism.[148] According to Baer, the privileged Jewish elites so absorbed the influences of their host cultures that they ultimately abandoned their loyalties to Judaism and the Jewish people.[149] They had not, in Strauss's terms, maintained a necessary state of unease with *galut*.

Baer's *History of the Jews in Christian Spain* was surely both ambitious and innovative, but the boldest attempt by a Weimar Jew to revise scholarly opinion about the Jewish Middle Ages was made by Gershom Scholem. Scholem presented his pioneering views in a 1938 lecture series at the Jewish Institute of Religion in New York, and published them three years later as *Major Trends in Jewish Mysticism*. For both Strauss and Scholem, medieval—not ancient—Jewish thought contained the most powerful currents. In *Major Trends in Jewish Mysticism*, Scholem laid out a tripartite scheme of the history of Judaism. In opposition to other periodizations, which relegated mysticism to an irrational and primitive historical stratum, Scholem sought to capture the centrality and vitality of mysticism in the belief system of Judaism. The first period of religious development in Judaism is mythical. It is distinguished by the lack of a consciousness regarding the alienation of man from God. The second period, which still "knows no real mysticism," nevertheless signals the "creative epoch in which . . . the break-through of religion occurs." In classical Judaism, this meant the fulfillment of "religion's supreme function": to destroy a harmonious view of the relation among man, universe, and God. The second period is marked by the confrontation of the "vast gulf which can be crossed by nothing but the *voice*."[150] The third stage of religious development is essentially romantic and signals the emergence of mysticism. Mysticism begins by confronting the abyss among God, man, and the universe, but "proceeds to a quest for the secret that will close it in, the hidden path that will span it. It strives to piece together the fragments broken by the religious cataclysm, to bring back the old unity which religion has destroyed, but on a new plane, where the world of mythology and that of revelation meet in the soul of man." Thus, the third stage marks a conscious return and transformation of myth.[151]

An example of the importance of this periodization is Scholem's attitude toward one of the central texts of Jewish mysticism, the *Zohar*. In the 1930s, Scholem reversed his earlier position regarding the antiquity of the *Zohar*.[152] In 1925, Scholem delivered his opening lecture at the newly established Institute for Jewish Studies in Jerusalem. Scholem rejected the claim put forward by such prominent nineteenth-century historians as Heinrich Graetz (1817–1891) that the central mystical text of the *Zohar* was a medieval forgery written by Moses de Leon, the thirteenth-century mystic.[153] While Scholem did not establish an alternative author of the *Zohar*, he emphasized its authentic ancient roots. In 1938, however, Scholem argued that Moses de Leon wrote most of the *Zohar*. For Scholem, this later periodization of the *Zohar* did not diminish its religious authenticity. Even though Moses de Leon ascribed the *Zohar* to antiquity, Scholem defended this pseudepigraphical move as a legitimate device "far removed from forgery." Attributing one's words to a past writer can be understood as an expression of one's understanding and genuine esteem for predecessors who embarked on the same religious quest. "The further a man progresses along his own road in this Quest for Truth," reflected Scholem, "the more he might become convinced that his own road must have already been trodden by others, ages before him."[154] David Biale aptly summarized Scholem's position:

> The pseudepigrapher identifies himself with a former age because he believes in the eternal significance of his message. Pseudepigraphy is not forgery, but a proclamation of the continuity of a hidden tradition. The Kabbala as a whole, even when it did not engage in pseudepigraphy, was metaphorically pseudepigraphical, Scholem intimates, because it claimed to be an ancient esoteric tradition (Kabbala). The Kabbala considered itself "old as the hills" even as it generated new interpretations because it defined itself as a mystical reinterpretation of tradition which had always been implicit in the tradition. Even when the Kabbala recognized that its sources were recent, it regarded them as revivals of a genuine hidden tradition and therefore authentically ancient.[155]

This explanation of Scholem's attitude toward medieval pseudepigraphers also sheds light on Strauss's habit of attributing secret heretical viewpoints to a lineage of premodern political philosophers.[156] Scholem and Strauss were both engaged in recovering medieval intellectual traditions that laid claim to ancient roots; that is, medieval religious and philosophical paradigms that deployed a necessary myth of ancient and divine sanction.

Both Scholem and Strauss focus on esoteric traditions centered on a pragmatic philosophy intended for the elect. The doubly esoteric character of Jewish mysticism was elucidated by Scholem as follows: "It treats of the most deeply hidden and fundamental matters of human life; but it is secret also because it is confined to a small elite of the chosen who impart the knowledge to their disciples."[157] While Scholem pioneered investigations into mystical traditions that remained aristocratic in form and content (such as Abulafia's doctrine of prophetic kabbalah), he was not merely interested in ecstatic experiences of the elite. Scholem's eyes searched Jewish history for discrete moments when a text such as the *Zohar* sprung forth in the language of one "who has experienced the common fears of mankind as profoundly as anyone." It is precisely because the *Zohar* tapped into the common existential experience that it "struck a chord which resounded deeply in human hearts and assured it a success denied to other forms of early Kabbalism."[158]

Although Scholem acknowledged that Jewish rationalism and mysticism were, to a certain extent, "interrelated and interdependent," he argued that only Jewish mysticism resonated with the deepest concerns of Jewish existence. Jewish mysticism succeeded and rationalist philosophy failed because only the former spoke to the most urgent needs of religious man. Kabbalah "deeply" tapped into the "main forces active in Judaism" while Jewish rationalism turned its "back upon the primitive side of life, that all-important region where mortals are afraid of life and in fear of death." The Kabbalists had "a strong sense of the reality of evil and the dark horror that is about everything living. They do not, like the philosophers, seek to evade its existence with the aid of a convenient formula."[159]

Strauss expressed his gratitude to Scholem for his "sweeping and forceful condemnation of our medieval philosophy." Even though Scholem's criticisms may have been "unusually ruthless," they refine the implicit perspective of seemingly more sympathetic treatments offered by modern Jewish philosophers—Julius Guttmann, for one. Strauss argues that both Scholem and Guttmann would agree that the medieval Jewish philosophers adopted Greek ideas in place of biblical conceptions of God and the world. Gutmann saw modern Jewish philosophy as decisively superior to its medieval counterpart because it was able to safeguard the original spirit and purpose of Jewish belief. Strauss highlighted modern Jewish philosophy's dismissal of its medieval predecessor by stating boldly that his venerated mentor, Franz Rosenzweig, held Hermann Cohen's *Religion of Reason* to be superior to Maimonides's *Guide of the Perplexed*. Strauss argued that modern philosophy has not approached medieval Jewish philosophy with the necessary seriousness: the moderns never contemplate the real possibility that medieval Jewish philosophy imparts the true teaching.

Thus, Strauss does not address "the gravest issue" of betrayal. Ultimately Strauss agrees that these figures were guilty of harboring secret heterodox positions and questions. What is required is the serious conviction that medieval philosophy is superior to modern philosophy in that the former might be "simply true." Strauss argued that medieval philosophy can be understood "only if we are prepared to learn something, not merely *about* the medieval philosophers, but *from* them."[160]

Strauss appeals to those interested in historical understanding when arguing for a more audacious project. One who is interested in "a true historical understanding" must be prepared to embark upon a journey to an unfamiliar territory. Strauss's deepened appreciation for medieval philosophy evolved during his own peregrinations through Europe and then the United States. Strauss's own reorientation to conditions of exile converges with the advice he offers to potential students who are preparing for intellectual journeys into medieval thought. As an émigré, Strauss did not simply assimilate and adopt the norms and conventions of his new host environments. Instead, he accommodated to the existing regimes under which he lived with one foot always firmly planted in a different home: the world inhabited by his fellow exiled and persecuted thinkers who were forced to make homes for themselves under difficult circumstances: Socrates, Xenophon, Plato, Aristotle, Lucretius, Cicero, Averroës, al Farabi, Maimonides, Machiavelli, Spinoza, Lessing, and Nietzsche.

Likewise, in the dark and foreign world of medieval Jewish and Islamic philosophy, the traveler should not try to take his bearings by modern assumptions and normative presuppositions. Rather, he should be guided by "the signposts which guided the thinkers of old."[161] But even this preliminary task is exceedingly difficult and requires a clearing of modern presuppositions. Strauss's historian must experience "utter bewilderment" and "perplexity" before undergoing the transformative experience of a conversion to philosophy:

> These old signposts are not immediately visible: they are concealed by heaps of dust and rubble. The most obnoxious part of the rubble consists of the superficial interpretations by modern writers, of the cheap clichés which are offered in the textbooks and which seem to unlock by one formula the mystery of the past. The signposts which guided the thinkers of the past, must be *recovered* before they can be used. Before the historian has succeeded in recovering them, he cannot help being in a condition of utter bewilderment, of universal doubt: he finds himself in a darkness which is illumined exclusively by his knowledge that he knows nothing. When engaging in the study of the philosophy of the past, he must know that he embarks on a journey whose end is completely hidden from him: he is not likely to return to the shore of his time as the same man who left it.[162]

While acknowledging a debt to the historical scholarship of Salomon Munk, David Kaufmann, and Harry A. Wolfson, Strauss held that such historical scholarship has "not yet crossed the threshold" of Yehuda Halevi's *Kuzari* and Maimonides's *Guide*. Strauss's judgment on the state of contemporary scholarship is levied in his appropriation of the Talmudic phrase that was employed by Maimonides: *Ben Zoma 'adayin bahutz* (Ben Zoma is still outside).[163] In other words, modern scholarship has not come close to uncovering the secret wisdom buried between the lines of medieval Jewish philosophy. Strauss veiled his bold expeditions to recover these forgotten treasures with cautious ambiguity in order to ensure that only the student who possesses rare and necessary qualities will be able to follow his quest for wisdom.

In his European exile Strauss already began to reset the battle between ancients and moderns in his attempt to trace the contours of the restorative orientation of Platonic politics. In America, his descriptive project turned into a modern renewal of this tradition. This project of reclamation obligates the modern philosopher to follow after the medieval Islamic and Jewish philosophers in respect to the Law. Just as the medieval philosopher reinforced the sanctity of the Law and placed that founding document (Torah or the Koran) beyond all question, so too must the modern philosopher elevate the timeless truth and wisdom of his or her country's founding legal document. In a liberal democracy such as the United States, this source text of legal founding is the Constitution.

In 1949 Leo Strauss gave a series of lectures at the University of Chicago, a series that would mark the beginning of a new phase of his American career. Strauss chose to open his famous lecture series, later published as *Natural Right and History* (1950), by invoking the Declaration of Independence. If we remember Strauss's convictions regarding a natural aristocracy and ranking of men, it is difficult to see how he could embrace the principle that "all men are created equal," unless such a rhetorical affirmation reinforces the unquestionable nature of the political order under whose law he now lives. It is fitting that Strauss's first words at the University of Chicago should pronounce the timeless wisdom of America's founding fathers and link America's rising wealth and power to the foundational truths that must be placed beyond question and examination. In order to justify his own ruminations on controversial and potentially subversive philosophical and political matters, however, Strauss follows Maimonides in establishing the necessity of such a disclosure based upon an imminent crisis. We close our investigation into Strauss's journey from Germany to America with the opening words that appeared in *Natural Right and History*:

> It is proper for more reasons than the most obvious one that I should open this series of Charles R. Walgreen Lectures by quoting a passage from the Declaration of Independence. The passage has frequently been quoted, but, by its weight and its elevation, it is made immune to the degrading effects of the excessive familiarity which breeds contempt and of misuse which breeds disgust. "We hold these truths to be self-evident, that all men are created equal, that they are endowed by their Creator with certain unalienable Rights, that among these are Life, Liberty, and the pursuit of Happiness." The nation dedicated to this proposition has now become, no doubt partly as a consequence of this dedication, the most powerful and prosperous of the nations of the earth. Does this nation in its maturity still cherish the faith in which it was conceived and raised? Does it still hold those "truths to be self-evident"?[164]

# Conclusion: Looking Back on Weimar and the Politics of Exile

*E*very now and then, a historian comes across small scraps of paper that had lain in obscurity and darkness until that point. Soon after Strauss's death on October 18, 1973, Gershom Scholem scrawled a series of reflections that most likely served as the basis of his public remarks delivered at the Van Leer Institute in Jerusalem in October 1974.[1] Scholem, who pioneered the academic study of Jewish mysticism, met Strauss in 1927; they soon thereafter developed a lifelong friendship.[2] In providing the biographical building blocks of the young Strauss, Scholem portrays a man tarrying with the most profound issues of philosophy, theology, and politics, with rare and determined rigor. Scholem wastes no time in attempting to capture an appropriate epitaph. Scholem's very first observation was that Strauss was a man "*benaftulav*." Scholem's brilliantly succinct assessment is also hopelessly untranslatable. Modern Hebrew dictionaries do not capture the resonating meaning of this phrase. The literal definition of "*naftul*" connotes confusion and convolution. Scholem certainly did not intend these pejorative associations. Rather, his epithet is a wonderfully mimetic instantiation of Strauss himself. One flexible and more apt rendering would be that Strauss was a man caught in the coil of his theological and existential wrestlings.[3] And the prepositional syllable in "*benaftulav*" could also mean that Strauss himself was constituted by his existential and intellectual agitations.

Scholem's description of his friendly intellectual sparring partner captures Strauss's self-description, which appears in the opening lines of Strauss's "semi-autobiographical" intellectual portrait, his preface for an English translation of his first book *Die Religionskritik Spinozas* (1930).[4] Writing in August 1962, Strauss reflects backs upon the unique historical context of Weimar Germany and its profound impact upon his emergence as a Jewish intellectual.[5] The Preface opens in stark fashion: "This study on Spinoza's *Theologico-political Treatise* was written during the years 1925–28 in Germany. The author was a young Jew

118

born and raised in Germany who found himself in the grip of the theologico-political predicament."[6]

The preface to *Spinoza's Critique of Religion* is a dialectic of historically grounded philosophical positions circling around the Jewish problem—or more extensively "the theologico-political predicament." Strauss's analysis reveals the inner complexities and seriousness with which he had engaged this dominant reality. Yet its consequences for his own philosophic and political perspectives can only be interpreted by following the clues he leaves for the careful reader.

Rather than simply provide some autobiographical comments for the sake of nostalgia, Strauss produced a carefully constructed and singularly peculiar work of modern political thought. Focusing on the predicament of modern German Jewry and various Jewish responses, Strauss explicates the dynamics of modern German-Jewish history by dialectically fusing them into an extraordinary mélange of apparent contradictions, unexpected omissions, unnecessary repetitions, and perplexing ambiguities. An unmediated reading of this text would doubtlessly result in much confusion and some vague impression that Strauss wants to critique modern thought's siege against religious orthodoxy. However, all of the aforementioned literary devices serve as guiding clues for a second layer of textual meaning that is qualitatively different from that which appears on the surface. Still, these pieces are exemplifications of exoteric rather than esoteric writing/speech; the reader can gain access to them without too much effort.[7]

Strauss's analysis of the situation of Jewry in Germany in the last two centuries focuses on the highly charged cultural and political forces that guided and shaped German-Jewish historical consciousness. After teasing out the inner contradictions of various solutions to the Jewish problem—the most manifestly intransigent form of the theologico-political problem for Strauss—Strauss's argument appears to culminate in a call for a return to Jewish Orthodoxy as the only viable solution to the Jewish problem for the modern Jew. There is no direct answer, however, to the question of whether or not such a return to faith is possible for the modern Jewish intellectual. I argue that Strauss's call for an unqualified return to Orthodoxy is not meant for intellectuals, but rather should be understood as appropriate for "the many." For the select few, Strauss points toward a continuation of the political project initiated by the prophets in the Hebrew Bible: the task of creating or sustaining a community in which a moral code of conduct is obeyed by all members. The prophets are understood by Strauss as possessing the political wisdom necessary to bind a people to a moral code. The role of the prophet, therefore, is appropriate only for a philosophic elite who can properly respond to the challenge of knowing that providence does not guide the unfolding of history.[8]

In February 1962, Strauss gave a lecture at the B'nai B'rith Hillel Foundation of the University of Chicago entitled "Why We Remain Jews: Can Jewish Faith and History Still Speak To Us?"[9] Access to this text does not require the same degree of interpretive acumen as does the Preface to *Spinoza's Critique of Religion* (for reasons related to the limited public nature of a lecture at the University's Hillel House as well as Strauss's stated lack of "proper" preparation, which left less time for carefully inserting obstacles to a clear understanding).[10] Because this lecture was not intended to be distributed as a polished written text, Strauss may have felt less inhibited to be forthright. Here Strauss points toward a unique, if not radical, historical vision of modern Jewish identity in which a philosophical meaning is explicitly attached to the condition of *galut* or exile. In making this connection, Strauss transforms the traditional notion of Jewish "chosenness" into a national symbol affirming the universal absence of redemption in the world. After arguing that Jewish chosenness necessarily entails the eternal separation of the Jew from the divine, Strauss universalizes this condition for all humankind: we are unable to effectuate a perfectly just political order and utopia is impossible to realize. It is my contention that this perceived ontological pessimism became a primary source of Strauss's intransigent conservativism and utter disdain for liberal and progressive politics throughout his adult life.[11]

The figure of Leo Strauss understood as conservative prophet of Chicago appears to be at odds with the way he was understood by his Jewish contemporaries from German academia. I cite two intriguing accounts of Strauss's perspectives on Judaism, both of which are drawn from private letters of prominent German Jewish contemporaries and scholarly colleagues. In them, Strauss is depicted as an unabashed atheist—a characterization that may surprise many who are familiar with his far more prevalent image as a (reactionary) believer who centered his philosophy on a rigid religious and political orthodoxy (understood in its literal etymological meaning as correct or right opinion).

In 1954, upon reading the original German edition of *Spinoza's Critique of Religion*, Karl Jaspers asked Hannah Arendt about the author whom he assumed to be "an orthodox Jew of strong rational powers."[12] Arendt had incidentally been an acquaintance of Strauss while attending Heidegger's lectures in Freiburg and Giessen. She informed Jaspers that Strauss was a "highly respected professor of political philosophy at the University of Chicago" who possessed a "truly gifted intellect." After listing some of his "notable works," Arendt gives a striking portrayal of Strauss as "a convinced orthodox atheist." The passage ends with her terse personal judgment: "I don't like him."[13] Perplexed by Arendt's unexpected description of Strauss as an atheist, Jaspers asks, "An atheist now? In his earlier books he appears as an Orthodox Jew who is providing justification for authority."[14] Did this inquiry of Jaspers about a dramatic shift from believer to nonbeliever in Strauss's thought have substance?[15]

We recall that some twenty years earlier, Strauss had been described as a brilliantly provocative atheist by Scholem in a letter to Benjamin.[16] The enigmatic character of Strauss provides an intriguing backdrop to the study of his intellectual development presented in earlier chapters. The comment by Jaspers in

1954 that *Spinoza's Critique of Religion* seemed to be an argument for religious authority does not necessarily mean that Strauss was a true adherent to Orthodox beliefs. Perhaps Strauss found religious authority desirable quite apart from motives of personal theological commitment.

Strauss begins his preface with staccato notes: "This study on *Spinoza's Theologico-political Treatise* was written during the years 1925–28 in Germany. The author was a young Jew born and raised in Germany who found himself in the grip of the theologico-political predicament."[17]

Several questions immediately arise upon reading this passage. Perhaps the most pressing question regards the meaning of "the theologico-political predicament." How and why did Strauss find himself in its "grip," the condition Scholem referred to in the word *benaftulav?* What is the significance of a German Jew writing a book on Spinoza in the mid- to late 1920s? Strauss does not answer these questions in the direct fashion one might expect from a traditional preface—but perhaps by now, we have already come to recognize Strauss's mercurial intellectual character.

While Strauss "intended to bridge the gulf between 1930 Germany and 1962 U.S.A." with the Preface, it cannot be read as a simple autobiography.[18] Gershom Scholem's only criticism of the text is that it seems "to leap over several stages" in Strauss's autobiography.[19] And Strauss responded to Scholem that he had indeed "omitted in a way everything which comes after 1928."[20] The text, according to Strauss, "comes as close to an autobiography as is possible *within the bounds of propriety.*"[21] We wonder what if anything substantive falls outside those bounds? After all, the Preface opens the door to many sensitive issues in Strauss's biography. He points to his earlier engagement with and attraction to thinkers who eventually joined the Nazi Party such as Heidegger and Schmitt. One wonders how many English readers of Strauss would have been alerted to Strauss's critique of Schmitt from the right, that Schmitt did not fully extricate himself from the "systematics" of liberalism. As for suspect religious and ethical positions, Strauss presents a strong philosophical case for the internal necessity of atheism and even nihilism as the final ends of modern rationalism. Yet Strauss emphasizes that revelation taken on its own terms can neither be successfully refuted by philosophical critique nor successfully recast by philosophical rationalizations. While he offers incisive and devastating critiques of the shortcomings of the German-Jewish "return movement" from Hermann Cohen to Franz Rosenzweig, he does present what he found to be most compelling about them, and he did hold back his severe personal judgments of someone like Martin Buber.[22] And finally, he limits the status of Jewish chosenness to the event of revelation, but undermines any philosophical grounding and understanding— that is, on the sole basis of autonomous human reason—for the miraculous occurance of divine intervention into this world.

Stopping at 1928 does make a certain amount of sense considering the book was originally completed then. However, the Preface actually ends in 1932 with his explicit mentioning of his critique of Carl Schmitt's *Concept of the Political*.[23] The historical narrative of the Preface offers a brief tour of Jewish attempts to respond to the exclusionary and sometimes violent expression of anti-Jewish sentiments that have permeated Christian European history. This narrative relates the dynamically complex battle for recognition and drive toward freedom by a group continuously defined as "other." The options for relief of the Jewish problem appear to be individual assimilation, political liberalism, communism, fascism, political Zionism, cultural Zionism, religious Zionism, and the personal return to Orthodoxy.

An immediate response to the problem of discrimination and persecution is individual assimilation. A primary impulse for assimilation was put forward by Henrich Heine, the German-Jewish poet who converted to Christianity, saying, "Judaism is not a religion but a misfortune." The practical implications for the individual Jew, according to Strauss, was the position of complete assimilation: "Let us get rid of Judaism as fast as we can and as painlessly as we can."[24] To place such a position in historical perspective, Strauss turns to the Middle Ages, when many Jews pursued this possibility by simply converting to Christianity. We learn that such a solution "was not quite easy even then." Pointing to the Spanish Expulsion in 1492 and the "extra-legal but not illegal" distinction between old Christians and new Christians, Spaniards of pure blood (the old Spaniards) and Spaniards of impure blood (*conversos*), Strauss uses history to demonstrate the difficulty of the path for individual assimilation. In Spain, the Jews were forced to become Christian but paradoxically were also "forced to remain Jews" regardless of stated theological beliefs. The Spanish identification of the Jew by blood thus sets forth the historical precedent of the futility of the individual Jew who attempts to pursue this path of assimilation.

For Strauss, as illustrated in his first book, the situation of the Marrano is paradigmatic not only of medieval Jewry, but of philosophy as well. Both must keep their true beliefs concealed from public comprehension while publicly affirming current regimes of order. The next response was to seek the political solution offered by political liberalism: secular assimilation. It was reasonable to assume that "a society which is not legally a Christian society, a society beyond the difference between Judaism and Christianity," should be indifferent to individual religious preferences.[25] But in an argument that might be viewed as a truncated form of Marx's critique of liberalism in his 1843 essay "On the Jewish Question," Strauss turns the logic of liberalism against itself. Because a liberal society is dependent on the distinction between autonomous public and private spheres, a liberal society cannot legally prohibit private discrimination; such would be deemed an illegitimate encroachment of the state into society and thus obliterate the fundamental autonomy of the private realm, culminating in the dissolution of the liberal state.[26]

Additionally, the Nazi regime's triumph over the Weimar Republic might offer additional insight into some shortcomings of an abstract notion of liberalism.

As Strauss relates: "The German Jews owed their emancipation to the French Revolution or its effects. They were given full political rights for the first time by the Weimar Republic. The Weimar Republic was succeeded by the only German regime—the only regime ever anywhere— which had no other clear principle than murderous hatred of the Jews, for 'Aryan' had no clear meaning other than 'non-Jewish.'"[27] According to Strauss, the committment of Weimar to the principle of equality met with a dialectical response: the emphasis on a tradition of the unique superiority of German traditions. This clash set the stage for an explosive potentiality that determined the uncertainty of the Weimar project.[28]

For Strauss, the link between Weimar's weak liberal regime and its authoritarian successor is explained by the collapse of the liberal foundation: belief in modern rationalism. The uncertainty that followed this collapse was felt most acutely by that group who had the most to gain by the success of the liberal project: the Jews. The analysis offered by Strauss vividly expresses the unstable status of Jews in Germany and the ways in which they searched for some sense of security: "At a time when German Jews were politically in a more precarious situation than Jews in any other country, they originated 'the science of Judaism,' the historical-critical study by Jews of the Jewish heritage."[29] The application of the methods and tools of German historicism to the Jewish tradition could uncover the rationalist pillars of Jewish culture and religion while rejecting the less rationally inclined tendencies (such as creation of the world out of nothing, resurrection of the dead, messianic promise, and any mystical elements) as aberations.

The modern idealized redefinition of Judaism as the religion of reason is seen by Strauss as the product of the dynamic interaction of a diaspora culture leading to a continuous reshaping of the Jewish tradition. But direct absorption of an external culture can be extremely dangerous if brought to a point of absolute dependence, especially when the original status of "other" is not overcome:

> The emancipation of Jews in Germany coincided with the greatest epoch of German thought and poetry, the epoch in which Germany was the foremost country in thought and poetry. One cannot help comparing the period of German Jewry with the period of Spanish Jewry. The greatest achievement of Jews during the Spanish period were rendered possible partly by the fact that Jews became receptive to the influx of Greek thought, which was understood to be Greek only accidentally. During the German period, however, the Jews opened themselves to the influx of German thought, the thought of the particular nation in the midst of which they lived—a thought which was understood to be German essentially: political dependence was also spiritual dependence. This was the core of the predicament of German Jewry.[30]

To illustrate the precarious situation of the Jews in Germany who were so dependent on a cultural matrix permeated with hostility toward Jews, Strauss refers to statements made by the German intellectual icons Goethe, Nietzsche, and Heidegger. All three had enormous influence on Strauss's own thinking. Strauss refers to expressions of anti-Jewish sentiments in the works of these figures starting with a mere discomfort for German Jews but culminating in Heidegger's infamous statement regarding "the inner truth and greatness of National Socialism."[31]

Let us grant that liberalism does not account for cultural forces of intolerance. Why not then pursue other political programs that would rise upon the destruction of liberal society if this be the only way in which to eliminate discrimination as a significant social phenomena? After all, as late as 1932, in his review of Carl Schmitt's *Concept of the Political,* Strauss rebukes Schmitt for not being radical enough in his critique of liberalism. There, Strauss argued for an exploration into a truly postliberal political theory, one that can only be understood by uprooting the liberal tradition espoused by Thomas Hobbes. At such a turbulent time in Germany's political scene, Strauss's entrenched antipathy for "pacifist internationalism" centers his political orientation.[32]

In 1962, however, Strauss rejects any possibility of a conservative postliberal society and confines his exploration to the Soviet Union as the case study to see how the destruction of liberal society affects the fate of the Jews. He argues that the history of the USSR's brutal anti-Jewish policies cannot be ignored as inessential for communism. To seek an "essence of communism" outside of its historical reality is an unallowable breach of orthodox Communism.[33] Thus Trotsky's communism, which did not contain any such similar anti-Jewish element, had been "refuted by his [Trotsky's] highest authority, history. A Trotskiite is a living contradiction." Indeed, Strauss explains that the Soviet Union could not have survived World War II had Stalin not rejected Trotsky's vision of a revolution founded on the support of a revolutionary proletariat:

> The USSR owes its survival to Stalin's decision not to wait for the revolution of the Western proletariat, i.e. for what others would do for the USSR, but to build up socialism in a single country where his word was the law, by the use of any means however bestial, and these means could include, as a matter of course, certain means successfully used previously, not to say invented by Hitler: the large-scale murder of party members and anti-Jewish measures.[34]

The second lesson Stalin learned from Hitler regarded the functional utility of anti-Jewish policies. Prior to World War I, when there was no visible distinction in Western socialist movements between Bolshevism and Menshevism, "it was an axiom, 'Anti-semitism is the socialism of the fools,' and therefore incompatible with intelligent socialism." But Strauss's belief that the majority of humankind is composed of the vulgar masses inverted this old adage: "The fact that anti-Semitism is the socialism of fools, is an argument not against but for anti-Semitism; given the fact that there is such an abundance of fools, why should one [not] steal that very profitable thunder." While Hitler, according to

Strauss, became a prisoner of absurd racial theories, Stalin "judicially" used anti-Jewish policies to govern the many different national groups that constituted the Soviet Union. This judicious practice was much easier than treating Jews fairly.[35] Strauss concludes that such implications "confirm *our* contention that the uneasy 'solution of the Jewish problem' offered by the liberal state is superior to the Communist 'solution.'"[36]

But it is not necessarily an either/or choice between liberalism and communism. There are still the options of different brands of Zionism. As a modern political movement, Zionism's unique character is ascertained by Strauss in its first expressions: Leon Pinsker's *Autoemancipation* and then Theodor Herzl's *The Jewish State*. Although Pinsker and Herzl started from the failure of the liberal solution in Europe, they still operated under the modern prejudice that the Jewish problem was merely a human problem that could be solved through human means. Nevertheless, as Strauss states, Pinsker and Herzl "radicalized this purely human understanding": "The terrible fate of the Jews was in no sense to be understood any longer as connected with divine punishment for the sins of our fathers or with the providential mission of the chosen people and hence to be borne with the meek fortitude of martyrs. It was to be understood in merely human terms, as constituting a purely political problem which as such cannot be solved by appealing to the justice or generosity of other nations, to say nothing of a league of nations."

Thus, political Zionists were concerned primarily with "cleansing the Jews of their millennial degradation, with the recovery of Jewish dignity, honor or pride." In other words, they aimed at the negation of the political condition of *galut* that had plagued Jewish existence for two millennia.

> The failure of the liberal solution meant that Jews could not regain their honor by assimilating as individuals to the nations among which they lived or by becoming citizens like all other citizens of the liberal states: the liberal solution brought at best legal equality, but not social equality; as a demand of reason it had no effect on the feelings of non-Jews. Only through securing the honor of the Jewish nation could the individual Jew's honor be secured. *The true solution* to the Jewish problem requires that the Jews become 'like all the nations' (I Samuel 8), that the Jewish nation assimilate itself to the nations of the world or that it establish a modern, liberal, secular (but not necessarily democratic) state. Political Zionism then strictly understoood was the movement of an elite on behalf of a community constituted by common descent and common degradation, for the restoration of their honor through the acquisition of statehood and therefore of a country—of any country: the land which the strictly political Zionism promised to the Jews was not necessarily the Land of Israel.[37]

The political Zionist project of securing Jewish honor and pride by founding a secular soveriegn state "implied a profound modification of traditional

Jewish hopes, a modification arrived at through a break with these hopes." In a succinct analysis of political Zionism's relation to the Jewish past, Strauss returns to the motto of Pinsker's pamphlet, which quotes Hillel: "If I am not for myself, who will be for me? And if not now, when?" Strauss incisively points out that Pinsker significantly omitted the sentence that forms the center of Hillel's statement: "And if I am only for myself, what am I?" Through his critique of the isolating self-reference of political Zionism, Strauss might be seen as embracing an affirmative conception of assimilation. Here we see one of Strauss's most valuable insights into the dynamics of Jewish history: that Jewish tradition and culture do not develop within a historical vacuum.

Pinsker diagnosed Judeophobia in Europe and sought to overcome the Jewish condition of diasporic passivity. Strauss comments: "He saw the Jewish people as a herd without a shepherd to protect and gather it; he did not long for a shepherd, but for the transformation of the herd into a nation that could take care of itself." Pinsker's perception of Jewish identity and aspirations eliminated all traditional theological substance, a point brought to the forefront when one follows Strauss's reference to an often misinterpreted sentence of Spinoza: "If the foundations of their religion did not effeminate the minds of the Jews, I would absolutely believe that they will at some time, given the occasion (for human things are mutable), establish their state again."[38] The Zionist mission to perpetuate the physical existence of the Jewish people through the establishment of a sovereign state, according to this analysis, can only be made possible by gutting Judaism of its foundation in divine law and messianic redemption.

The deficiencies of political Zionism are addressed by cultural Zionism. The foundation of Zionism is reformulated as a Jewish cultural heritage, that is, "as a product of the national mind, of the national genius." Cultural Zionism finds itself unable to escape internal contradiction because "the foundation, the authoritative layer, of the Jewish heritage presents itself, not as a product of the human mind, but as a divine gift, as divine revelation."[39] Cultural Zionism failed to acquire the necessary determined ability to arrive at a balance between the two extremes of politics (that is, power politics) and divine revelation.

"When cultural Zionism understands itself, it turns into religious Zionism." But any attempt to handle the Jewish problem, a divine matter, with humanly imposed solutions must be regarded as "blasphemous." "Zionism may go so far as to regard the establishment of the state of Israel as the most important event in Jewish history since the completion of the Talmud, but it cannot regard it as the arrival of the Messianic age, of the redemption of Israel and of all man." The line of argument Strauss expounds here finds its original inspiration in his early writings on the centrality of *galut.* "The establishment of the state of Israel is the most profound modification of the Galut which has occurred, but it is not the end of the Galut." In a spiritual and political sense, the state of Israel is subsumed under the *galut* because "[f]inite, relative problems can be solved, absolute problems cannot be solved. In other words, *human beings will never create a society which is free of contradictions.*"[40]

Thus, if the Jewish people come to this recognition and see that humans are unable to accomplish the task of creating a perfectly free and just society, they may be identified as "the chosen people in the sense, at least, that the Jewish problem is the most manifest symbol of the human problem as a social or political problem."[1]

Strauss uses this possibility of limiting human hubris for the purposes of promoting acceptence of the contradictions inherent in the liberal state. This concern to counter anthropocentric arrogance can clearly be seen in his call for a return to Orthodoxy. While he had previously argued that the Jewish problem is insoluble,[42] Strauss suddenly states that "[t]here is a Jewish problem that is humanly soluble,[43] the problem of the Western Jewish individual who or whose parents severed his connection with the Jewish community in the expectation that he would thus become a normal member of a universal human society, and who is naturally perplexed when he finds no such society." Western European Jews lived with this anguish and despair when social discrimination seemed as though it were intensifying in the early twentieth century. "The solution to this problem is return to the Jewish community, the community established by the faith and the Jewish way of life." This notion of return and repentance is embodied in the Hebrew term *teshuvah*.[44]

But is *teshuvah* a viable option for the Jewish intellectual? Strauss does not directly answer this question. "While admitting that their deepest problem would be solved by that return," skeptical intellectuals "assert that intellectual probity forbids them to sacrifice intellect in order to satisfy even the most vital need. Yet they can hardly deny that a vital need legitimately induces a man to probe whether what seems to be an impossibility is not in fact only a very great difficulty."[45]

It appears that Strauss indirectly builds toward an affirmative answer to this question. He demonstrates the self-destruction of Orthodoxy's archenemy in the modern era: modern rationalism.[46] Then Strauss distances himself from his early work on Spinoza by stating that it was "based on the premise, sanctioned by powerful prejudice, that a return to pre-modern philosophy is impossible."[47] But premodern philosophy should not be understood as philosophy reconciled with revelation. Indeed, Strauss claims that his article on Schmitt marked the beginning of his journey to rediscover "the manner in which heterodox thinkers of earlier ages wrote their books."[48] These heterodox thinkers of earlier ages are none other than such religious philosophic icons as Maimonides and al Farabi. The brilliant concealment of heterodox ideas throughout their writings, according to Strauss, was achieved by "a forgotten kind of writing": esoteric writing. Strauss attempts to implement the lost art, concealing his heterodox ideas in this text that appears to affirm *teshuvah* as the ultimate refuge for modern individuals.

To illustrate this concealment, let us take up Strauss's other argument about assimilation. In both texts, Strauss refers to a striking passage from Nietzsche on the highest possibilities of Jewish assimilation. In the lecture, Strauss reads aloud an extended version of the following passage:

> Among the spectacles to which the coming century invites us is the decision as to the destiny of the Jews of Europe. That their die is cast, that they have crossed their Rubicon, is now palpably obvious: all that is left is for them either to become the masters of Europe or to lose Europe. They themselves know that a conquest of Europe, or any kind of violence, on their part is not to be thought of: but they also know that at some future time Europe may fall into their hands like a ripe fruit if only they would just extend them. To bring that about they need, in the meantime, to distinguish themselves in every domain of European distinction and to stand everywhere in the first rank until they have reached the point at which they themselves determine what is distinguishing. . . . Then, when the Jews can exhibit as their work such jewels and golden vessels as the European nations of a briefer and less profound experience could not and cannot produce, when Israel will have transformed its eternal vengeance into an eternal blessing for Europe: then there will again arrive that seventh day on which the ancient Jewish God may *rejoice* in himself, his creation and his chosen people—and let us all, all of us, rejoice with him!"[49]

Strauss states that this passage is "the most profound and most radical statement on assimilation" he has read. Although Nietzsche did write this with a certain degree of irony, its significance should not be overlooked:

> Assimilation cannot mean abondoning the inheritance but only giving it another direction, transforming it. And assimilation cannot be an end, it could only be a way toward that. Assimilation is an intermediate stage in which it means distinguishing oneself in pursuits which are not as such Jewish but, as Nietzsche would say, European, as we would say, Western.[50]

After understanding what assimilation could mean in its highest possibility, "one trembles" to see how assimilation has been actualized. "There exists a kind of Jewish glorification of every clever or brilliant Jewish mediocrity which is as pitiable as it is laughable. It reminds one of villagers who have produced their first physicist, and hail him for this reason as the greatest physicist that ever was." The perception that there are so many respected Jews is not due to any Jewish greatness, but rather only "to the general decline, to a general victory of mediocrity." Strauss does not see it as difficult to be considered a great man in such a swamp of mediocrity: "Among the blind the one-eyed is king."[51]

Strauss ends his lecture by recasting Judaism in light of a noble myth that ought to be perpetuated. Strauss rejects Heine's characterization of Judaism as a misfortune and prefers instead to call it a "*heroic delusion*" that consists of righteousness or charity. These two words are synonomous in Strauss's view of Judaism and constitute the only requisite of Judaism. But the defensibility of Judaism's primary requisite appears to be contingent on the existence of a loving God. "The root of injustice and uncharitableness which abounds is not in God but in the free acts of his creatures; in sin. The Jewish people and their fate are the living witness for the absence of redemption." The meaning of the chosen people is that "*the Jews are chosen to prove the absence of redemption.*"[52] The *Alenu* prayer becomes the greatest monument to this recast vision of faith in an all-powerful, righteous, and loving Lord whose stature is not compromised by the given fact of immutable human evil.[53]

Thus, for Strauss, "No nobler dream was ever dreamt" than the naïve loyalty to a conception of a just deity: "It is surely nobler to be victim of the most noble dream than to profit from a sordid reality and to wallow in it."[54] In both the Preface and the public lecture "Why We Remain Jews," Strauss offers a tightly spun interrogation of modern Jewish attempts to respond to the Jewish question. In the latter talk (sponsored by the University of Chicago Hillel organization), Strauss offered a peculiar definition of what it means to be Jewish; his definition was accompanied by a playfully provocative appropriation of Nietzsche and ironic appreciation for pieces of Jewish liturgy. These last elements he excised from its revised state in the Preface, probably because he did not want his "semi-autobiographical" text to be considered a Jewish text. And yet, as Harold Bloom has noted, there are few texts in modern Jewish intellectual history that resonate more adroitly with the problematics of Jewish politics, hermeneutics, and existence.[55]

While I reject many of Strauss's fundamental convictions about humanity and politics, there is no doubt that he has forced me to take seriously problems inherent within modern religion and politics. He has widened my own horizons for understanding the radical possibilities and limitations of modern Jewish existence and politics. Ultimately, his lifelong struggle with the entanglements of exile have helped me to see the shallow and hubristic contours of current debates about Jewish existence and politics. Reconstructing modern Jewish politics on the foundation of exile may follow Strauss's stress on political resignation in light of the dangers of radical change, but not necessarily.

We have seen Strauss's penetrating treatments of the Jewish problem and critique of Zionism in the companion texts of the Preface and "Why We Remain Jews." Let us compare those treatments to that found in his 1956 public defense of the State of Israel (on grounds of "conservatism") that appeared in the *National Review*. Strauss's article originated as a letter to Wilmoore Kendall (November 19, 1956) following Strauss's year as a visiting professor in political science at the Hebrew University. While generally supportive of the *National Review*, Strauss finds it "incomprehensible" why all of the magazine's contributors on Israel are so uniformly and unqualifiedly opposed to the state. Given their lack of knowledge and reasoned argumentation, "anti-Jewish animus" is raised as one possible reason. Strauss was most likely correct in sensing an anti-semitic undertone driving the *National Review*'s anti-Israel stance up to that point, but the argument he presents is one of the most unpersuasive publications of his career. Strauss argues that American conservatives ought to support the young state for some of the following reasons: (1) it serves as a "western outpost" by educating immigrants from the East in the ways of the West; (2) the "heroic austerity" of the Israeli national ethos—which is "supported by the nearness of biblical antiquity"—coincides with the conservative appreciation for ancient heritage; and (3) as for concerns that socialists run the state, Strauss states that they are more Western pioneers than socialists. This piece, just as his public affirmation of those "self-evident" principles of the Declaration of Independence in the opening of *Natural Right and History* are examples of Strauss's conservative strategy of accommodation, which ends up approximating a modern version of the premodern strategy of Jews to ally themselves with the holders of power: the Jewish royal alliance.

But this accommodation is certainly not the only direction in which exilic politics can proceed. Indeed, there is another side of Strauss in which I see a progressive and radical alternative. Acknowledging exile as a starting point means keeping in mind how unjust and imperfect current political orders are when compared to the very principles and ideals of those states and societies. The urgent attempts to redress these intolerable injustices, indeed, can be seen in many peoples' attempts to make whole that which is broken and fragmented. While past utopian solutions may rightly be received with a certain degree of skepticism, it is no improvement that chauvinistic narcissism and cynicism seem to have won the day. Acknowledgment of exile carries with it a heightened concern for the fragility of human life under stressed and impoverished conditions; it also makes one wary of the growing coercive and invasive power of the modern state in the name of national security. But the direction and contours of such a politics have yet to be fully engaged. And it is this unexamined legacy of Strauss I offer for rediscovery.

# Abbreviations

"CCM"      Leo Strauss, "Correspondence Concerning Modernity," trans. Susanne Klein and George Elliot Tucker, *Independent Journal of Philosophy* 4 (1983): 105–119.

*EPLJ*     Leo Strauss, *Das Erkenntnisproblem in der philosophischen Lehre Fr. H. Jacobis*, in *GS*, 2.

*EW*       *Leo Strauss: The Early Writings (1921–1932)*, trans. and ed. Michael Zank (Albany: State University of New York Press, 2002).

"GA"       Leo Strauss, "A Giving of Accounts," with Jacob Klein. Originally published in *The College*, 22, no. 1 (April): 1–5. Republished in *Jewish Philosophy and the Crisis Of Modernity in Modern Jewish Thought*, ed. Kenneth H. Green (Albany: SUNY Press, 1997), 457–466.

"gLG"      Leo Strauss, "Die geistige Lage der Gegenwart," in *GS*, 2:441–464.

*GS*, 1    Leo Strauss, *Gesammelte Schriften*, vol. 1, *Die Religionskritik Spinozas und zugehörige Schriften*, ed. Heinrich Meier (Stuttgart: J. B. Metzler, 1996).

*GS*, 2    Leo Strauss, *Gesammelte Schriften*, vol. 2, *Philosophie und Gesetz: Frühe Schriften*, ed. Heinrich Meier (Stuttgart: J. B. Metzler, 1997).

*GS*, 3    Leo Strauss, *Gesammelte Schriften*, vol. 3, *Hobbes' politische Wissenschaft und zugehörige Shriften—Briefe*, ed. Heinrich Meier (Stuttgart: J. B. Metzler, 2001).

"IHE"      Leo Strauss, "An Introduction to Heideggerian Existentialism," in *The Rebirth of Classical Political Rationalism*, ed. Thomas Pangle (Chicago: University of Chicago Press, 1989), 27–45.

*JPCM*     Kenneth Hart Green, ed., *Jewish Philosophy and the Crisis of Modernity* (Albany: State University of New York Press, 1997).

*LSTH*     Carl Schmitt, *Der Leviathan in der Staatslehre des Thomas Hobbes: Sinn und Fehlschlag eines politischen Symbols* (Cologne: Hohenheim, 1982).

"NCP"      Leo Strauss, "Notes on the Concept of the Political," in Heinrich Meier, *Carl Schmitt and Leo Strauss: The Hidden Dialogue*, trans. J. Harvey Lomoz Meier (Chicago: University of Chicago Press, 1995).

*NRH*      Leo Strauss, *Natural Right and History* (Chicago: University of Chicago Press, 1952).

"OAPT"     Leo Strauss, "On Abravanel's Philosophical Tendency and Political Teaching," in *Isaac Abravanel*, ed. J. B. Trend and H. Loewe (Cambridge: Cambridge University Press, 1937), 93–129. Reprinted in *GS*, 2:195–228.

*PG*       Leo Strauss, *Philosophie und Gesetz: Beiträge zum Verständnis Maimunis und seiner Vorläufer* (Berlin: Schocken, 1935), as reprinted in *GS*, 2.

| "PKJ" [EPLJ] | Leo Strauss, "Das Erkenntnisproblem in der philosophischen, Lehre Fr. H. Jacobis," Ph.D. diss., 1921 (Hamburg) in *GS* 2:237–292 (trans. as "The Problem of Knowledge in the Philosophical Doctrine of Fredrich Heinrich Jacobi)." |
|---|---|
| *PL* | Leo Strauss, *Philosophy and Law: Contributions to the Understanding of Maimonides and his Predecessors*, trans. Eve Adler (Albany: State University of New York Press, 1995). |
| *PPH* | Leo Strauss, *The Political Philosophy of Thomas Hobbes: Its Basis and Genesis*, trans. Elsa M. Sinclair (Oxford: Clarendon Press, 1936; Chicago: University of Chicago Press, 1952). |
| *RkS* | *Die Religionskritik Spinozas als Grundlage seiner Bibelwissenschaft Untersuchungen zu Spinozas Theologisch-Politischem Traktat* (Berlin: Akademie-Verlag, 1930), as reprinted in *GS*, 1:1–362. |
| "RLG" | Leo Strauss, "Religiöse Lage der Gegenwart" (1930), in *GS*, 2:377–91. |
| "RMF" | Leo Strauss, "Some Remarks on the Political Science of Maimonides and Farabi," trans. Robert Bartlett, *Interpretation* 18, no. 1 (fall 1990): 3–30. |
| *SCR* | Leo Strauss, *Spinoza's Critique of Religion*, trans. E. M. Sinclair of *RkS* (New York: Schocken Books, 1965); reprinted in abbr. format (Chicago: University of Chicago Press, 1997). |
| *SdE* | *Stern der Erlösung* in *Franz Rosenzweig: Der Menschen und sein Werk: gesammelte Schriften*, band 2 (1918–1929). II, *Der Stern der Erlösung* (Haag: Martinus Nihoff, 1979–1984). |
| *SoR* | Franz Rosenzweig, *The Star of Redemption*, 2nd edition, 1930, trans. William W. Hallo (Notre Dame, Ind.: Notre Dame University Press, 1985). |
| *SPPP* | Leo Strauss, *Studies in Platonic Political Philosophy*, with introduction by Thomas Pangle (Chicago: University of Chicago press, 1983). |
| "SRPS" | Robert Bartlett, "Some Remarks on the Political Science of Maimonides and Farabi," *Interpretation* 18, no. 1 (Fall 1990): 3–30. |
| "SSTX" | Leo Strauss, "The Spirit of Sparta; or, A Taste of Xenophon," *Social Research* 6, no. 4 (November 1939): 502–536. |
| StAM | Staatsarchiv Marburg |
| "WWRJ" | Leo Strauss, "Why We Remain Jews," in *JPCM* (lecture, Hillel House, University of Chicago, 1962). |
| WPP | Leo Strauss, *What Is Political Philosophy and Other Studies* (Chicago: University of Chicago Press, 1988). |
| "ZAW" | Leo Strauss, "Zur Auseinandersetzung mit der europäischen Wissenschaft," *Der Jude* 8, no. 10 (October 1924): 613–17; reprinted in *GS*, 2: 341–350. |
| "ZN" | Leo Strauss, "Der Zionismus bei Nordau," in *GS*, 2. |

# Notes

## Introduction (pp. 1–8)

1. The most recent book on this subject is Anne Norton's *Leo Strauss and the Politics of American Empire* (New Haven: Yale University Press, 2004). Norton's book engages the political tentacles connecting Straussian academics, conservative think tanks, and government. The book, however, openly confesses not to approach the subject of Strauss himself.

2. See the opinion piece by James Atlas, "The Nation: Leo-Cons; A Classicist's Legacy: New Empire Builders," *New York Times*, May 4, 2003, sec. 4, p. 1. This article, complete with a flowchart attempting to show the links between top Bush officials and Strauss evoked a strong response by critics. Similar pieces have appeared in the *New Yorker, Le Monde,* the *Boston Globe, The Economist,* the *International Herald Tribune,* the *Washington Post, Vanity Fair,* and *The Nation.* Perhaps it is not surprising that the conspiratorial organs of Lyndon LaRouche have also picked up on Leo Strauss as "The Fascist Godfather of Neo-Conservatism." The strongest case for such a view was made by Alain Franchon and Daniel Vernet in *Le Monde,* "Le Stratège et le philosophe," (April 15, 2003). Most of these pieces point to central broad themes of Strauss's American writings without ever touching a nuanced and accurate portrait of Strauss's core intellectual concerns and theories. The same may be said of the defensive responses by self-proclaimed disciples and offspring. See for example, Steven Lenzner and William Kristol, "What Was Leo Strauss Up To?" *Public Interest* 153 (Fall 2003): 19–40. It is important to note a response to some of these charges by Jenny Strauss Clay, Strauss's adopted daughter, who published "The Real Leo Strauss" in the *New York Times* (June 7, 2003, p. A15).

3. Mark Lilla, "Leo Strauss: The European," *New York Review of Books* 51, no. 16 (October 21, 2004) and "The Closing of the Straussian Mind," *New York Review of Books* 51, no. 17 (November 4, 2004). One can detect a significant difference even in the titles. The first is a sober subject of analysis, while the second mobilizes a pun on Allan Bloom's *The Closing of the American Mind* (New York: Simon and Schuster, 1987). The second title also signals the shift toward the personal and polemical.

4. Shadia Drury, *Leo Strauss and the American Right* (New York: St. Martin's, 1997).

5. Kenneth Hart Green, *Jew and Philosopher: The Return to Maimonides in the Jewish Thought of Leo Strauss* (Albany: State University of New York Press, 1993).

6. Leo Strauss, *Jewish Philosophy and the Crisis of Modernity: Essays and Lectures in Modern Jewish Thought,* ed. Kenneth Hart Green (Albany: State University of New York Press, 1997).

7. Leo Strauss, *Gesammelte Schriften,* vol. 1, *Die Religionskritik Spinozas und zuge-*

*hörige Schriften;* ed. Heinrich Meier (Stuttgart: J. B. Metzler, 1996); Leo Strauss, *Gesammelte Schriften,* vol. 2, *Philosophie und Gesetz; Frühe Schriften,* ed. Heinrich Meier (Stuttgart: J. B. Metzler, 1997).

8. Heinrich Meier's first comparative study of the two was *Carl Schmitt, Leo Strauss und "Der Begriff des Politischen": zu einem Dialog unter Abwesenden* (Stuttgart: J. B. Metzler, 1988); translated into English as *Carl Schmitt & Leo Strauss: The Hidden Dialogue,* trans. J. Harvey Lomax, foreword by Joseph Cropsey (Chicago: University of Chicago Press, 1995). Cropsey's endorsement is indicative of a larger Straussian embrace of Meier's interpretive renderings of Strauss as a "political philosopher" in opposition to Schmitt's status as a "political theologian." See also Meier's *Die Lehre Carl Schmitts: vier Kapitel zur Unterscheidung politischer Theologie und politischer Philosophie* (Stuttgart: J. B. Metzler, 1994); translated into English as *The Lesson of Carl Schmitt: Four Chapters on the Distinction Between Political Theology and Political Philosophy,* trans. Marcus Brainard (Chicago: University of Chicago Press, 1998). Meier has in turn published, under the auspices of the Catholic conservative C. F. von Siemens Stiftung, a slew of translations of Straussian works into German.

9. See Heinrich Meier's *Das theologisch-politische Problem: zum Thema von Leo Strauss* (Stuttgart: J. B. Metzler, 2003). See his earlier *Die Denkbewegung von Leo Strauss: die Geschichte der Philosophie und die Intention des Philosophen* (Stuttgart: J. B. Metzler, 1996).

10. Daniel Tanguay, *Leo Strauss: Une biographie intellectuelle* (Paris: Bernard Grasset, 2003).

11. Michael Zank, *Leo Strauss: The Early Writings (1921–1932)* (Albany: State University of New York Press, 2002); henceforth cited as *EW.*

12. Leo Strauss, *Yerushalayim ve-atunah: mivhar ketavim,* ed. and introd. Ehud Luz (Jerusalem: Mossad Bialik: Leo Baeck Institute, 2001).

13. John Gunnell, "Strauss before Straussianism: Reason, Revelation, and Nature," *Review of Politics* 51 (1990): 53–74.

14. Heinrich Meier has published a slim volume that attempts to lay out Strauss's views on this imposing theme: *Das theologisch-politische Problem: Zum Thema von Leo Strauss* (Stuttgart: J. B. Metzler, 2003). There is now an English edition, *Leo Strauss and the Theologico-Political Problem,* trans. Marcus Brainard (Cambridge: Cambridge University Press, 2006).

15. See, for example, Leo Strauss, review of Karl Löwith's *Von Hegel bis Nietzsche,* in *Social Research* 8, no. 4 (Nov 1941): 512–515. Reprinted in *What Is Political Philosophy?*

16. See the editor's preface in David Biale's *Cultures of the Jews* (New York: Schocken Books, 2002), xxi.

17. I am appropriating the phrase from Harold Bloom's *The Anxiety of Influence: A Theory of Poetry* (New York: Oxford University Press, 1973).

### Chapter 1. Antisemitism and Neo-Kantianism: From Kirchhain to Marburg (1899–1920) (pp. 9–16)

1. Stephen Lowenstein's general analysis of Germany's rural Jewry has been slightly augmented here with the specific case of Kurhessen in mind. Most recently, see his comments in *Jewish Daily Life in Germany, 1618–1945,* ed. Marion A. Kaplan (New York: Ox-

ford University Press, 2005), 144f. Also see *Jüdisches Leben auf dem Lande: Studien zur deutsch-jüdischen Geschichte,* ed. Monika Richarz and Reinhardt Rürup (Tübingen: Mohr Siebeck, 1997). There is nonetheless a "quasi-urban character" ascribed to the *Landjuden* who settled in the towns and villages surrounding Marburg. Gerald L. Soliday noted the "quasi-urban" qualities of early modern Marburg Jewry; see his "The Jews of Early Modern Marburg, 1640s–1800: A Case Study in Family and Household Organization," *The History of the Family* 8, no. 4 (2003): 495–516. For the centrality of the university to the Jewish population in the surrounding district (*Landkreis*), see the overview in Axel Erdmann, *Die Marburger Juden—ihre Geschichte von den Anfängen bis zur Gegenwart: dargestellt anhand der staatlichen Quellen unter besonderer Berücksichtigung des 19. Jahrhundert* (Ph.D. diss., University of Marburg, 1987).

2. See the sketch of Kirchhain's Jewish communal history by Paul Arnsberg, *Die jüdischen Gemeinden in Hessen* (Frankfurt am Main: Societäts Verlag, 1971), 1:444–47. See also Uta Löwenstein's three-volume *Quellen zur Geschichte der Juden im Hessischen Staatsarchiv Marburg, 1267–1600* (Wiesbaden: Kommission für die Geschichte der Juden in Hessen, 1989).

3. In an unpublished letter to Joseph Meisl dated September 10, 1923, Strauss offered his fellow Zionist *Bundesbruder* a shrewd political analysis of the differences in Hessen Jewry as a result of various constitutional changes and regional inclinations toward assimilation or orthodoxy. Cf. David Peal, "Antisemitism and Rural Transformation in Kurhessen: the Rise and Fall of the Böckel Movement" (Ph.D. diss., Columbia University, 1985), 18f.

4. Accounting for 8.2 percent of the population. See the population data in the Hebrew encyclopedia of German Jewish communities, *Pinkas ha-Kehilot. Germanyah: Entsiklopedyah shel ha-yishuvim ha-Yehudiyim le-min hivasdam ve-'ad le-ahar sho'at milhemet ha-'olam ha-sheniyah,* ed. Baruch Z. Opher (Jerusalem: Yad Vashem, 1991), 1:345.

5. The other two centers of Jewish life in the *Landkreis* were Neustadt and Wetter. See Bernd Klewitz, *Kirchhain: Alltag im Dritten Reich* (Marburg: SP-Verlag, 1990), 18–19.

6. See Yeshayahu Wolfsberg, "Popular Orthodoxy," *Leo Baeck Institute Yearbook* (henceforth *LBIYB*) 1 (1956): 237–54.

7. For a general overview of Orthodox Jewry in imperial Germany, see Mordechai Breuer, *Modernity Within Tradition: The Social History of Orthodox Jewry in Imperial Germany,* trans. Elizabeth Petuchowski (New York: Columbia University Press, 1992).

8. The more dominant countercase of a German-Jewish modernist subculture advanced by "the ideologues of emancipation" has been a primary object of study by David Sorkin. For a succinct formulation of his provocative thesis regarding the emergence of a subculture that was invisible to its participants, see *The Transformation of German Jewry 1780–1840* (New York: Oxford University Press, 1987), 3–9.

9. Steven Lowenstein, "Pace of Modernization of German Jewry in the Nineteenth Century," *LBIYB* 21 (1976): 41–56.

10. Ibid.

11. Hirsch successfully championed the secession law of 1876, which permitted withdrawal (*Austritt*) from the official Jewish community without abandoning Judaism. He argued that the differences between Reform and Orthodox are greater than those between Catholicism and Protestantism. Hirsch was also reported to have said that he would rather be buried in a Christian cemetery than to commune with reformers. He went so

far as to speculate that upon death, the first question God addresses is whether or not one had left the liberal community. Unlike the mainstream of German Orthodoxy under the leadership of Seligmann Bamberger, Hirsch rejected all cooperation with non-Orthodox movements and organizations. His Society of Orthodox Rabbis denied membership to anyone who also maintained an affiliation with the General Association of German Rabbis because they grouped both Orthodox and Liberal rabbis together. See Robert Liberles, *Religious Conflict in Social Context: The Resurgence of Orthodox Judaism in Frankfurt am Main, 1838–1877* (Westwood, Conn.: Greenwood, 1985), 208.

12. Cf. David Sorkin's explorations into the links between Jewish emancipation, the development of German-Jewish public subculture, the decline of a traditional autonomous community, and the rise of a Jewish self-cultivated bourgeoisie (*Bildungsbürgertum*) in the nineteenth century. See, for example, his essay, "The Impact of Emancipation on German Jewry: A Reconsideration," in *Assimilation and Community: The Jews in Nineteenth-Century Europe*, ed. Jonathan Frankel and Steven J. Zipperstein, (New York: Cambridge University Press, 1992), esp. 184–98. See also his *The Transformation of German Jewry.*

13. Steven Lowenstein, "Pace of Modernization of German Jewry," 42.

14. Ibid.

15. See Richard Simon Levy, *The Downfall of Antisemitic Political Parties in the German Empire* (New Haven: Yale University Press, 1970), esp. chap. 2, "The Outsiders: Antisemitism in Hessenland, 1883–1890" (55–91).

16. David Peal, "Antisemitism by Other Means? The Rural Cooperative Movement in the Late Nineteenth-Century Germany," *LBIYB* 32 (1987): 136.

17. Böckel was first elected to the Reichstag in February 1887. For a concise overview of the populist antisemitism of the period, see David Blackbourn, "The Politics of Demagogy in Imperial Germany," *Past and Present,* no. 113 (November 1986): 152–84. See also Paul Massing's *Rehearsal for Destruction: A Study of Political Anti-Semitism in Imperial Germany* (New York: H. Fertig, 1967).

18. In 1878–79 Bismarck pulled together the Catholic Center Party (*Zentrum*) and the right wing of the National Liberal Party. For Catholic antisemitism, see David Blackbourn, "Roman Catholics, the Centre Party, and Anti-Semitism in Imperial Germany," in *Nationalist and Racialist Movements in Britain and Germany before 1914,* ed. Anthony Nicholls and Paul Kennedy (Oxford: Oxford University Press, 1981), 106–29.

19. Strauss, "Why We Remain Jews." Such a possibility, Strauss says, "went to my bones." Published in *JPCM,* 143.

20. Staatsarchiv Marburg (StAM) 165/724. 180 Kirchhain/499. See Peal, "Antisemitism by Other Means?" (142).

21. Cited in Peal, "Antisemitism by Other Means?" (147 n. 44).

22. Strauss, "Why We Remain Jews," in *JPCM,* 313.

23. StAM, Bestand 300 Kirchhain, Nr. 5310. See also Joachim Lüders, and Ariane Wehner, *Mittelhessen—eine Heimat für Juden? Das Schicksal der Familie Strauss aus Kirchhain* (Gymnasium Philippinum, Marburg, 1989). After Jenny Strauss died, Hugo remarried Johanna (Hanna) Strauss (1886–1942). Johanna was born in the Eastern corridor of Hessen in Eschwege. After being deported on May 31, 1942, to the Lublin Ghetto along with thirty-five other Jews from the Landkreis Marburg, she was eventually murdered in either the Majdanek or Sobibor death camps. See Händler-Lochmann and Schütt,

*Purim, Purim,* 227f. including a heartwrenching oral testimony of her holding a baby in her arms on the transport train from Kirchhain. The order of the second deportation of thirty-five Jews from Landkreis Marburg is kept at StAM, Bestand 180 LA Mbg, Nr. 3593.

24. The Strauss name appeared in Kirchhain since the early nineteenth century in the wake of Napoleonic inroads and in accord with an 1809 edict requiring the Jews of Kirchhain to adopt surnames.

25. Strauss referred to his family's roots in Kirchhain in a letter to Joseph Meisl, dated September 10, 1923. The letter is preserved in Joseph Meisl's papers at the Central Archives for the History of the Jewish People (CAHJP) in Jerusalem, P35. One can find limited, but not wholly accurate information about the various strands of the Strauss family in Händler-Lachmann and Schütt, *"unbekannt verzogen" oder "weggemacht"—Schicksale der Juden im alten Landkreis Marburg, 1933–1945* (Marburg: Hitzeroth, 1992): 97–99.

26. The 1809 edict requiring Jews in Kirchhain to acquire surnames.

27. "GA." Reprinted in *JPCM,* 459–60.

28. Records from 1915 of the Gymnasium Philippinum at Marburg are held at StAM. See for example, *Jahresbericht des König. Gymnasium Philippinum zu Marburg für das Schuljahr 1914* (LXXXii)—Staatliches Gymnasium Philipinum zu Marburg (Lahn), 1915.

29. The Marburg Gymnasium's population during Strauss's years of attendance was more representative of the confessional differences in the smaller town of Kirchhain. See the population data in the Hebrew encyclopedia of German Jewish communities, *Pinkas ha-Kehilot. Germanyah: Entsiklopedyah shel ha-yishuvim ha-Yehudiyim le-min hivasdam ve-'ad le-ahar sho'at milhemet ha-'olam ha-sheniyah.* ed. Joseph Walk (Jerusalem: Yad Vashem, 1991), 2:32f. Cf. the historical sketch of Marburg's Jewish community in Arnsberg, 48–60.

30. Strauss to Scholem, November 22, 1960. National Library at the Hebrew University.

31. "GA," 460.

32. "WWRJ," 319. Strauss continued by estimating the intellectual life of some of his former comrades who were quite passionate, some of whom had since become officials in Israel, as being limited to "concern for people like Balzac"; ibid. For a portrait of Jabotinsky as a nationalist *and* European cosmopolitan, see Michael Stanislawski, *Zionism and the Fin de Siècle: Cosmopolitanism and Nationalism from Nordau to Jabotinsky* (Berkeley and Los Angeles: University of California Press, 2001).

33. Cf. Rivka Horwitz, "Voices of Opposition to the First World War among Jewish Thinkers," *Leo Baeck Institute Year Book* 32 (1988): 233–59.

34. Edward C. Banfield bases this account on what Strauss had told him. See his "Leo Strauss (1899–1973)," in *Remembering the University of Chicago: Teachers, Scientists, and Scholars,* ed. Edward Shils (Chicago: University of Chicago Press, 1991), 490–501.

35. Cohen held his chair at the University of Marburg from 1876 to 1912. See Bernhard Breslauer, *Die Zurürcksetzung der Juden an den Universitäten Deutschlands. Denkschrift im Auftrage des Verbandes der Deutschen Juden* (Berlin: Berthold Levy, 1971).

36. See "GA," in *JPCM,* 460. The text is transcribed from an event featuring Strauss and Jacob Klein held at St. John's College, Annapolis, Md., on January 30, 1970.

37. Ibid., 462.

38. Hermann Cohen, *Religion der Vernunft aus den Quellen des Judentums* (1919). Strauss wrote an introduction to its English translation, *Religion of Reason Out of the Sources of Judaism,* trans. Simon Kaplan (New York: Ungar, 1972).

39. Strauss, introductory essay to Hermann Cohen, *Religion of Reason Out of the Sources in Judaism* (New York: Schocken, 1965), 1–31. Reprinted in *JPCM,* 267.

40. Leora Batnitzky has explored the centrality of Strauss's repeated and sometimes distorted engagements with Cohen in *Leo Strauss and Emmanuel Levinas: Philosophy and the Politics of Revelation* (Cambridge: Cambridge University Press, 2006). In particular, Batnitzky uncovers how Strauss's well-known mature critique of Hermann Cohen's interpretive strategy of idealization rested on a series of incorrect quotations that began in Strauss's essay on Cohen's *Ethics of Maimonides* and culminated in his introduction to the English translation of Cohen's *Religion of Reason Out of the Sources in Judaism.* See chapter 5 in Batnitzky.

41. According to Strauss's later reflections, he "converted to Zionism—to simple, straightforward political Zionism" at the age of seventeen. "GA," 2; reprinted in *JPCM.*

42. See Matriculation Records of Marburg University beginning in 1917–18, Marburg City Archives, Bestand 305a Acc. 1950/9, Nr. 777; Bestand 305q, Nr. 8, Matriculation Records, 315a, Acc. 1963/13 Nr. 1. See also the biographical statement (*Lebenslauf*) Strauss attached to his dissertation (1921), reprinted in *GS,* 2:298.

43. Ibid. For the central role of Plato in Marburg neo-Kantianism, see Karl-Heinz Lembeck, *Platon-Rezeption und Philosophiegeschichtsphilosophie bei Cohen und Natorp* (Würzburg: Königshausen & Neumann, 1994).

44. See Matriculation Records of Marburg University from winter semester of 1917 through spring semester of 1920. StAM, Bestand 305a Acc. 1950/9, Nr. 777.

45. *SPPP,* 167.

46. "GA," 460.


## Chapter 2. The Formation of a Weimar Conservative Jew (1921–1932) (pp. 17–53)

1. For Strauss's place as a Weimar Jewish critic of historicism, see David Myers's *Resisting History: Historicism and Its Discontents in German-Jewish Thought,* esp. the chapter on Leo Strauss, "Anti-Historicism and the Theological-Political Predicament in Weimar Germany: The Case of Leo Strauss," 106–29. Also see the generational portrait of radicalized Jewish thinkers in Steven Aschheim, "German Jews Beyond *Bildung* and Liberalism," in his *Culture and Catastrophe: German and Jewish Confrontations of National Socialism and Other Crises* (New York: New York University Press, 1997), 31–44.

2. "ZAW," *GS* 2:341.

3. This Socratic question appears throughout Strauss's work after the late 1920s; see for example, "RLG" in *GS* 2:380–89. The Greek "pôs biôeon" is employed here on 388–89 in particular.

4. Karl Mannheim's (1893–1947) theory of intellectuals purports to be neutral in regard to political orientation, which is one reason why Strauss would eventually attack it for being relativistic. Mannheim attributes the phrase "free-floating intellectual" and its liberal-minded critical openness to Alfred Weber. Isaiah Berlin captures the pedigree of intellectuals, viewed as a whole social class, in an interview: "The intelligentsia, historically, are people who are united around certain social ideas, who believe in progress, in reason . . . free criticism, individual liberty, in short oppose reaction, obscurantism, the

Church and the authoritarian state, and see each other as fellow fighters in a common cause—above all for human rights and a decent social order." Isa Ramin Jahanbegloo, *Conversations with Isaiah Berlin: Recollections of an Historian of Ideas* (London: Phoenix, 1992), 183. Strauss set out to problematize exactly this presumed set of convictions. Strauss offers a critique of Mannheim's "sociology of knowledge" in "Der Konspectivismus" (1929), published posthumously in *GS*, 2:365–75. Mannheim's *Ideologie und Utopie* first appeared in English as *Ideology and Utopia*, trans. Louis Wirth (London, K. Paul, Trench, Trubner; New York, Harcourt, Brace, 1936).

5. See the different accounts of the "conservative revolution" or radical conservativism during the Weimar Republic: Stefan Breuer, *Anatomie der Konservativen Revolution* (Darmstadt: Wissenschaftliche Buchgesellschaft, 1995); *The Weimar Dilemma: Intellectuals in the Weimar Republic,* ed. Anthony Phelan (Manchester, U.K.: Manchester University Press, 1985); Roger Woods, *The Conservative Revolution in the Weimar Republic* (New York: St. Martin's, 1996).

6. Oswald Spengler (1880–1936), *Der Untergang des Abendlandes: Umrisse einer Morphologie der Weltgeschichte,* 2 vols. (Munich: Beck, 1920–23). Spengler is of an older generation than the one that was so captivated by him, and for this reason is sometimes not included in the so-called conservative revolution.

7. Ironically, what has been described as "the generation of 1914" is a generation younger than Spengler himself, who lived from 1880 to 1936. Strauss considered the impact of Spengler on his generation in his lecture "German Nihilism," delivered at the New School for Social Research; see my discussion in chap. 3. For a comparative European cultural study of this generation, see Robert Wohl, *The Generation of 1914* (Cambridge, Mass.: Harvard University Press, 1979). For Strauss's generation of intellectuals in France, who were decisively influenced by Heidegger, see Ethan Kleinberg's provocative study, *Generation Existential: Heidegger's Philosophy in France, 1927–1961* (Ithaca, N.Y.: Cornell University Press, 2005).

8. See Stephen Aschheim's review of George Mosse's *German Jews Beyond Judaism* in Aschheim, *Culture and Catastrophe.* Also see David Biale's remarks on contextualizing Strauss within a larger group of Weimar Jewish intellectuals with whom he "shared a common discourse, a common background, and ultimately common fate." Biale notes that for Strauss, "Jewish thought today constitutes, as it did in the Middle Ages, a mode of opposition to conventional opinion and that it preserves truth in a world dominated by the insidious philosophies" that have a Christian veiled character. David Biale, "Leo Strauss: The Philosopher as Weimar Jew," in *Leo Strauss's Thought: Toward a Critical Engagement,* ed. Alan Udoff (Boulder, Colo.: Lynne Rienner, 1991), 32. Michael Löwy articulated a model of radicalized Jewish intellectuals—that could theoretically cut to the right as well as to the left—in "Jewish Messianism and Libertarian Utopianism in Central Europe," (1900–1933)," *New German Critique,* no. 20, special issue 2 (Spring–Summer 1980): 105–15. The argument appeared in a book-length but no less general formulation in *Redemption and Utopia: Jewish Libertarian Thought in Central Europe: A Study in Elective Affinity,* trans. Hope Heaney (Stanford, Calif.: Stanford University Press, 1992).

9. See the general overview provided by Hagit Lavsky in *Before Catastrophe: The Distinctive Path of German Zionism* (Detroit, Mich.: Wayne State University Press; Jerusalem: Magnes, 1996)

10. "RLG," *GS*, 2:382, 386.

11. The three late Weimar texts in which Strauss formulates this task of breaking free from present presupposition are the speech offered at a Zionist youth camp, "RLG"; "Besprechen von Julius Ebbinghaus, *Über die Fortschritte der Metaphysik*" (1931); and "Anmerkungen zu Carl Schmitt, *Der Begriff des Politischen*" (1932). Compare Strauss's attitude toward rupture from the present (discussed in chapter 3).

12. Cf. Daniel Krochmalnik, "Modelle jüdischen Philosophierens," *Trumah* 11 (2001): 89–107. Krochmalnik offers a wide spectrum of modern Jewish philosophers who make use of central antinomies such as Athens and Jerusalem, Schem and Japhet, and Torah and Wisdom (*hochmah*).

13. Kenneth Hart Green has conveyed an anecdote told by Marvin Fox (to Harry Jaffa) about an unidentified "famous Talmudic scholar" at the Jewish Theological Seminary in New York who reacted to a lecture Strauss had just given there by exclaiming: "Such a terrible loss! Such genius! What a great talmudist he would have made, had he not wasted his life on philosophy!" Quoted in *JPCM*, 58 n. 19.

14. Cf. the account of Jewish hermeneutics in Simon Rawidowicz's essay "On Interpretation" originally published in the *Proceedings of the American Academy for Jewish Research* 26 (1957): 83–126. This posthumous essay can be found in a shortened form in Simon Rawidowicz, *Studies in Jewish Thought*, ed. Nahum N. Glatzer (Philadelphia: Jewish Publication Society of America [1974]).

15. Strauss, "Cohens Analyse der Bible-Wissenschaft Spinozas," in *GS*, 1:363; "Cohen's Analysis of Spinoza's Bible Science," *EW*, 140.

16. Strauss's matriculation records held at the Marburg City Archive mentioned above in note 42.

17. See matriculation records of Marburg University from 1917 to 1918 through the spring semester of 1920. StAM Bestand 305a Acc. 1950/9, Nr. 777. Fittingly enough, one of Strauss's first courses was on Plato. Strauss developed a relationship with Jacob Klein (who studied with Natorp at Marburg in 1919) and then later continued to study with Heidegger. Hans-Georg Gadamer would later follow the same trajectory in the 1920s. Strauss's sister Bettina also attended Marburg from 1918 to 1921. For Natorp's relationship to Marburg neo-Kantianism, see his published lecture "Kant und die Marburge Schule" in *Kant Studien* 17 (1912). Also see Vasilis Politis, "Anti-Realist Interpretations of Plato: Paul Natorp," *International Journal of Philosophical Studies* 9, no. 1 (2001): 47–61. See Strauss's letter to Gadamer, dated February 26, 1961, in which he alludes to Natorp's seminars. The correspondence was first published in the second edition of Hans Georg Gadamer's *Wahrheit und Methode: Grunddzüge einer philosophischen Hermeneutik* (Tübingen: Mohr, 1965), 503–12. See the dual German-English version, which first appeared in the lost treasure trove of the *Independent Journal of Philosophy / Unabhängige Zeitschrift für Philosophie* 2 (1978): 5–12.

18. For an overview of the different schools of neo-Kantianism in Germany, see Manfred Pascher, *Einführung in den Neukantianismus: Kontext, Grundpositionen, praktische Philosophie* (Munich: Fink, 1997). See also Klaus Christian Köhnke, *The Rise of Neo-Kantianism: German Academic Philosophy between Idealism and Positivism*, trans. R. J. Hollingdale. (New York: Cambridge University Press, 1991).

19. See "GA," in *JPCM*, 460–61.

20. Leo Strauss, "An Unspoken Prologue to a Public Lecture at St. John's College in Honor of Jacob Klein" (1959) first published in *Interpretation* 7 (1978); republished in *JPCM*, 450. Cf. "GA." 461.

21. *JPCM*, 450.

22. Leo Strauss, *Das Erkenntnisproblem in der philosophischen Lehre Fr. H. Jacobis.* The oral defense of the dissertation took place on December 17, 1921.

23. Jacobi was appointed as director of the Bavarian Academy of Sciences by Frederick II in 1805, a position he held for seven years. Figures such as Hamann, Herder, Lessing, and Mendelssohn were all acquainted with Jacobi but, given Jacobi's penchant for provocation and controversy, relations with each of these figures (with the exception of Hamann) either became strained or simply hostile.

24. Ernst Cassirer, *Das Erkenntnisproblem in der Philosohie und Wissenschaft der neueren Zeit* (Berlin: B. Cassirer, 1922–23).

25. Ibid, 2–3.

26. For an understanding of the liberal social democratic orientation of Marburg neo-Kantianism, see Bernard Tucker, *Ereignis: Wege durch die politische Philosophie des Marburger Neukantianismus* (Frankfurt am Main: Lang, 1984). Also see the edited volume *Ethischer Sozialismus: zur politischen Philosophie des Neukantianismus,* ed. Helmut Holzhey (Frankfurt am Main: Suhrkamp, 1994).

27. The handwritten additions are found on the dissertation held in the Leo Strauss Papers, held at the University of Chicago; reprinted in *GS*, 2:297 and *EW*, 58.

28. "GA" and Strauss's 1965 preface to *Hobbes Politische Wissenschaft* (Berlin: Luchterhand, 1965). See the English version in *JPCM*, 453.

29. Benjamin Lazier argues: "More than any of his contemporaries, Strauss seemed to inhabit the two epochs at once, and serves witness to the peculiar hermeneutic fusion of the 1780s and '90s with the 1920s and '30s." In "Redemption through Sin: Judaism and Heresy in Interwar Europe" (Ph.D. diss., University of California, 2002), 148. I would only qualify this statement about a fusion occurring; for Strauss many times noticed the stark differences of the eighteenth century from his own period as an entry point for his own critique of the present. See also David Janssen's analysis on this question: "The Problem of the Enlightenment: Strauss, Jacobi, and the Pantheism Controversy," *Review of Metaphysics* 56, no. 3 (March 2003): 605–32.

30. In the twentieth-century movements of crisis theology and dialectical theology, Scheleiermacher was held as a key culprit. Walter Benjamin's early ruminations on experience also blame the constriction of experience on Kant and/or his neo-Kantian successors. Martin Jay directs our attention to such essays as "On Perception" (1917) and "On Language as Such and on the Language of Man" (1916), where Benjamin emphasizes the inability of the Kantian and neo-Kantian traditions "to recover a robust notion of experience prior to its modalization"; *Songs of Experience: Discourses of Experience in Modern Thought* (Berkeley and Los Angeles: University of California Press, 2005), 319. For Benjamin's relationship to Cohen and neo-Kantianism, see Astrid Deuber-Mankowsky, *Der frühe Walter Benjamin und Hermann Cohen: Jüdische Werte, kritische Philosophie, vergängliche Erfahrung* (Berlin: Vorwerk 8, 2000).

31. See Zank's gloss on *Literalismus* as referring "to the position that affirms the irrational quality of God, and hence an utter dependence of human reason on positive, revealed religion"; *EW*, 60 n. 7. For both thinkers, the Church did not recognize the unavailability of God and the word of God as the foremost problem. Barth's position against the Catholic Church can be seen already in his interpretation of Paul's Epistles to the Romans (in the 1919 edition of the *Römerbrief* and even more strongly in the thoroughly revised second edition of 1922) as well as in his later *Church Dogmatics* (1928).

Barth argued that it is only in and through crisis that the fundamental *decision* regarding God and true religious authority must be made ever anew. The papal church seeks to evade this essential requirement due to its hubristic view that it continues revelation and is the sole and infallible voice for the kingdom of God; see *Die christliche Dogmatik im Entwurf,* vol. 1, *Die Lehre vom Worte Gottes* (Munich: C. Kaise, 1927), 348–49.

32. *GS,* 2:288–89; my emphasis. The English translation can be found in *EW,* 56–57. Note that in the same paragraph of the dissertation's section "Zur Philosophie der Religion," Jacobi is also set between the forces of "relativism" and "rationalism."

33. Ibid.

34. Ibid, 286. Compare to Kant's position that reason gains knowledge of something it produces in nature "according to a plan of its own" (*selbst nach ihre Entwürfe*). Kant, *Critique of Pure Reason,* trans. Norman Kemp Smith, 2nd printing (London: Macmillan, 1933), B xiv.

35. See Janssen, "The Problem of the Enlightenment," esp. 608–11. Janssen alerts us to the following passage from the dissertation: "Autonomism is the ethical form of general doubt, of the principle of modern culture, which invokes the autonomy of religious conscience, of scientific reason and of moral legislation (*sola fides, sola ratio,* 'only a good will'). In opposition, Jacobi emphasizes that, in ethical matters, it is simply unnecessary for the acting subject to understand the norm and to affirm it out of its own insight. It is not the case that insight precedes and obedience follows, but precisely the reverse: only out of obedience, as a result of following the norm, from the penetration of the norm into the center of our lives as a consequence of obedience, does moral insight emerge"; *EPLJ,* in *GS,* 2:281.

36. This is one reason why he is sometimes seen as a proto-existentialist.

37. See Strauss, "Existentialism," *Interpretation* 22 no. 3 (Spring 1995): 304–5. I quote from this publication rather than the redacted version included in *SPPP.*

38. Ibid. Note that the transcription to the lecture emphasizes "problem."

39. Strauss, "Das Erkenntnisproblem," *GS,* 2:251–52. See Michael Zank's rendering of this term, *EW,* 59 n. 5. Samuel Moyn makes this exacting insight about the import of Strauss's use of *Deskription:* it points to "Edmund Husserl's early project of the analysis of intentional states of consciousness (as distinguished from his interwar idealism) as providing a route to extrasubjective knowledge." In "From Experience to Law" (forthcoming), Moyn's larger argument about Strauss's developing ideas about the possibilities of finding an extrasubjective knowledge of the divine is a crucial insight into both the ideational context in which the young Strauss operated as well as the points of continuity and transition in his post-Weimar thought. While the full argument is beyond the scope of the current discussion, the diligent reader will notice that the title of Moyn's article points to a transition in Strauss's thought in *Philosophy and Law* (1935) where his turn to law provides a framework for philosophy, religion, and politics.

40. Strauss, *EPLJ,* in *GS,* 2:283.

41. Letter of August 15, 1946, to Karl Löwith in *GS,* 3:663–64. See Moyn, "From Experience to Law," which teases out the full import of Strauss's comment.

42. See Strauss's statement in "GA" that Husserl's primary orientation belonged to a "pre–World War I world." The defining "characteristic of the post–World War I world was the resurgence of theology"; *JPCM,* 460.

43. In a 1970 public lecture Strauss called it "a disgraceful performance"; "GA." He also never returned to the subject in his American career.

44. See the chapter on Leo Strauss in Lazier, "Redemption through Sin." See also Lazier, "Overcoming Gnosticism: Hans Jonas, Hans Blumenberg, and the Legitimacy of the Natural World," *Journal of the History of Ideas* 64, no. 4 (2003): 619–37.

45. See George di Giovanni's introductory essay to *Friedrich Heinrich Jacobi: The Main Philosophical Writings and the Novel Allwill* (Montreal: McGill-Queen's University Press, 1994).

46. "PKJ," in *GS*, 2:252.

47. For a fuller description of what I have vaguely referred to as liberal idealist traditions running through the nineteenth and early twentieth centuries, see Jay, *Songs of Experience,* 78–130.

48. John J. Gunnel points out that Jacobi introduced the term *Nihilismus* into modern German philosophy; see his "Strauss before Straussianism," *The Review of Politics* 53, no. 1 (winter 1991): 53–74.

49. Strauss's *Lebenslauf* is reprinted in *GS*, 2:298. The *Lebenslauf* is missing from the two copies of the dissertation deposited in the library of the University of Hamburg.

50. "ZAW." All citations refer to the reprinted version in *GS*, 2:341–50.

51. Strauss responds to Ernst Cassirer's *Die Begriffsform im mythischen Denken* (Leipzig: Teubner, 1922).

52. "ZAW," 348. English translation in *EW*.

53. "ZAW," 349.

54. Ibid., 349.

55. Ibid., 358.

56. Ibid.

57. See Samuel Moyn's chapter "Weimar Revelations: Rosenzweig, Barth, and the Theological Other," in *Origins of the Other: Emmanuel Levinas Between Revelation and Ethics* (Ithaca, N.Y.: Cornell University Press, 2005) for a brilliant exposition of Rosenzweig's similar emphasis on an absolute gulf that separates the sources of revelation and the potential modern believer.

58. I have been unable to determine when exactly Strauss first read or met Rosenzweig. Based upon one of Strauss's later recollections in "On Existentialism," however, we can safely presume that Strauss had already become well acquainted with Rosenzweig before 1923. Having grasped something concrete from Heidegger's treatment of the beginning of Aristotle's *Metaphysics,* Strauss stopped at Rosenzweig's house in Frankfurt am Main to convey his enthusiasm for Heidegger's brilliance. Heidegger served as Husserl's teaching assistant from 1919 to 1923, and was in the midst of writing his book on Aristotle in 1922; he received his appointment at Marburg in 1923. See Strauss, "Existentialism," 343.

59. Quoted in *GS*, 2:358.

60. *GS*, 2:359.

61. "Soziologische Geschichtschreibung?" *Der Jude* 8, no. 3 (March, 1924): 190–92; reprinted in *GS*, 2:333–37. Strauss reviewed the first set of Dubnow's *Weltgeschichte des jüdischen Volkes,* 10 vols. (Berlin: Jüdischer Verlag, 1925–29).

62. *GS*, 2:335.

63. Martin Buber, "Jüdischer Renaissance," *Ost und West* 1 (January 1901): cols. 7–10; reprinted in Buber, *Die Jüdische Bewegung: Gesammelte Aufsätze und Ansprachen, 1900–1914* (Berlin: Jüdischer Verlag, 1916).

64. Leon Pinkser (1821–91), *Auto-Emancipation* (New York: Federation of American Zionists, 1916).

65. Buber, *Die Jüdische Bewegung,* 14.

66. Martin Buber, "Jewish Religiosity" (1916); reprinted in his *On Judaism* (New York: Schocken Books, 1967), 79–94.

67. Buber, "Judaism and Mankind" (1911), *On Judaism,* 29.

68. Buber, "Holy Way" (1918), *On Judaism,* 147–48.

69. This is not to deny Buber's affirmation of the "admixture" of German-Jewish identity. See Paul Mendes-Flohr, *German Jews: A Dual Identity* (New Haven: Yale University Press), 41–44 and note 70.

70. Writing of the joint Rosenzweig-Buber German translation of the Bible, Paul Mendes-Flohr explains Rosenzweig's Jewish humanism thus: "The Jew resides on the banks of two cultures, that of the world and that of Judaism. This dual allegiance is the ground of an authentic pluralism, a pluralism that preserves the Jew's integrity as both a Jew and a citizen of the world" *German Jews,* 44.

71. Rosenzweig, *SdE,* 450; *SoR,* 368.

72. See part III. sec. 1 of *SoR,* entitled "The Holy Land," 300.

73. Rosenzweig, "Zeit ists . . ." (Ps 119:126). "Gedanken über das Bildungsproblem des Augenblicks," reprinted in *Gesammelte Schriften,* vol. 3, *Zweistromland: Kleinere Schriften zu Glauben und Denken,* ed. Reinhold Mayer and Annemarie Mayer (Dordrecht: Martinus Nijhoff, 1984).

74. For a history of the founding and closing of this institution, see David Myers, "The Fall and Rise of Jewish Historicism: The Evolution of the *Akademie für die Wissensschaft des Judentums* (1919–1934)," *Hebrew Union College Annual* 58 (1992): 107–44.

75. Translation from the *JPS Hebrew-English Tanakh,* 2nd ed. (Philadelphia: Jewish Publication Society, 1999), 1569.

76. Rosenzweig, *Der mensch und sein werk,* vol. 3, *Zweistromland: Kleinere Schriften zu Glauben und Denken,* ed. Reinhold Mayer and Annemarie Mayer (Dordrecht: Martinus Nijhoff, 1984), 78.

77. Other fellows included Fritz (Yitzhak) Baer, David Baneth, Selma Stern, and Chanoch Albeck. See Michael Zank, "Leo Strauss' Rediscovery of the Esoteric," in *Religious Apologetics—Philosophical Argumentation,* ed. Yossef Schwartz and Volkhard Krech (Tübingen: Mohr Siebeck, 2004), 190.

78. Franz Rosenzweig, *On Jewish Learning,* ed. Nahum Glatzer (New York: Schocken Books, 1965), 78.

79. Myers, "The Fall and Rise of Jewish Historicism: The Evolution of the Akademie für die Wissenschaft des Judentums (1919–1934)," *Hebrew Union College Annual* 63 (1992), 107–144.

80. For a fuller account of the responses by Cohen, Rosenzweig, Strauss, and Isaac Breuer to the crisis of historicism, see David Myers, *Resisting History: Historicism and Its Discontents in German-Jewish Thought* (Princeton: Princeton University Press, 2003). Ernst Simon employed this phrase in "Franz Rosenzweig und das jüdische Bildungsproblem," *Korrespondenzblatt* 11 (1930): 12.

81. See the English translation of this essay in Rosenzweig, *On Jewish Learning,* 55–71.

82. Ibid., 99–100.

83. See Nahum Glatzer's early presentation in *Franz Rosenzweig: A Life* (New York, 1945).

84. See Leora Batnitzky, *Idolatry and Representation: The Philosophy of Franz Rosenzweig Reconsidered* (Princeton: Princeton University Press, 2000), 188–98. Batnitzky quotes a few passages in which Rosenzweig partially endorses Ahad Ha-am's vision of a Jewish spiritual center in Palestine that would radiate a transformed Jewish culture to the diaspora. Rosenzweig stated that Ahad Ha-am's vision was "unconsciously correct"; see Rosenzweig, *Der Mensch und sein Werk: Gesammelte Schriften—Briefe und Tagebücher,* vol. 2 (The Hague: Martinus Nijhoff, 1974–84).

85. Peter Gordon, *Rosenzweig and Heidegger: Between Judaism and German Philosophy* (Berkeley and Los Angeles: University of California Press, 2003), esp. 219.

86. Franz Rosenzweig letters to Rudolf Hallo in 1921 and 1922, quoted in Gordon, *Rosenzweig and Heidegger,* 219. Note that "golus" is simply an Ashkenazi rendering of the Hebrew *galut.*

87. See Rosenzweig, *The Star of Redemption* (Madison: University of Wisonsin Press, 2005), 426–28; *SdE,* 449–51. See Gordon's argument about the process of "constriction" (*Engigkeit*), in *Rosenzweig and Heidegger,* 219–20. For a phenomenological reading of the dynamics entailed in such liturgical practice, see Almut Sh. Bruckstein, "Zur Phänomenologie der jüdischen Liturgie in Rosenzweigs Stern der Erlösung. Ein Versuch über das Schweigen mit Husserl," in *Rosenzweig als Leser: Kontextulle Kommentare zum "Stern der Erlösung,"* ed. Martin Brasser (Tübingen: Max Niemeyer, 2004), 357–68.

88. This concern is explicitly recognized in the title of two of Strauss's Weimar writings. Strauss's lecture "Religiöse Lage der Gegenwart" (The religious situation of the present [1930]) was first delivered as a lecture at the German Zionist camp Kadima in Brieselang. "Die geistige Lage der Gegenwart" (The spiritual situation of the present [1932]) is a manuscript dated February 6, 1932. Both texts were first published thanks to Heinrich Meier's efforts as editor of Strauss's complete writings. The texts are found in *GS,* 2:377–91 and *GS,* 2:441–64, respectively.

89. The Frankfurt Lehrhaus was founded in 1920 and boasted an impressive list of instructors. Among the most notable were Gershom Scholem; Martin Buber; Rabbi Leo Baeck; the sociologist Leo Löwenthal; Ernst Simon; the Hebrew writer S. Y. Agnon; the enigmatic champion of women's rights, Bertha Pappenheim; the journalist and cultural critic, Siegfried Kracauer; an orthodox representative of the Orthodox Agudat Yisrael, Nathan Birnbaum; archaeologist Rudolf Hallo; and the biochemist, Eduard Strauss. See Michael Brenner's excellent discussion of the *Lehrhaus* in *The Renaissance of Jewish Culture in Weimar Germany* (New Haven: Yale University Press, 1996), 69ff. See also Nahum Glatzer, "The Frankfort Lehrhaus," *Leo Baeck Institute Year Book* 1 (1956): 105–22. For a list of other prominent lecturers at the *Lehrhaus,* see Nahum Glatzer, "Das Frankfurter Lehrhaus," in *Der Philosoph Franz Rosenzweig (1886–1929), Internationaler Kongress-Kassel,* ed. Wolfdietrich Schmied-Kowarzik (Munich: Karl Alber Freiburg, 1986), 1:303–27. Strauss's participation at the *Lehrhaus* was mentioned by Franz Rosenzweig in a letter to Ernst Simon dated December 6, 1924; see Rosenzweig's *Briefe und Tagebücher,* ed. Rachel Rosenzweig and Edith Rosenzweig-Scheinmann, vol. 2, *1918–1929.* (The Hague: Martinus Nijhoff, 1979) 107.

90. According to Nahum Glatzer, this "analytic reading" of Cohen took place during

the 1923–1924 program. See his article "The Frankfort Lehrhaus," *Leo Baeck Institute Year Book*, 1 (1956): 116.

91. The Blau-Weiss was at first a Jewish offshoot of the German *Wandervogel* that emphasized hiking excursions as a way to commune with nature and as an antidote to decadent bourgeois life. The quest and demand of the Blau-Weiss for "Jewish content," inspired by figures such as Martin Buber, while based on a rejection of assimilation, remained in the eyes of Strauss and contemporaries mere decorative gestures (such as replacing the German greeting of "Heil" with "Shalom"). For the Zionist disputes between Blau-Weiss and other German Zionist groups, see Jörg Hackeschmidt, *Von Kurt Blumenfeld zu Norbert Elias: die Erfindung einer jüdischen Nation* (Hamburg: Europäische Verlagsanstalt, 1997). Glenn Richard Sharfman, "Between Identities: The German-Jewish Youth Movement Blau-Weiss, 1912–1926," *Forging Modern Jewish Identities: Public Faces and Private Struggles,* ed. Michael Berkowitz, Susan L. Tananbaum, and Sam W. Bloom (Portland, Ore.: Vallentine Mitchell, 2003), 198–228. Michael Zank provides notes on the factional positions mentioned in Strauss's essay; *EW*, 71–75. For an overview of German Zionist movements and their relative strengths, see Jehuda Reinharz, "Ideology and Structure in German Zionism, 1882–1933," *Jewish Social Studies,* 42, no. 2 (Spring 1980): 119–47. Also see Michael Berkowitz's broader analysis in *Western Jewry and the Zionist Project, 1914–1933* (Cambridge: Cambridge University Press, 2002), 149f.

92. See *EW*, 73–74. The Rosenzweig letter to Simon is dated December 6, 1924, and appears in *Briefe und Tagebücher,* 2:1007.

93. Strauss, *Jüdische Rundschau* 28, no. 9 (January 30, 1923): 45–46. Published in *GS,* 2:299–306, and *EW* as "Response to Frankfurt's 'Word of Principle'" (64–75).

94. "Ein prinzipielles Wort zur Erziehungsfrage," *Jüdische Rundschau* 27, nos. 103–4 (December 29, 1922): 675–76. It was signed by Ernst Simon, Ernst Michalis, Erich Fromm, and Fritz Gothein.

95. *GS,* 2:300 and *EW,* 66. In the 1930s, Strauss changes his mind about this issue. Cf. Strauss's exchange of letters with Karl Löwith in 1946 about this very issue in *GS* 3:658–70; see esp. the letter dated August 15, 1963, from Strauss to Löwith where Strauss states; "one cannot overcome modernity with modern means, but only insofar as we also are still natural beings with natural understanding; but the way of thought of natural understanding has been lost to us, and simple people such as myself and those like me are not able to regain it through their own resources: we attempt to *learn* from the ancients"; *GS,* 3:661. "Correspondence Concerning Modernity," *Independent Journal of Philosophy* 4 (1983): 107.

96. Leo Strauss, "Cohens Analyse der Bibel-Wissenschaft Spinoza's," *Der Jude* 8, nos. 5–6 (May–June 1924): 295–314. Reprinted in *GS,* 1:363–86. Strauss's essay was an extended review of Cohen's "Spinoza über Staat und Relgion, Judentum und Christentum" (1915) originally published in *Jahrbuch für jüdische Geschichte und Literatur* 18:56–150, and reprinted in Herman Cohen's *Jüdische Schriften* (Berlin: Schwetschke, 1924).

97. See Isaac Husik, "Joseph Albo, the Last of the Jewish Philosophers," *Proceedings of the American Academy for Jewish Research* 1 (1930): 61–72. For the general background to Albo's Maimonidean revival as a response to disputations, see Colette Sirat, *A History of Jewish Philosophy in the Middle Ages* (Paris: Maison des Sciences de l'Homme; Cambridge: Cambridge University Press, 1985), 374–81.

98. While participating in Guttmann's seminar, Strauss is reputed to have often

discussed his excitement for Heidegger's teaching with fellow students. See Alan Udoff, "On Leo Strauss: An Introductory Account," in *Leo Strauss's Thought: Toward a Critical Engagement*, (Boulder, Colo.: Lynne Rienner, 1991), 26–27 n. 63. According to Udoff, the biblical scholar Nehama Leibowitz (1905–97) had taken the course with Strauss and the two entered into an agreement regarding their respective fields of strength and deficiency. She tutored the older Strauss in the Hebrew text of Saadya Gaon's *The Book of Beliefs and Opinions* in exchange for his help in working through the Greek text of Plato's *Gorgias*. Leibowitz also reported that Strauss repeatedly spoke about Heidegger with enthusiasm during this two-year period.

99. Strauss's eulogy for Rosenzweig (1929) was a public rebuke of Guttmann's directorship of the Akademie in that it abandoned Rosenzweig's vision of the Akademie serving the interests of contemporary Jewish existence; *GS*, 2:363–64. Also see Meier's comments on the disagreements between Strauss and Guttmann in *GS*, 2:xxxi.

100. There is little documentation of the specific revisions Guttmann expected. See Strauss's letter to Krüger, October 3, 1931, now published in *GS*, vol. 3. Based on the differences between Strauss's articles in the 1920s and the book, along with Strauss's explicit acknowledgment of Guttmann's input, we might infer that the second section of the first part, devoted to Uriel da Costa, might have been one place of contestation. Guttmann could have expected Strauss to pursue more deeply the connection between Uriel da Costa and Michael Servetus, contemporaries within currents of skepticism, especially regarding the status of Moses and Christ as sources of divine revelation, and the critique of the immortality of the soul. But this suggestion is based primarily on comments made by Strauss in the published book. See for example, *SCR*, 276 n. 25, where Strauss expresses his indebtedness to Guttmann for indicating the significance of the connection. Successive notes 26–29 compare Servetus's Bible criticism with Uriel da Costa's on the aforementioned issues, which push both figures into the Epicurean tradition of *Religionskritik* that Strauss constructs. The Spanish heretic Servetus was eventually put to death by the Inquisition for his heretical criticisms of such central dogma as the doctrine of the trinity. Here, however, Strauss draws attention to how da Costa's critique of the immortality of the soul was thoroughly conditioned by Servetus. Servetus's scientific views on physiology formed the basis for such ideas as his theory of the soul's mortality. Compare to Strauss's earlier essays on this question. But this small section certainly would not seem to merit a two-year delay in publication.

101. Rosenzweig pointed to Strauss's unique status in this regard in a letter to Gustav Bradt, October 9, 1926, in *Briefe und Tagebücher*, 1107. He states that Strauss was in keeping with Cohen's "founding spirit."

102. Ibid.

103. On the history of the K.j.V. see Walter Gross, "The Zionist Student Movement," in *Leo Baeck Institute Year Book* 4 (1959): 143–64. The K.j.V. officially came into existence in 1914. Strauss is also listed in the address book for the K.j.V. produced in Palestine during the 1940s, but is not listed in a later version. Strauss referred to his experience as a recruiter in "Bemerkung zu der Weinbergschen Kritik," *Der jüdische Student* 22 (1925): 15–18.

104. Leo Strauss, "Bemerkung zu der Weinbergschen Kritik," and "Die Zukunft einer Illusion," *Der jüdische Student* 26, no. 4 (1928): 17–21. The Berlin publication of *Der jüdische Student* first appeared in 1902 (sponsored by the Kartell zionistische Verbindungen) and ran until 1933.

105. See, for example, "RLG" and "gLG."

106. In addition to Meisl's career as an essayist for such journals as *Der Jude,* he also became the archivist of the Berlin Jewish community; after emigrating to Palestine, he became the founding director of the Central Archives for the History of the Jewish People in Jerusalem.

107. Letter from Leo Strauss to Joseph Meisl, September 10, 1923. The letter is preserved in Joseph Meisl's papers at the Central Archives for the History of the Jewish People in Jerusalem, P35. One landmark act was the law of December 31, 1823, which coordinated rabbinical appointments to four provinces of Kurhessen.

108. In 1925 Strauss explained his use of the term *politics* as connoting "a will sustained by the consciousness of responsibility of the existence and dignity of a people, whereby such existence is seen as depending on purely 'natural' . . . conditions"; "Bemerkung zu der Weinbergschen Kritik," 17.

109. *SoR,* 104; *Stern der Erlösung* in *Franz Rosenzweig. Der Menschun und sein Werk. Gesammelte Schriften,* 4 vols. (Dordrecht, The Netherlands: Martinus Nijhoff, 1976–84), 2:118.

110. The situation started to change in the 1920s, with a sharp increase in the number of Jewish schools, especially in urban areas. For a brief summary of this change, see Paul Mendes-Flohr, "Jewish Cultural and Spiritual Life," in *German Jewish History in Modern Times,* ed. Michael A. Meyer (New York: Columbia University Press, 1998), 4:135–36.

111. Leo Strauss, "Cohens Analyse der Bibel-Wissenschaft Spinozas," *Der Jude* 8 (1924): 295–314; reprinted in *GS,* 2:111; *SCR,* 174.

112. Strauss, "Franz Rosenzweig und die Akademie für die Wissenschaft des Judentums," *Jüdische Wochenzeitung für Kassel, Hessen und Waldeck* 6, no. 49 (December 13, 1929); reprinted in *GS,* 2:363–64; in English, in *EW,* 212–13. See also Strauss's words in the section dedicated to Rosenzweig's "circle" in *Franz Rosenzweig, eine Gedenkschrift,* ed. Eugen Mayer (Frankfurt am Main: Israelitischen Gemeinde Frankfurt am Main, 1930).

113. *GS,* 2:364 and *EW,* 212.

114. Karl Löwith makes this claim in his provocative essay, "M. Heidegger and F. Rosenzweig; or, Temporality and Eternity," *Philosophy and Phenomenological Research* 2, no. 1 (September 1942): 53–77. His earlier book, written under Heidegger's direction, was *Das Individuum in der Rolle des Mitmenschen* (Munich: Drei Masken, 1928). Löwith only read Rosenzweig following 1933 along with Hermann Cohen's essays on Spinoza. *GS,* 2:689, letter no. 58. Also compare to Karl Löwith's interpretation of the polemical character of Schmitt's Weimar writings in an article written under the pseudonym Hugo Fiala: "Politischer Decisionismus" (1935), reprinted in Löwith's *Sämtliche Schriften,* vol. 8 (Stuttgart: Metzler, 1984). Translated as "The Occasional Decisionism of Carl Schmitt," in *Martin Heidegger and European Nihilism,* ed. Richard Wolin, trans. Gary Steiner (New York: Columbia University Press, 1995), 138.

115. Franz Rosenzweig, "Vertauschte Fronten," *Der Morgen* 6, no. 6 (April 1930): 85–87; reprinted in his *Zweistromland: Kleinere Schriften* (Berlin: Schocken, 1937). and in Franz Rosenzweig, *Der Mensch und sein Werk. Gesammelte Schriften* 3:235–38. See the recent English translation "Transposed Fonts" with a helpful editorial introduction in *Franz Rosenzweig: Philosophical and Theological Writings,* trans. and ed. Paul W. Franks and Michael L. Morgan (Indianapolis, Ind.: Hackett, 2000), 146–52. Peter Gordon has made Rosenzweig's comparison the departure point for his own study, *Rosenzweig and Heidegger.*

116. According to Gadamer, "we" referred to Heidegger's teaching assistants: Löwith, Krüger and Gadamer. The wider circle of initiates might be expanded to include Walter Broecker, Jacob Klein, Hans Jonas, and Hannah Arendt. Gadamer, *Philosophische Lehrjahre* (Frankfurt am Main: Klohstermann, 1977), 47f.

117. Löwith acquired Rosenzweig's letters (which had been published in 1935) before leaving Europe for Japan in the autumn of 1936. But it was not until 1939 that he read them. They made such an impact that Löwith read through *The Star of Redemption* as well as his *Kleinere Schriften,* more than 1000 pages in toto, "at one stretch." Löwith refers to his interest in Rosenzweig in his fascinating 1942 essay, "M. Heidegger and F. Rosenzweig: A Postscript to *Being and Time,*" reprinted in *Nature, History and Existentialism,* ed. Arnold Levison (Evanston, Ill: Northwestern University Press, 1966), 51.

118. Less well known than Heidegger's "crisis of faith" and subsequent atheism is that the Catholic Church excommunicated Schmitt from 1926 to 1950 for following through with an ecclesiastically improper second marriage. See Gopal Balakrishnan, *The Enemy: An Intellectual Portrait of Carl Schmitt* (New York: Verso, 2000), 62. Balakrishnan also provides a compelling analysis of the complex relations between Schmitt and Catholic politics, 42–52.

119. "GA" and Leo Strauss, *The Rebirth of Classical Political Rationalism* (Chicago: University of Chicago Press, 1989), 27ff. Heidegger lectured at Freiburg in the summer semester of 1922 on the subject of phenomenological interpretations of Aristotle's ontology and logic and continued to lecture on Aristotle during the following academic year. See Theodore Kisiel, *The Genesis of Heidegger's Being and Time* (Berkeley and Los Angeles: University of California Press. 1993), 227–75.

120. This term has also been rendered as "orphan child," in "GA," 3.

121. "Existentialism," 304. Cf. "GA," 461.

122. See Strauss's published version of his memorial lecture for Kurt Riezler which appeared as "Kurt Riezler" in *Social Science Research* in 1956 and then republished in *What is Political Philosophy?* (Chicago: University of Chicago Press, 1959), 233–60. Strauss first met Riezler in the United States in 1938 at the New School for Social Research (noted on p. 233 of the article). In the academic year 1944–45, Strauss taught a joint seminar with S. E. Asch and Kurt Riezler on Aristotle's *On the Soul* and Descartes's *The Passion of the Soul;* and a joint seminar with Riezler on Plato's *Theatatus.* See the *New School Bulletin of the Graduate Faculty Catalogue* (1944–45), 16, 17.

123. See Peter Eli Gordon, "Continental Divide: Ernst Cassirer and Martin Heidegger at Davos 1929: An Allegory of Intellectual History," *Modern Intellectual History* 1, no. 2 (2004): 219–48.

124. This passage is found in "Kurt Riezler," 246. See Virgil, *Aenid,* book I, lines 151–52.

125. Virgil, *Aeneid,* Book I (lines 148–54). The Latin reads:

> ac veluti magno in populo cum saepe coorta est
> seditio, saevitque animis ignobile vulgus,
> iamque faces et saxa volant—furor arma ministrat—
> tum pietate gravem et meritis si forte virum quem
> conspexere, silent arrectisque auribus adstant;
> ille regit dictis animos, et pectora mulcet:
> sic cunctus pelagi cecidit fragor.

126. Charles R. Bambach, *Heidegger, Dilthey, and the Crisis of Historicism* (Ithaca, N.Y.: Cornell University Press, 1995), 197–98. Heidegger appropriated *Destruktion* from Luther's use of the Latin term *destruere*. Bambach's expanded discussion of this philosophical etymology refers to notes taken from Heidegger's course in the summer semester of 1920, "Phänomenologie der Anschauung und des Ausdrucks: Theorie der philosophischen Begriffsbildung" (July 26, 1920).

127. Martin Heidegger, *Sein und Zeit* (1927): part I, chap. 2, sec. 6, paragraphs 19–27; *Being and Time*, trans. John Macquarrie and Edward Robinson (New York: Harper and Row, 1962), 43.

128. See Dana R. Villa, *Arendt and Heidegger: The Fate of the Political* (Princeton, N.J.: Princeton University Press, 1996), 9–11. Villa argues that Heidegger, Arendt, and Benjamin each used destruction as a way to "shatter the complacency of the present." Arendt had met Heidegger at Marburg in 1924 and began a four-year love affair the following year. See Peter Baehr's introduction to *The Portable Hannah Arendt*, ed. Peter Baehr (New York: Penguin Books, 2000), viii.

129. Strauss, "An Unspoken Prologue to a Public Lecture at St. John's," 2; reprinted in *JPCM*, 450.

130. "Existentialism," 305.

131. Ibid., 306. There are several other places where this condemnation takes place. See "GA."

132. Well before his later reflections on Weimar, Strauss's correspondence from the 1930s and 1940s is replete with references to Heidegger's actions, thought, and writings after *Being and Time;* see *GS*, 3:619–20, 633, 674–77. The moral condemnations, which are only slightly harsher than what he says about Nietzsche, are always undercut by Strauss's insistence that Heidegger's thought must be engaged rather than ignored. "The most stupid thing I could do would be to close my eyes or to reject his work" ("Existentialism," 306).

133. Rosenzweig, "Vertauschte Fronten," in *Zweistromland*, 235–37.

134. See K. Gründer, "Cassirer und Heidegger in Davos 1929" in *Über Ernst Cassirers Philosophie der symbolischen Formen*, ed. Hans-Jürg Braun, Helmut Holzhey, and Ernst Wolfgang Orth (Frankfurt: Suhrkamp, 1988). David R. Lipton, *Ernst Cassirer: The Dilemma of a Liberal Intellectual in Germany, 1914–1933* (Toronto: University of Toronto Press, 1978), 155–59.

135. Calvin O. Schrag, "Heidegger and Cassirer on Kant," *Kant-Studien* 58, no. 1, (1967): 87–100. The two primary published texts involved are Heidegger's *Kant und das Problem der Metaphysik* (Bonn: F. Cohen, 1929) and Cassirer's review, "Kant und das Problem der Metaphysik . . . ," *Kant-Studien* 36, nos. 1–2 (1931) 1–16.

136. Reported in Jean Grondin, *Hans-Georg Gadamer: A Biography*, trans. Joel Weinsheimer (New Haven: Yale University Press, 2003). Jean Grondin lists Strauss as one of the Heideggerian circle from Marburg who attended the Davos conference. See his *Hans-Georg Gadamer*, 146. Cf. the official registry of attendees.

137. Rosenzweig, "Vertauschte Fronten," 236.

138. For Strauss's later reflections on Davos, see the posthumously published lecture, "An Introduction to Heideggerian Existentialism," in *The Rebirth of Classical Political Rationalism* (Chicago: University of Chicago Press, 1989), 28.

139. Ibid.

140. Strauss, "Biblische Geschichte und Wissenschaft" (1925), *GS*, 2:360.

141. Strauss, "IHE," 28.

142. Strauss's critique of Cohen's approach to Spinoza appears to have secured him a position at the Akademie für Wissenschaft des Judentums in Berlin. Julius Guttmann assigned Strauss to the history of Jewish philosophy. While in Berlin, Strauss struck up friendships with the young Jewish historians Gershom Scholem, Fritz Bamberger, and Fritz (Yitzhak) Baer. Strauss worked on the academy's collaborative publication of Moses Mendelssohn's complete writings. Strauss wrote introductions contextualizing Mendelssohn's pantheism dispute with Jacobi. Mendelssohn is portrayed as incapable of seeing the significance of Jacobi's elusive and provocative style.

143. Strauss, *SCR*, 178–82.

144. Ibid., 181.

145. Herzl, "Mauschel," *Die Welt* 20 (October 15, 1897).

146. *EW*, 82, n. 2.

147. Franz Rosenzweig, "Apolegetsches Denken: Bemerkungen zu Brod und Baeck," reprinted in *Kleinere Schriften* (Berlin: Schocken, 1937), 677–86. English translation found in *Franz Rosenzweig: Philosophical and Theological Writings*.

148. "Anmerkung zur Discussion ueber 'Zionismus und Antisemitismus'" originally appeared in *Jüdische Rundschau* 28, nos. 83–84 (September 28, 1923): 501; reprinted in *GS*, 2:311–313. Translated into English by Michael Zank as "A Note on the Discussion on 'Zionism and Anti-Semitism,'" 81–82.

149. *GS*, 3:361–362.

150. Such a position would not surprise readers were the author a pious traditional Jew from Eastern Europe. It is worth remarking that Strauss recovers that traditionalist perspective on world politics.

151. See "Die Zukunft einer Illusion" (1928), reprinted in *GS*, 2:431–39 (2nd ed.).

152. "ZN," *GS*, 2:321.

153. Ibid., 2:318.

154. Despite valuable intellectual exchanges, Gadamer and Strauss were apparently never close. See the interview with Gadamer in which he claims to have remained circumspect with Strauss: "We were on good terms and talked now and then but otherwise had little contact with each other." "An Interview," *Interpretation: A Journal of Political Philosophy* 12, no. 1 (1984): 2. Grondin reports that in Marburg in the 1920s, Strauss was considered an outsider while Gadamer was an insider. "Gadamer, the reserved insider at Marburg, had a friendly, though distant relationship to him [Strauss]." Although gossip is not the focus of this study, it is pertinent to mention that in this same account, Gadamer was given reason to believe that Strauss harbored some type of "animosity toward him." Because Strauss was a "mistrustful sort of person," Gadamer remained "circumspect with him, careful not to give his mistrust any nourishment"; *Hans-Georg Gadamer*, 173.

155. See Habermas's early treatment of Schmitt and Hobbes on this very point as a decisive innovation in regarding the conscience as a private opinion rather than as a direct window on truth (as was, for example, the view of Ambrose). Jürgen Habermas, *The Structural Transformation of the Public Sphere: An Inquiry into a Category of Bourgeois Society*, trans. Thomas Burger (Cambridge, Mass.: MIT Press, 1991), 81–85.

156. See Strauss's use of this expression in his 1965 preface to *Spinoza's Critique of Religion*, reprinted in *JPCM*, 173.

157. Heinrich Meier, *Carl Schmitt and Leo Strauss: The Hidden Dialogue*, trans. J. Harvey Lomax (Chicago: University of Chicago Press, 1995). William Scheuerman has pointed to the influence of another German Jew who exercised unacknowledged influence on Schmitt: Hans Morgenthau. William E. Scheuerman, *Carl Schmitt: The End of Law* (Lanham, Md.: Rowman and Littlefield, 1999), 225–51.

158. "NCSCP," 101 (my emphasis).

159. Ibid., 101.

160. Ibid., 104–5.

161. Ibid., 101–2.

162. Ibid., 106.

163. Ibid., 108

164. Ibid., 119.

165. Strauss, "Die Zukunft einer Ilusion," *Der jüdische Student* 25, no. 4 (1928): 16–21; reprinted in a supplement to *GS*, vol. 2.

166. Klatzkin translated Spinoza into Hebrew, edited the German *Encyclopaedia Judaica* (1928–34) and compiled a thesaurus and compendium to medieval Hebrew philosophical terms.

167. Jakob Klatzkin, *Krisis und Entscheidung im Judentum: der Probleme des modernen Judentums* (Berlin: Jüdischer Verlag, 1921), 57. He edited the *Encyclopaedia Judaica: das Judentum in Geschichte und Gegenwart,* (Berlin: Eschkol [1928–34]). Klatzkin received his doctorate at the University of Bern in 1912.

168. Strauss, "Die Zukunft einer Ilusion," 17–18.

169. Max Joseph published three separate critiques of Strauss's "Future of an Illusion" essay in the same journal, *Der jüdische Student:* "Zur atheistischen Ideologie des Zionismus," *Der jüdische Student* 25, nos. 6–7 (October 1928): 8–18; "Ist die Religion wirklich eine Illusion?" *Der jüdische Student* 26, no. 8 (December 1928): 6–17; and "Wissenschaft und Religion" *Der jüdische Student* 26, no. 5 (May 1929): 15–22.

170. Strauss, "Zur Ideologie des politischen Zionismus," *Der jüdische Student* 26, no. 5 (May 1929): 22–27; reprinted in *GS*, 1:441–48.

171. Strauss makes this argument in several Zionist writings.

172. Strauss, "Der Zionismus bei Max Nordau," *GS*, 2:318–19.

173. Leo Strauss, "Ecclesia militans," *Jüdische Rundschau* 20, no. 36 (May 8, 1925): 334–36; reprinted in *GS*, 2:351–56.

174. Isaac Breuer was the son of Salomon Breuer (1849–1926) who became the son-in-law of the founder of the Frankfurt separatist community (*Austrittsgemeinde*), Raphael Samson Hirsch (1808–1888).

175. "Ecclesia militans," *GS*, 2:355.

176. Strauss, "Cohens Analyse der Bibel-Wissenschaft Spinozas" originally appeared in *Der Jude* and was reprinted in *GS*, 1:362–86.

177. Hermann Cohen, "Ein ungedruckter Vortrag Hermann Cohens über Spinozas Verhältnis zum Judentum," in *Festgabe zum Zehnjährigen Bestehen der Akademie für die Wissenschaft des Judentums, 1919–1929* (Berlin: Akademie, 1929), 59.

178. *GS*, 2:367.

179. *SCR*, 112; *RkS*, 155–56.

180. *SCR*, 115; *RkS*, 157.

181. Hans-Georg Gadamer, *Wahrheit und Methode* (Tübingen: Mohr, 1960), 223f.;

see the English translation, *Truth and Method* (New York: Continuum, 1993), 271 n. 189. See the correspondence in *Wahrheit und Methode*, 503–12. See the dual German-English in "Correspondence Concerning *Wahrheit und Methode*," *Independent Journal of Philosophy*, 2 (1978): 5–12.

182. See *RkS*, in *GS*, 1:233; *SCR*, 181.

183. Leo Strauss, "Das Testament Spinozas," *Bayerische Israelitische Gemeindezeitung*, 8, no. 21 (November 1, 1932): 322–26; reprinted in *GS*, 1:415–22.

184. Ibid., 416–17.

185. Ibid., 419.

186. *GS*, 1:422.

187. *SCR*, 163–64; *RkS*, 213–14.

188. *SCR*, 165; *RkS*, 214.

189. *SCR*, 53.

190. Strauss, preface to *Spinoza's Critique of Religion*, reprinted in *JPCM*, 140.

191. "RLG" (1930) and "Cohen und Maimuni" (1931) in *GS*, 2:393–436 are emblematic of this shift.

192. "RLG," 384.

193. Strauss, "Besprechung von Julius Ebbinghaus, *Über die Fortschritte der Metaphysik*" (1931) in *GS*, 2:439.


*Chapter 3. European Exile and Reorientation (1932–1937) (pp. 54–80)*

1. "RLG," 382 and 386.

2. Leo Strauss, "Notes on Carl Schmitt, *The Concept of the Political*" first appeared in *Archiv für Sozialwissenschaft und Sozialpolitik* 67, no. 6 (August–September 1932): 732–49. All citations here refer to the reprinted English translation in Heinrich Meier, *Carl Schmitt and Leo Strauss: The Hidden Dialogue*, trans. J. Harvey Lomax, with a foreword by Joseph Cropsey (Chicago: University of Chicago Press, 1995), 91–119. Minor changes in translation are based on the German version in Heinrich Meier, *Carl Schmitt, Leo Strauss und "der Begriff des Politischen": Zu einem Dialog unter Abwesenden* (Stuttgart: J. B. Metzler, 1988).

3. Dr. Ludwig Feuchtwanger, the head of Duncker and Humbolt publishing house, had been friendly with Carl Schmitt since World War I. Schmitt wrote a letter (June 10, 1932) to Feuchtwanger stating that out of some hundred reviews of *Concept of the Political*, Strauss's was the only noteworthy one. It should, Schmitt wrote, therefore be published in *Archiv für Sozialpolitik*, a journal published by Feuchtwanger's company. Feuchtwanger would later write to Strauss (dated April 15, 1935) upon the publication of *Philosophie und Gesetz* that "the author of *Der Begriffe de Politscher* had spoken of Strauss in high esteem" ever since Strauss's first book, *Die Religionskritik Spinozas* (1930). Schmitt's letter to Feuchtwanger is quoted in *Carl Schmitt and Leo Strauss*, 8 n. 7. Feuchtwanger's letter is in the Leo Strauss Papers at the University of Chicago Special Collections, box 1, folder 13.

4. For a detailed study of Schmitt's incorporation of Strauss's commentary, see Meier, *Carl Schmitt and Leo Strauss*. Cf. William E. Scheuerman, *Carl Schmitt: The End of Law* (New York: Rowman and Littlefield, 1999), 226–30, where Meier's chronol-

ogy is called into question and Hans Morgenthau appears as a more decisively influential critic for the most significant changes in the different early editions of the *Concept of the Political*.

5. Schmitt joined the Nazi party in Cologne, while Heidegger did so in Freiburg. For Schmitt's decision to join the party, see Andreas Koene, *Der Fall Carl Schmitt: Sein Auftieg zum "Kronjuristen des Dritten Reiches"* (Darmstadt: Wisssenschaftliche Buchgesellschaft, 1995), 6–9. See also Rüdiger Safranski, *Martin Heidegger: Between Good and Evil*, trans. Ewald Osers (Cambridge, Mass.: Harvard University Press, 1998), 88f.

6. Leo Strauss to Carl Schmitt, dated July 10, 1933. Strauss makes particular reference to Louis Massignon and André Siegfried. Strauss's three extant letters to Schmitt are published in Meier's *Carl Schmitt and Leo Strauss*, 123–28.

7. Charles Maurras was the co–founding editor of the *Action Française* (1908–44), welcomed the Vichy government, and was jailed for treason in 1945. Maurras began his career as a classical scholar and railed against the decadence of modern republican romanticism. His "integrative nationalism" sought to protect French society by stripping unassimilated aliens such as Protestants, Jews, and "métèques" (a term he coined in 1894), of all civic rights. His royalism and idiosyncratic anticlerical Catholicism were later currents adapted to his overall reactionary political and cultural philosophy. See Eugen Weber, *Action Française: Royalism and Reaction in Twentieth-Century France* (Stanford: Stanford University Press, 1962). Pierre Birnbaum situates Maurras and his continuous antisemitic nationalist diatribes at the center of the Franco-Catholic right: a front that included Edouard Drumont, Pierre Gaxotte, and Léon Daudat. *The Jews of the Republic: A Political History of State Jews in France from Gambetta to Vichy*, trans. Jane Marie Todd (Stanford: Stanford University Press, 1996), esp. 156–78.

8. According to Heinrich Meier, Strauss was not aware of Schmitt's "abrupt about-face" after the Enabling Act of March 23, 1933. Indirect evidence of this position is supported by a letter dated October 9, 1933, in which Strauss asked Jacob Klein why Schmitt has stopped replying to his letters: "Is that generally the case now?" Klein wrote to Strauss on October 21 that Schmitt "is joining the crowd in an *inexcusable* way. In the official position he now holds, no doubt he *cannot* very well answer. . . . And I would certainly not write to him again." Strauss had apparently put the same question to Karl Löwith. In a letter dated December 6, 1933, Löwith informed Strauss that one of Schmitt's former doctoral students, a Dr. Werner Becker, "regards it out of the question that Schmitt—despite his anti-Semitism in principle—has not answered you *for that reason*." Schmitt is reputed to have shown Strauss's letters to various visitors and to have claimed that he continued to receive letters from Strauss as late as 1934 from England. No letters dated after the summer of 1933 have been found in Schmitt's or Strauss's holdings. There is an extant letter that contains an explicit mention of Schmitt as a Nazi, but that is in a letter to E. I. J. Rosenthal dated May 10, 1935. Strauss would later complain that Schmitt had taken many of his ideas and not acknowledged him appropriately.

9. In a letter from Jacob Klein to Leo Strauss dated April 27, 1933, Klein informed Strauss how Heidegger has chosen this course with his students and colleagues and even his former mentor Edmund Husserl, in an attempt to be appointed rector at the University of Freiburg; Leo Strauss Papers at the University of Chicago Special Collections, box 8, file 4. Strauss's awareness of the climate of censorship and persecution in Germany is revealed in his 1933 correspondence with H. G. Gadamer. Gadamer and Strauss

seemingly limit their discussions to interpretive issues around Platonic texts. But these interpretive debates center on issues of political and ethical dilemmas that have a striking resonance to the events which surrounded them. See the Gadamer-Strauss 1933 correspondence held in the Leo Strauss Papers, box 1, file 14.

10. Letter from Klein to Strauss dated October 9, 1933.

11. Letter from Strauss to Schmitt dated July 10, 1933.

12. Letter from Strauss to Schmitt dated March 13, 1932. Quoted in Meier, *Carl Schmitt and Leo Strauss,* 123; translation altered.

13. I claim that Schmitt was considered by Strauss and his contemporaries to be a figure of the right even though some see Schmitt's Weimar writings as interested in salvaging the liberal-democratic regime from its enemies and self-imposed deficiencies. While Schmitt's pronouncements in the wake of his entrance into the Nazi Party assume new qualities, his disdain for the inadequacies of liberalism remains continuous with his earlier career. See Gopal Balakrishnan, *The Enemy: An Intellectual Portrait of Carl Schmitt* (New York: Verso, 2000).

14. Vicki Caron, *Uneasy Asylum: France and the Jewish Crisis, 1933–1942* (Stanford, Calif.: Stanford University Press, 1999), 4.

15. Koyré's 1932–33 seminar on Hegel's religious philosophy was attended by Strauss, Georges Bataille, Henry Corbin, Aron Gurvitsch, Raymond Queneau, and Eric Weil. See Michael Roth, *Knowing and History: Appropriations of Hegel in Twentieth-Century France* (Ithaca: Cornall University Press, 1988), 95. Kojève's seminar was attended by Raymond Queneau, Henri Corbin, Geroges Bataille, Jacques Lacan, Eric Weil, Maurice and Jacques Merleau-Ponty, Denyse Mosseri, André Breton, and Jean Hyppolite. See Dominique Auffret, *Alexandre Kojève: la philosophie, l'Etat, la fin de l'Histoire* (Paris: B. Grasset, 1990), 238.

16. *PPH,* 8. *GS,* 3.

17. *PPH,* 1.

18. Cf. the presentation in *SCR* where Strauss states that Hobbes, in contradistinction to Spinoza, believes that "the political allegiance of all the subjects of the state is a bond whose origin lies in reason alone." Hobbes therefore goes well beyond Spinoza in providing a strictly rationalist theory of obligation wherein religion is no longer needed. "According to Spinoza, the commandment 'thou shalt love thy neighbor' takes its force as commandment for the multitude only from the belief that the commandment is the directly 'revealed' word of God, but from Hobbes' position this commandment is sufficiently binding upon men by virtue of the fact that God has created men as reasonable beings. The distinction between the wise and the vulgar does not enter into the matter at all. Because that distinction does not come into consideration, there is no necessity for recourse to religion"; *SCR,* 101.

19. *PPH,* 155.

20. *PPH,* 152–53.

21. *PPH,* 125 (my emphasis).

22. One can also draw parallels with Heidegger's conception of "resolve" and his thundering pronouncements at the Davos conference.

23. See Schmitt's *Concept of the Political,* trans. George Schwab (New Brunswick, N.J.: Rutgers University Press, 1976), 62. Strauss perceived that Schmitt's target was actually Hegel's "first polemical-political definition of the bourgeois." This figure was char-

acterized by Hegel in *Über die wissenschaftlichen Behandlungsarten des Naturrechts* as he "who does not want to leave the sphere of the unpolitical, risk-free, who in possession and in the justice of private possession behaves as an individual against the whole, who 'finds' the substitute for his political nonentity in the fruits of peace and acquisition and, above all, 'in the perfect *security* of the enjoyment of those things,' who consequently wants to remain exempt from courage and removed from the danger of a violent death" (emphasis Schmitt's). English translation found in Georg Wilhelm Friedrich Hegel, *Natural Law: The Scientific Ways of Treating Natural Law, Its Place in Moral Philosophy, and Its Relation to the Positive Sciences of Law,* trans. T. M. Knox (Philadelphia: University of Pennsylvania Press, 1975). Cf. Strauss's lecture, "German Nihilism," treated in the next chapter.

24. *PPH,* 125 n. 2.

25. Strauss to Löwith, May 19, 1933, in *GS,* 3:625. I thank Jeffrey Barash for alerting me to this letter. The quotation from Virgil appears to have been corrupted; thus the passage I quote has a slightly altered syntax. Strauss's original letter reads as follows:

> Zwar kann ich nicht für irgend ein anderes Land "optieren"—eine Heimat und, vor allem, eine Muttersprache wählt man sich nicht, ich jedenfalls werde keine andere als deutsch schreiben *können,* ob ich gleich in anderer Sprache werde schreiben *müssen*—; andererseits sehe ich keine annehmbare Möglichkeit, unter dem Hakenkreuz zu leben, d.h. unter einem Symbol, das mir nichts anderes sagt als: du und deinesgleichen, ihr seid φυσει Untermenschen und darum rechtens Parias. Es gibt hier nur *eine* Lösung. Wir müssen uns immer wieder sagen: wir "Männer der Wissenschaft"—so nannten sich unseresgleichen im arabischen Mittelalter—non habemus locum manentem, sed quaerimus. . . . Und, was die *Sache* betrifft: darum, dass das rechts-gewordene Deutschland uns weg . . . , folgt schlechterdings nichts gegen die rechten Prinzipien. Im Gegenteil: nur von den rechten Prinzipien aus, von den fascistischen, autoritären, *imperialen* Prinzipien aus lässt sich mit Anstand, ohne den lächerlichen und jämmerlichen Appell an die *droits imprescriptibles de l'homme,* gegen das meskine Unwesen protestieren. Ich lese Caesars Commentarien mit tieferem Verständnis, und ich denke an Vergils: In regni imperio . . . parcere subjectis et detellare superbos. Es gibt keinen Grund[,] zu Kreuze zu kriechen, auch nicht zum Kreuz des Liberalismus, solange noch irgendwo in der Welt ein Funke des *römischen* Gedankens glimmt. Und auch dann: lieber als jegliches Kreuz das Ghetto.

26. Löwith often expressed surprise at Strauss's background and interest in matters Jewish. Löwith once earned Strauss's ire by referring to him as an Orthodox Jew. In a personally revealing letter, dated September 25, 1962, Löwith responded to a draft of Strauss's preface to *Spinoza's Critique of Religion.* He remarked how the clarity and depth with which Strauss addressed the complex issues relating to German Jewry and the crisis of modern thought was completely new to him as he had been raised outside the Jewish tradition, and probably never would have engaged any of these issues were it not for Hitler. Löwith explains that his father was born out of wedlock to a Jewish mother and a non-Jewish Viennese baron.

27. Karl Löwith, *Mein Leben in Deutschland vor und nach 1933: ein Bericht* (Stuttgart: J. B. Metzler, 1986). Franz Rosenzweig, *Briefe,* no. 364 (letter to Rudolf Hallo, end of January 1923) (Berlin: Schocken, 1935), 472–75. Regarding Rosenzweig's story, see

Peter Gordon, *Rosenzweig and Heidegger: Between Judaism and German Philosophy* (Berkeley and Los Angeles: University of California Press, 2003), introduction.

28. See Löwith's sharp response to Strauss, dated May 28, 1933, in which Löwith emphasizes the crude reactionary *völkisch* nationalism and racism not only in Germany, but in France and England. Löwith sees the convergence of left and right, as the seeds of fascism are planted in democratic societies. He closes his letter with a query and then defiance.

> Was das Zukreuzekriechen betrifft so denke ich zwar auch nicht daran
> es in irgend einer Form zu tun, aber umgekehrt ist die Welt der
> Gegenwart nicht so dass sie Märtyrer hervorbringen könnte—sondern
> nur Mitmachende und Abseitsstehende.
> Was meinen *Sie* zu alldem?
> Dixi et animam meam slavavi!
> Einen herzlichen Gruss
> Ihr K. Löwith

Note that Löwith's invocation of Ezekial 3:18–19 in Latin (I have spoken and saved my soul) references Marx's biting sarcasm in his 1875 epilogue to his "Critique of the Gotha Programme."

29. Robert Weltsch, "Tragt ihn mit Stolz, den gelben Fleck," *Jüdische Rundschau*, no. 27 (April 4, 1933). See the English translation by Robert Wistrich in Yad Vashem's SHOAH Resource Center: http://www1.yadvashem.org/about_holocaust/documents/part1/doc 14.html

30. *GS*, 3:512.

31. Ibid., 512–13.

32. Ibid., 519.

33. Ibid., 516.

34. Ibid., 517.

35. Ibid., 527.

36. Ibid., 516.

37. Thus, whenever secular political authority bows to the power of the church, it becomes viewed as "crawling to the cross."

38. *Thus Spoke Zarathustra*, "The Apostates," part 3, chap. 52, sec. 1. See also an aphorism where Nietzsche cries out against how, like Don Quixote, most spirits are crushed with a disgraceful crawl to the Cross. One also thinks of the third act of Wagner's *Parsifal* as perhaps the most notable dramatic version of the more pious legacy of this phrase, reset as Teutonic myth.

39. Nietzsche, *Will to Power*, trans. Walter Kaufmann and R. J. Hollingdale, ed. Walter Kaufmann (New York: Random House, 1967).

40. *PPH*, 71. Cf. Strauss's earlier comparisons between Spinoza's and Hobbes's Bible criticism: "Cohens Analyse der Bible-Wissenschaft Spinozas," reprinted in *GS*, 1:367 n. ii; "Cohen's Analysis of Spinoza's Bible Science," *EW*, 144 n. 2. *RkS* in *GS*, 1:146–48/*SCR*, 101–104.

41. *PPH*, 76. Strauss claims that, like Spinoza, Hobbes too was influenced by the Socinians in the critique of theological traditions. *PPH*, 76 n. 3; Cf *RkS*, where Strauss limits the Socinian influence only to Spinoza.

42. *PPH*, 74.

43. The definite article is missing in the original English translation.

44. See Hobbes, *Leviathan*, chap. 35.

45. "On the Basis of Hobbes's Political Philosophy," 188.

46. Ibid.

47. Ibid., 188, the citations to Lessing in note 21. Note that in the 1936 version, only Hermann Samuel Reimarus is mentioned by name. For Lessing's bold but veiled writings in this controversy, see *Sämtliche Schriften,* ed. Karl Lachmann and Franz Muncker (Stuttgart, 1886–1924), 12:254–71. For historical background, see Henry E. Allison, *Lessing and the Enlightenment: His Philosophy of Religion and Its Relation to Eighteenth-Century Thought* (Ann Arbor: University of Michigan Press, 1966), 83f.

48. *LSTH.* The English translation is *The Leviathan in the State Theory of Thomas Hobbes: Meaning and Failure of a Political Symbol,* trans. George Schwab and Erna Hilfstein (Westport, Conn.: Greenwood, 1996).

49. These mythic symbols reappear in Schmitt's masterly analysis of naval power, *Land und Meer: Eine weltgeschichtliche Betrachung,* 4th ed. (Klett-Cotta, 2001).

50. *LSTH,* 38n.

51. Ibid., 18.

52. *PPH,* 72.

53. See Miguel Vatter, "Strauss and Schmitt as Readers of Hobbes and Spinoza: On the Relation between Political Theology and Liberalism," *New Centennial Review* 4, no. 3 (2004): 161–214. Vatter illuminates the connections between Strauss and Schmitt's reading of the seventeenth-century figures of Spinoza and Hobbes as mediated through Mendelssohn and especially Lessing. The reader should be cautioned that the chronology of this debate is crucial in determining who is responding to what and the original publication dates of these writings becomes a sine qua non for a clear attempt to reconstruct a back-and-forth between Schmitt and Strauss.

54. *PPH,* 189.

55. For Mendelssohn's worship, see Sorkin, "The Impact of Emancipation on German Jewry: A Reconsideration," in *Assimilation and Community: The Jews in Nineteenth-Century Europe,* ed. Jonathan Frankel and Steven J. Zipperstein (New York: Cambridge University Press, 1992), 186f.

56. Strauss's contributions to the jubilee edition of Moses Mendelssohn's *Gesammelte Schriften* were published in 1931, 1932, and 1974. Heinrich Meier recounts the delayed publication of Strauss's essays written in the 1930s; see *GS,* 2:xxxi. The 1974 edition of Mendelssohn's *Gesammelte Schriften* included Strauss's most extensive writings on Mendelssohn and taps into his earlier interest in Jacobi and increasing appreciation of Lessing: his introduction to "Morgenstunden" and "An die Freunde Lessings," was published in 1974 under the direction of Alexander Altmann; reprinted in *GS,* 2:528–605.

57. See Strauss's account in his letter to Jacob Klein, dated June 26, 1930, where he referred to this project on Gersonides, "the Jewish scholastic," as pure "Lehrnarbeit." Strauss also expressed frustration in pursuing the type of work that interested him most when his employer attempted to force his work in different directions. Cf. Strauss's letter to Krüger, December 7, 1933, in which he describes the essay, "Maimunis Lehre von der Prophetie und ihre Quellen," which was supposed to appear in the 1931 *Korrespondezblatt der Akademie für die Wissenschaft des Judentums;* because of that organ's financial difficulties, however, the essay did not appear until the publication of *Philosophy and*

*Law* (1935). It formed the third chapter, "The Philosophic Foundation of the Law: Maimonides's Doctrine of Prophecy and its Sources," as a preliminary outline to a medieval theory of prophetology based on a study of Gersonides's *Wars of the Lord* and Averroes's (Ibn Rushd) commentaries on Aristotle (e.g., the *Decisive Treatise*).

58. See Strauss's letter to Karl Löwith, dated June 23, 1935, published in *Independent Journal of Philosophy* 5–6 (1988): 182–83.

59. In a letter dated December 31, 1933, Strauss wrote to Krüger: "Everything speaks for England." In this same letter Strauss disclosed with a tone of despair that the more senior scholar, Simon Rawidowicz, applied for the chair in medieval Jewish philosophy at the Hebrew University in Jerusalem. Apparently, Strauss assumed that Guttmann, who was teaching in the United States at this time, was not a candidate for the Jerusalem position. Strauss's assessment of his situation earlier that month was that the Hebrew University was a real possibility; Strauss letter to Krüger, dated December 7, 1933, *GS*, 3:436–37.

60. Strauss's letter to Kojève undated, published in Strauss, *On Tyranny* (New York: Free Press of Glencoe, 1963), 222.

61. *On Tyranny*, 222.

62. *PG*. Reprinted in *GS*, 2:3–124. The revised English translation is cited here as *PL*.

63. *PL*, 21; *PG*, in *GS*, 2:9. In *Spinoza's Critique of Religion*, Strauss argued that "prejudice" was a "modern historical category" that became the antipode to "freedom." Strauss wrote: "The word 'prejudice' is the most appropriate expression for the dominant theme of the Enlightenment movement, for the will to free, open-minded investigation. . . . [T]he struggle of the Enlightenment against prejudice has an absolute meaning. For this reason, the age of prejudice and the age of freedom can stand in opposition to one another. For the age of freedom, it is essential that it be preceded by the age of prejudice. 'Prejudice' is an historical category. This precisely constitutes the difference between the struggle of the Enlightenment against prejudices and the struggle against appearance and opinion with which philosophy began its secular journey"; *SCR*, 181.

64. Strauss first pointed to these elements in his unpublished review of Karl Mannheim's *Ideologie and Utopie* [1929] in "Konspektivismus" (1929), posthumously published in *GS* 2:363–76. Strauss subsequently saw Mannheim as an example of the "sophistry of our times." See Strauss's letter to Krüger, dated February 27, 1931, and the two handwritten pages written under the title "Sophistik der Zeit" in the Strauss Papers, box 8, folder 4.

65. Cf. Strauss's earlier formulation of belief and unbelief in "Die Zukunft einer Illusion," *Der jüdische Student* 25, no. 4 (1928): 16–21.

66. Cf. Strauss's earlier employment of this phrase in *RkS*, 230; *SCR*, 194 and 229.

67. Strauss quotes Lessing's *Gedanken über die Herrnhuter*, *PG*, 18; *PL*, 28.

68. Strauss had already pointed to this shift in his first book. Strauss contrasted Nietzsche's courageous atheism to premodern felicitous atheism; *RkS*, 266 n. 276.

69. *PG*, 13–14 n. 2; *PL*, 112 n. 2.

70. *PL*, 22.

71. Ibid., 19.

72. Ibid., 55.

73. *PG*, 46; *PL*, 59.

74. *PL*, 90–91.

75. Ibid., 92.

76. Ibid., 102–3.

77. Ibid., 103.

78. *Briefwechsel 1933–1940/Walter Benjamin, Gershom Scholem*, ed. Gershom Scholem (Frankfurt am Main: Suhrkamp, 1980), 192–97; *The Correspondence of Walter Benjamin and Gershom Scholem, 1932–1940*, trans. Gary Smith and André Lefevere (New York: Schocken, 1989), letter 72, 155–58. Strauss had already come to Benjamin's attention. See Benjamin's letter to Scholem, dated February 14, 1929, where Benjamin states: "I won't deny that he awakens my trust and I find him sympathetic. I will soon intercept him once again at the state library, at which time I hope to get his reports from the theatre of war." Benjamin was unable to find Strauss in Berlin the next month. On March 15, 1929, he reported to Scholem that "Strauss . . . has disappeared from sight. But I will send out a warrant for his arrest since he took with him an extensive bibliography on the nature of the fairy tale"; ibid., 347 and 349. This time coincides with the Davos congress and may present circumstantial piece of evidence regarding Strauss's possible attendence.

79. Ibid., letter of February 14, 1929, Scholem, like many of his contemporaries, was under stressful conditions at the time. In the same letter, Scholem informed Benjamin that he had just learned that his older brother Werner—a former leader of the German Communist Party—had been acquitted by a "People's Court" only to be "promptly taken into preventative custody and there has been no trace of him since." Scholem knew that this meant he had been taken to a concentration camp. Werner Scholem, after transferring from the Torgau concentration camp to Dachau, was murdered in Buchenwald, July 17, 1940.

80. Ibid. See *GS*, 2:xxvi–xxviii.

81. I have found nothing in the minutes of the Humanities Faculty of the Hebrew University that indicates Scholem's advocacy of Strauss for the position. However, Ilan Troen alerted me to the possibility that the minutes to these meetings were not necessarily accurate: some of the minutes to such faculty meetings are rumored to have been written before the meetings began.

82. Amos Funkenstein, one of the few individuals of his generation that could claim to rival the scholarly range of Strauss, elaborated upon the significance of "accommodation" in each of his major works. *Perceptions of Jewish History* (Berkeley and Los Angeles: University of California Press, 1993), chaps. 4 and 5 offer invaluable discussion of "accommodation" as a key element of medieval exegesis that demonstrates medieval historical consciousness; see in particular 88–98 and 140–152. See also *Theology and the Scientific Imagination from the Middle Ages to the Seventeenth Century* (Princeton, N.J.: Princeton University Press, 1986), 213–71. Funkenstein directly criticized Strauss's *Philosophy and Law* in "Gesetz und Geschichte: Zur historisierenden Hermeneutik bei Moses Maimonides und Thomas von Aquin," *Viator* 1 (1970): 147–48, 162 n. 60. That Funkenstein substituted "history" for "philosophy" provides much of the explanation regarding Funkenstein's animosity. Funkenstein devoted himself to recovering premodern forms of historical consciousness. Accordingly, Funkenstein deemed accommodation significant because of its historiographical richness: "Out of the exegetical *topos* (accommodation) grew various philosophies of history" that articulated "the adjustment of divine manifestations and divine institutions to the process of intellectual, moral and even political advancement of man"; *Perceptions of Jewish History* (Berkeley and Los Angeles: University of California Press, 1993), 88.

83. Strauss's efforts regarding a position in Jerusalem are recounted in letters he wrote to friends in the winter of 1933. See Strauss's letter to Fritz (Yitzhak) Baer dated September 24, 1933, as well as a letter to Gershom Scholem dated December 7, 1933. Archive 41500, Correspondence of Leo Strauss at the Department of Manuscripts and Archives at the Jewish National Library in Jerusalem. See also Strauss's letter to Gerhard Krüger dated December 7, 1933, in which Strauss refers to the possibility of obtaining a chair in medieval Jewish philosophy at the Hebrew University. In a letter to Jacob Klein dated December 7, 1933, Strauss thanked Klein, Krüger, and Gadamer for their assistance in this effort, referred to as the "Palestine-Buber-Action." See also *GS,* 2: xii–xiii.

84. The economic historian Henri Eugène Sée (1864–1936) provided a letter of introduction for Strauss. Simon Green, "The Tawney-Strauss Connection: On Historicism and Values in the History of Political Ideas," *Journal of Modern History* 67 (June 1995): 256.

85. See the letter from Walter Adams, general secretary of the Academic Assistance Council, to R. H. Tawney, dated July 3, 1936. Tawney had forwarded this letter to Professor John Nef at the University of Chicago. John U. Nef Jr. Papers held at the University of Chicago Library, box 42, folder 10. Cf. Letter of John Nef to Charles E. Merriam, October 13, 1936.

86. Letter from Conyers Read to John Nef, dated October 29, 1936. Held in the John University Nef, Jr. Papers at the University of Chicago Regenstein Library.

87. Leo Strauss, "Quelques remarques sur la science politique de Maïmonide et de Fârâbîs." (1936). Translated into English by Robert Bartlett as "Some Remarks on the Political Science of Maimonides and Farabi," in *Interpretation* 18, no. 1 (Fall 1990): 3–30; henceforth referred to as "SRPS." Rémi Brague has noted that this text was originally written in German and translated into French by Paul Kraus.

88. "SRPS," 4.

89. Ibid., 6. The Nietzschean disgust with which Strauss views the modern secularized Christian paradigm of philosophy is unmistakable in this passage.

90. Ibid., 14. See Maimonides's *Guide of the Perplexed,* I:15 and II:38; hereafter cited as *Guide.*

91. *Guide,* II:38, 376 (my emphasis).

92. "SRPS," 14.

93. *Guide,* II:35–38.

94. *Guide,* II:39. Strauss also looked to Maimonides's *Mishneh Torah* for clarification on the uniqueness of Mosaic prophecy. See "Foundational Laws of the Torah" (*H. Yesode ha-Torah*), IX, 2.

95. "SRPS," 15.

96. Ibid., 15–16.

97. Ibid., 16.

98. See *Guide,* I:5 and I:31–34.

99. *Guide,* I:72; "SRPS," 16.

100. "Not the mystery of its origin, the search for which leads either to theosophy or 'Epicureanism,' but its end, the comprehension of which guarantees obedience to the Torah, is accessible to human reason: "SRPS," 16.

101. Strauss, "On Abravanel's Philosophical Tendency and Political Teaching" (hereafter cited as "OAPT"), in *Isaac Abravanel,* ed. J. B. Trend and H. Loewe (Cambridge: Cambridge University Press, 1937), 93–129. Reprinted in *GS,* 2:195–228; "OAPT," 100.

102. "OAPT," 100.

103. Cf. Strauss's account of the Socratic *elenchus* in *The Political Philosophy of Hobbes:* "What men, in particular the Athenians, and in particular their spokesmen the Sophists, say is contradictory. The contradictions make necessary an investigation into which of the conflicting assertions is true. Whatever the result of the investigation, one of the conflicting endoxa must be given up, the opposite endoxon must be maintained. Thus the latter endoxon becomes truly paradoxical; but by making unanimity and understanding of each with himself and with others possible, it proves itself true" (*PPH,* 143).

104. *Guide* II:46.

105. "SRPS," 19.

106. Ibid., 19–20. Maimonides based this position on the teaching of the Jewish tradition and relying on a verse of Jeremiah (9:1); see *H. deot* VI, 1. Cf. *Acht Kapitel* IV, ed. Maurice Wolff (Leiden: Brill, 1903), 10–11; Farabi, *k. al-siyasat,* 50. Strauss noted that Falaquera refers to the same passage.

107. We might also place this reading of medieval responses to exile next to one of the many responses of German refugee intellectuals, especially that of entering an "inner migration" in their place of refuge. See for example Anthony Heilbut, *Kultur ohne Heimat: deutsche Emigranten in den USA nach 1933* (Reinbek bei Hamburg: Rowohlt 1991). See also the recent overview, David Ketter and Gerhard Lauer, eds., *Exile, Science, and Bildung: The Contested Legacies of German Emigré Intellectuals* (New York: Palgrave Macmillan, 2005). Cf. Mitchell G Ash and Alfons Söllner, eds., *Forced Migration and Scientific Change: Emigré German-Speaking Scientists and Scholars after 1933* (Cambridge: Cambridge University Press, 1996). Also see *Intellectual Migration and Cultural Transformation: Refugees from National Socialism in the English-Speaking World,* ed. Edward Timms and Jon Hughes (Vienna and New York: Springer-Verlag, 2003). However, note the paradoxical parallel to the claims of figures such as Schmitt, Heidegger, and Ernst Junger who, after lending their support to the Nazi regime in its early years, eventually claimed to have resorted to "internal migration" themselves. See for example Schmitt's post–World War II claims in *Ex Captivitate Salus. Erfahrungen der Zeit 1945–1947* that his book on the *Leviathan* (1938) and Ernst Jünger's novel *On the Marble Cliffs* (1939) were both veiled criticisms of the Nazis. Sympathetic treatments of figures in Nazi Germany, or in any totalitarian context, usually exonerate figures who made various accommodations to the new regime, whether on an elite level or that of everyday life, by employing some strain of this argument.

108. Scholem and Strauss would later debate the merits of Jewish mysticism versus Jewish philosophy. See for example Scholem's famous polemic against medieval Jewish philosophy in his *Major Trends in Jewish Mysticism,* where Scholem depicts the medieval Jewish philosopher, after the mold of Maimonides, as a destructive or at least acidic force in Jewish life. For Scholem, the philosopher can only carry through his felicitous tasks "after having successfully converted the concrete realities of Judaism into a bundle of abstractions. The individual phenomenon is to him no object of his philosophical speculation. By contrast the mystic refrains from destroying the living texture of religious narrative by allegorizing it." In contrast to the allegorical mode of philosophy, Scholem emphasizes the strictly "symbolical" mode of the kabbalah; *Major Trends in Jewish Mysticism* (New York: Schocken, 1946), 26. Strauss's response to this text can be seen in "How

to Begin the Study of Medieval Philosophy," published in *The Rebirth of Classical Political Rationalism: An Introduction to the Thought of Leo Strauss,* ed. Thomas L. Pangle (Chicago: University of Chicago Press, 1989).

109. "SRPS," 21.

110. In addition to Abraham Heschel's *Don Jizchak Abravanel* (Berlin, 1937), a special "Gedenkausstellung" was held in the Jewish Museum in Berlin. All of this attention, plus Valeriu Marcu's *The Expulsion of the Jews from Spain* (1934) provides some of the background to Carl Schmitt's engagement with Abravanel in his 1938 book on the *Leviathan* (*LSTH*) and again in the conclusion of his brilliant tract on the profound implications of challenges of modern naval power. *Land und Meer, eine Weltgeschichtliche Betreachtung* (Leipzig: Philipp Reclam, 1942). See Raphale Gross, *Carl Schmittt und die Juden—Eine deutsche Rechtslehre* (Frankfurt am Main, Suhrkamp, 2000), 276–77.

111. "SRPS," 21. Strauss points to *Guide* I:17 as a source text, but also adds a citation from *PL,* 133 n. 71, wherein Avicenna makes a similar remark.

112. See Peter M. Rutkoff and William B. Scott, *New School: A History of the New School for Social Research* (New York: Free Press, 1986).

## Chapter 4. Persecution and the Art of Writing: The New York Years (1938–1948) (pp. 81–117)

1. Strauss and his wife Miriam (Mirjam) were separated for long periods during 1936–38 when Strauss was searching for an appointment in the United States. I was not granted access to this part of Strauss's correspondence. They are held in the Leo Strauss Papers, box 4, folders 18–26, and box 5, folders 1–4.

2. Data published by *Reichsvertretung der Juden in Deuthschland* (October 1939 to September 1944) and reprinted in Helmut Genschel, *Verdraengung der Juden aus der Wirtschaft im Dritten Reich* (Ph.D. diss., University of Göttingen: 1966), 274–91. Out of an estimated 500,000 émigrés from Germany, some 270,000 to 300,000 were Jewish. See Herbert A. Strauss, *Jewish Immigrants of the Nazi Period in the USA; Essays on the History of, Persecution, and Emigration of German Jews* (New York: K. G. Saur, 1987), 6:151–52.

3. The correspondence between Strauss and his family in Kirchhain, Germany, during 1932–41 is held in the Strauss Papers in box 5. Here too, I was not granted access.

4. Kraus received his doctorate in semitics at the University of Berlin in 1929. He remained in Berlin as an assistant at the Berlin Forschungsinstitut für der Geschichte der Naturwissenschaften (later incorporated with the Institut für Geschichte der Medizen und der Naturwissenschaften as part of the University of Berlin). See Joel L. Kramer's illuminating biographical essay on Kraus, "The Death of an Orientalist: Paul Kraus from Prague to Cairo," in *The Jewish Discovery of Islam: Studies in Honor of Bernard Lewis,* ed. Martin Kramer (Tel Aviv: Moshe Dayan Center for the Middle Eastern and African Studies, Tel Aviv University, 1999), 181–223.

5. See Rémi Brague, "Paul Kraus: Person und Werk," in his edited volume of Kraus's writings, *Alchemie, Ketzerei, Apokryphen im fruehen Islam. Gesammelte Aufsaetze,* ed. Rémi Brague (Hildesheim: G. Olms, 1994). Strauss was under the impression that Kraus's death was not a suicide. Well into the following decades, he remained convinced

that Kraus was killed. See Strauss Papers, box 5, folders 15–17, for the correspondence concerning Kraus's death. Joel Kramer has explored and evaluated the events surrounding Kraus's tragic death in his "Death of an Orientalist," esp. 202–5.

6. Strauss Papers, box 5, folders 12–21, contain letters making arrangements for Jenny to come to the United States to live with Strauss. See his letter to Scholem dated June 1, 1958, in which he claims to have acquired evidence of foul play and a cover-up.

7. Strauss to Löwith, dated January 10, 1946. This letter was published in German accompanied by an English translation as "Correspondence Concerning Modernity" in the *Independent Journal of Philosophy* 4 (1983): 105. I have slightly altered the English translation.

8. Ibid.

9. The ambiguous use of this word is reflected in the title of a recent idiosyncratic intellectual biography written by Heinrich Meier, *Die Denkbewegung von Leo Strauss: Die Geschichte der Philosophie und die Intention des Philosophen* (Weimar: J. B. Metzler, 1996).

10. See Guy Stern, "In the Service of American Intelligence: German-Jewish Exiles in the War against Hitler," *LBIYB* 38 (1992): 461–77.

11. Barry M. Katz, "The Criticism of Arms: The Frankfurt School Goes at War," *Journal of Modern History* 59 (1987): 439–75. See also Robin W. Winks, *Cloak and Gown, 1939–1961: Scholars in the Secret War* (New York: Morrows, 1987), 85.

12. This context gave rise to the designation "the New York intellectuals." Terry A. Cooney summarized the *Partisan Review* circle's commitment to this cosmopolitan ideal as follows: "Cosmopolitan values demanded a resistance to particularisms of nationality, race, religion, or philosophy, and they celebrated richness, complexity, and diversity. Central to the ideal was a spirit of openness and striving—openness to variety and to change; striving for a fuller understanding of the world and for higher and more inclusive means of expression." *The Rise of the New York Intellectuals: Partisan Review and Its Circle* (Madison: University of Wisconsin Press, 1986), 5. But the transition of the New York intellectuals from self-conscious radicalism to cold war liberalism explains interesting points of overlap; ibid., 251–72.

13. George Mosse, *German Jews Beyond Judaism* (Bloomington: Indiana University Press; Cincinnati, Ohio: Hebrew Union College Press, 1985).

14. Steven Aschheim, "German Jews Beyond *Bildung* and Liberalism," in *Culture and Catastrophe: German and Jewish Confrontations of National Socialism and Other Crises* (New York: New York University Press, 1997), 31–44.

15. For treatments of the "elective affinities" of radicalized central European Jewish intellectuals, see Michael Löwy, *Redemption and Utopia: Jewish Libertarian Thought in Central Europe: A Study in Elective Affinity*, trans. Hope Heaney (Stanford, Calif.: Stanford University Press, 1992); and his *George Lukács: From Romanticism to Bolshevism*, trans. Patrick Camiller (London: New Left Books, 1979). See also Anson Rabinbach's "Between Enlightenment and Apocalypse: Benjamin, Bloch and Modern German Jewish Messianism." *New German Critique* 35 (1985): 78–124; and his introduction to *The Correspondence of Walter Benjamin and Gershom Scholem, 1932–1940*, ed. Gershom Scholem (New York: Schocken Books, 1989).

16. Cf. Yuri Slezkine, *The Jewish Century* (Princeton: Princeton University Press, 2004).

17. "ZN," in *GS*, 2:318; see chap. 2.

18. See Doron Niederland, "The Emigration of Jewish Academics and Professionals

from Germany in the First Years of Nazi Rule," *LBIYB* 33 (1988): 285–300. See also his *Defuse hagirah shel Yehude Germanyah, 1918–1938* (Ph.D. diss., Hebrew University, 1988).

19. On the creation of the position of high commissioner for refugees, see Michael R. Marrus, *The Unwanted: European Refugees in the Twentieth Century* (Oxford University Press: New York, 1985), 158–66.

20. See Herbert A. Strauss, ed., *Jewish Immigrants of the Nazi Period in the USA*, vol. 4, *Jewish Emigration from Germany, 1933–1942* (Munich: K. G. Saur, 1992), 289–315.

21. HICEM is an acronym taken from the initials of the three organizations that founded it in 1927: HIAS (Hebrew Sheltering and Immigrant Aid Society); JCA (Jewish Colonization Association); and the United Committee for Jewish Emigration (Emigdirect). The last group withdrew its involvement in 1934. From 1933 to 1936, HICEM helped more than fourteen thousand refugees to emigrate. After receiving a larger budget and joining with other groups such as the Hilfsverein der Juden in Deutschland and the British Council for German Jewry, HICEM helped to resettle some eighteen thousand additional refugees. See Marrus, *The Unwanted*, 67–68; see also the entry "HICEM" in *The Universal Jewish Encyclopedia*, ed. Isaac Landman (New York: Universal Jewish Encyclopedia, 1941), 5:356–57.

22. Claus-Dieter Krohn, *Intellectuals in Exile: Refugee Scholars and the New School for Social Research*, trans. Rita Kimber and Robert Kimber, with a foreword by Arthur J. Vidich (Amherst: University of Massachusetts Press, 1993), 29.

23. The London-based AAC helped directly or indirectly in placing 173 German-Jewish academics at English universities. In addition, AAC provided fares to Strauss and other refugee scholars for visits to American colleges and universities.

24. See Joachim Radkau, *Die Duetsche Emigration in den USA* (Düsseldorf: Bertelsmann Universitätsverlag, 1971).

25. For the particular success of placements at Ankara and Istanbul, see Horst Widman, *Exil und Bildungshilfe: Die deutsch-sprachige akademische Emigration in der Tuerkei nach 1933* (Bern: Herbert Lang; Frankfurt: Peter Lang, 1977). For immigration to Central and South America, see Herbert A. Strauss, *Jewish Immigrants of the Nazi Period*, 6:210–27; for the *Notgememeinschaft Deutscher wissencahftler im Ausland*, see 354.

26. For an intimate portrayal of Cassirer's history with the Warburg Institute, see Toni Bondy Cassirer, *Aus meinem Leben mit Ernst Cassirer* (Hildesheim: Gerstenberg, 1981). See also Martin Jesinghausen-Lauster, *Die Suche nach der symbolischen Form: der Kreis um die kulturwissenschaftliche Bibliothek Warburg* (Baden-Baden: V. Körner, 1985). For an institutional history of the German Warburg Institute, see Carl Hollis Landauer, *The Survival of Antiquity: The German Years of The Warburg Institute* (Ph.D. diss., Yale University, 1984).

27. See Löwith's posthumously published wartime autobiographical reflections, *Mein Leben in Deutschland vor und nach 1933* (Stuttgart: J. B. Metzler and Carl Ernst Pöschel, 1986). The "report" was translated into English by Elizabeth King under the title *My Life in Germany Before and After 1933* (Champaign: University of Illinois Press, 1994).

28. Löwith concluded a 1959 addendum to *My Life in Germany Before and After 1933*, "Curriculum Vitae," by reflecting upon the former and present members of the Heidelberg academy, which included Husserl, Jaspers, and Heidegger. "But, to be sure, those who mention these names and know their works will recall the verses from an ode by Horace in the light of their writings: Viler than grandsires, sires beget / Ourselves, yet

baser, soon to curse / The World with offspring baser yet. But we may console ourselves for this progressive decline with Kant by making the point that this 'now' or recent times, in which the demise of the world seemed to be nigh, is as old as history itself" (168).

29. Anne Klein's essay on Varian Fry's heroic rescue efforts provides a lucid contextual account of the difficult and urgent situation. See her "Conscience, Conflict and Politics. The Rescue of Political Refugees from Southern France to the United States, 1940–42," *LBIYB* 43 (1998): 287–311.

30. Bloch was a French Jew who taught history at the Sorbonne and cofounded as well as coedited (in 1929) the leading historical journal, the *Annales d'histoire économique et sociale*. Alvin Johnson had procured official transit documents and visas for Bloch and other members of his family so that they could come to New York. In the face of new policies that came into effect in June 1941, however, Bloch grew discouraged and decided to remain in France, joining the Resistance. Just weeks before the U.S. invasion of Normandy, in the early summer of 1941, the Gestapo captured and killed Bloch. See Carol Fink's *Marc Bloch: A Life in History* (New York: Cambridge University Press, 1989); and Ulrich Raulff, *Ein Historiker im 20. Jahrhundert: Marc Bloch* (Frankfurt am Main: S. Fischer, 1995).

31. See *The Correspondence of Walter Benjamin and Gershom Scholem, 1932–1940*, ed. Gershom Scholem, trans. Gary Smith and André Lefevere from the German volume, *Walter Benjamin/Gershom Scholem Briefwechsel, 1932–1940;* (New York: Schocken Books, 1989), 24, 156, 160, 179, 181.

32. See Anne Klein, "Conscience, Conflict and Politics."

33. See the letter from Frau Furland, one of Benjamin's companions, to Adorno, quoted in Frederic V. Grunfeld, *Prophets Without Honour: A Background to Freud, Kafka, Einstein, and Their World* (New York: Holt, Rinehart and Winston, 1979), 247–49.

34. See Krohn, *Intellectuals in Exile*, 59–61.

35. Prime examples included the Institute for Advanced Study at Princeton, Black Mountain College in North Carolina, Roosevelt University in Chicago, and of course, the Institute of Social Research, which left Frankfurt and then moved its center to Switzerland, France, and the United States (affiliated with Columbia University). Smaller institutions devoted to Jewish studies—such as the Hebrew College in Baltimore, the Hebrew College in Cleveland, Hebrew Union College in Cincinnati, the Jewish Institute of Religion in New York, the College of Jewish Studies in Chicago, Jewish Theological Seminary in New York, Graetz College, and Dropsie College—collectively absorbed several Jewish refugees in various disciplines associated with Jewish studies as well.

36. See Peter M. Rutkoff and William B. Scott, *New School: A History of the New School for Social Research* (New York: Free Press, 1986), 65–67, 80–82, and 87–90.

37. Ibid.

38. The *Institut für Sozialforschung* was originally conceived by Felix Weil in the fall of 1919 and established in 1923 as an affiliated institution of the University of Frankfurt am Main. Max Horkheimer became the director of the institute in 1931 after its first director, Carl Grunberg, retired. See the pamphlet *International Institute of Social Research. A Report on its History, Aims and Activities* (New York: Institute for Social Research, 1938). Also see Martin Jay, *The Dialectical Imagination: A History of the Frankfurt School and the Institute of Social Research, 1923–1950* (Boston: Little, Brown, 1973). Rolf Wiggershaus, *Die Frankfurter Schule: Geschichte, theoretische Entwicklung, politische Bedeu-*

*tung* (Munich: C. Hanser, 1986). Ulrike Migdal, *Die Frühgeschichte des Frankfurter Instituts für Sozialforschung* (Frankfurt: Campus Verlag, 1981).

39. For the various historical debates on these issues, see Krohn, *Intellectuals in Exile*, 189–97; Jay, *Dialectical Imagination*, 253–64; Lewis A. Coser, *Refugee Scholars in America: Their Impact and Their Experiences* (New Haven: Yale University Press, 1984), 84ff.

40. See Krohn, *Intellectuals in Exile*.

41. Rutkoff and Scott, *New School*, 91–103.

42. Ibid.

43. Krohn, *Intellectuals in Exile*, 79.

44. See chapter 3.

45. Krohn, *Intellectuals in Exile*, 85–86.

46. Ibid., 61–69.

47. Speier met Strauss in 1929. Speier's Jewish wife, Lisa, and Strauss's wife, Miriam, had been classmates and childhood friends in Erfurt. Speier had emigrated in 1933 after both he and his wife, who was a doctor, had lost their positions in Berlin. He was one of the first members recruited for the University in Exile. See Speier's introduction in *The Truth in Hell and Other Essays on Politics and Culture, 1935–1987* (New York: Oxford University Press, 1989), 9.

48. Rutkoff and Scott, *New School*, 104–5. From 1933 to 1937, the General Seminar consisted of twelve participants. After 1938, the number of participants hovered between eighteen and twenty-four.

49. For the ISR's ideal of research and presentation, see Martin Jay, "The Institute of Social Research between Frankfurt and New York," in his *Force Fields: Between Intellectual History and Cultural Critique* (New York: Routledge, 1993), 14–15.

50. Alvin Johnson, foreword to *War in Our Time*, ed. Hans Speier and Alfred Kaehler (New York: Norton, 1939), 9.

51. Cf. the inaugural issue of *Social Research*, which featured articles by Thomas Mann, Charles Beard, and so forth, decrying the current persecution of free thought and dissent in Europe.

52. For a contextual treatment of Central European Jewish homosocial intellectual circles in the 1930s, I have benefitted from reading Steven Wasserstrom's insightful yet to be published article, "Concubines and Puppies: Philologies of Esotericism in Jerusalem Between the World Wars." For a treatment of "young puppies" in Platonic scholarship, see Arlene W. Saxonhouse, "Comedy in Callipolis: Animal Imagery in the Republic," *American Political Science Review* 72, no. 3 (September 1978): 888–901.

53. Leo Strauss, "On a New Interpretation of Plato's Political Philosophy," *Social Research* 13, no. 3 (September 1946): 326–67. The book reviewed is John Wild, *Plato's Theory of Man: An Introduction to the Realistic Philosophy of Culture* (Cambridge, Mass.: Harvard University Press, 1946). Strauss's critical review notwithstanding, Wild's book has been reissued four times since its original publication.

54. Letter from Strauss to Löwith, January 10, 1946, published as "Correspondence Concerning Modernity," in *Independent Journal of Philosophy* 4 (1983): 108.

55. Leo Strauss, "Review of R. H. S. Crossman, *Plato Today*," *Social Research* 8 (May 1941): 251 n. 2.

56. See, for example, Strauss's letter to Löwith, dated August 20, 1946, "CCM," 111.

57. Leo Strauss, "The Spirit of Sparta; or, A Taste of Xenophon," *Social Research* 6, no. 4 (November 1939), 502–536.

58. "SSTX," 530. Strauss joined Xenophon's opposition to the public spirit of politics, which he viewed as Sparta. Thus, Strauss's reservations regarding the effects of political Zionism's wish to emulate Spartan politics in 1923 have become definitive.

59. Strauss awkwardly defines *sophrosynê* as bashfulness in this essay. Perhaps because from the viewpoint of public virtue, philosophical speculation that is tempered by moderation or prudence (typical definitions of *sophrosynê*) is perceived as bashful.

60. See Gerald Proietti, *Xenophon's Sparta: An Introduction* (Leiden: E. J. Brill, 1987). Proietti observed how Strauss's 1939 essay draws out Xenophon's "wry manner of referring quietly to the notoriously loose morals of the Spartan women in regard to sex and wine, the absence of any education of the women's souls, and the lack of a true education of the soul also for the Spartan boys and men." Proietti praises Strauss's exegetical subtlety in capturing Xenophon's ironic text: "Where Xenophon seems to be praising Spartan virtues, Strauss demonstrated his veiled criticisms of the superficial character of those virtues: instead of being educated in justice, wisdom, and true moderation, the Spartan citizens were trained in fearful and arbitrary obedience, shame, hypocrisy, and mere continence" (xv–xvii).

61. "SSTX," 530.

62. Ibid., 503.

63. Ibid.

64. Cf. Strauss's discussion of chapter heads in "The Literary Guide of the Guide for the Perplexed," in his *Persecution and the Art of Writing* (Glencoe, Ill.: Free Press, 1952), 77–78.

65. "Xenophon non excidit mihi, sed inter philosophos reddendus est"; Quintilian, *Institiones Oratoria* X, i, lines 74–75.

66. Quintilian treats historians in this section, but further on praises Xenophon as an Attic Orator, or in other words, a Greek philosopher; Ibid., X, i, lines 82–83.

67. Strauss, "Farabi's Plato," *Louis Ginzberg Jubilee Volume,* ed. Saul Liberman, Shalom Spiegel, Solomon Zeitlin, and Alexander Marx (New York: American Academy for Jewish Research, 1945), 375.

68. "SSTX," 535.

69. Strauss employs this phrase in a later article responding to criticisms of "Persecution and the Art of Writing." Reprinted in Leo Strauss, *What Is Political Philosophy?* (Chicago: University of Chicago Press, 1988), 221–32.

70. "SSTX," 534.

71. Ibid., 534.

72. Ibid., 535.

73. This phrase is used by Strauss in his prefaces to *SCR,* 26.

74. See Strauss's Weimar essays (*GS,* 2:333–38, 341–50, 365–76), "Soziogologische Geschichtschreibung?" (1924), "Zur Auseinandersetzung mit der europäischen Wissenschaft" (1924), and esp. "Der Konspektivismus" (1929), his direct comment upon Mannheim's sociology of knowledge.

75. See the introduction to Strauss, *Persecution and the Art of Writing.*

76. Rutkoff and Scott, *New School,* 137–43.

77. For a synoptic analysis of these studies, see Martin Jay, "The Institute's Analysis of Nazism," in *The Dialectical Imagination: A History of the Frankfurt School and the Institute of Social Research, 1923–1950* (Berkeley and Los Angeles: University of California

Press, 1973), 143–72. See, for example, Franz Neumann's *Behemoth: The Structure and Practice of National Socialism* (New York: Oxford University Press, 1942); Arkadij Gurland, Otto Kirchheimer, and Franz Neumann, *The Fate of Small Business in Nazi Germany* (Washington, D.C.: U.S. Government Printing Office, 1943). Theodor Adorno and Max Horkheimer, *Dialektik der Aufklärung: philosophische Fragmente* (Amsterdam: Querido, 1944); Otto Kirchheimer, "The Legal Order of National Socialism," *Studies in Philosophy and Social Science* 9 (1941): 456–475.

78. The 1934 inaugural issue of *Social Research* featured an article by a student of Benedetto Croce, Giuseppe Antonio Borgese's "The Intellectual Origins of Fascism"; and Paul Tillich's "The Totalitarian State and Claims of the Church," which grew out of General Seminar research projects. See *Social Research* 1 (1934): 405ff. and 475ff. Some of the works that emerged from these studies include Max Ascoli and Arthur Feiler, *Fascism for Whom?* (New York: Norton, 1938); Eduard Heinemann, *Communism, Fascism, or Democracy?* (New York: Norton, 1938); Adolph Löwe's pamphlet, *Price of Liberty* (London: L. and Virginia Woolf at the Hogarth Press, 1937). This pamphlet was originally written as a private letter to Paul Tillich and translated by Elsa Sinclair, the translator for Strauss's *The Political Philosophy of Thomas Hobbes* (*PPH*).

79. Leo Strauss, "German Nihilism." The lecture was to be delivered on February 26, 1941; I have found no records that confirm the paper was actually delivered. The lecture has recently appeared with careful editorial notes in *Interpretation* 26, no. 3 (Spring 1999): 353–78. The original manuscript can be found in the Leo Strauss Papers, box 8, folder 15.

80. Hermann Rauschning, *Die Revolution des Nihilismus; Kulisse und Wirklichkeit im dritten Reich* (Zurich: Europa Verlag, 1938). It appeared in an abridged version under the English title *The Revolution of Nihilism: Warning to the West*. Translated by E. W. Dickes (London: Alliance Book Corporation; Longmans, Green [c1939]). The English edition went through three printings in August 1939. See the opening comments by Golo Mann, editor, in the German edition (Zurich: Europa Verlag, 1964).

81. See the opening to the 1938 German edition of *Die Revolution des Nihilismus* entitled "Nationale Kritik" (5–13), where Rauchning describes how he was brought to National Socialism from the best of nationalist motives, only to be led astray.

82. Leo Strauss, "German Nihilism," 360.

83. See chapter 3.

84. The revitalization of German Jewry was seen by leading figures of Strauss's generation as being dependent on a break from the liberal aspirations that had been the hallmark of Germany's Jewish *Bildungsbürgertum*. Strauss's involvement with the German Zionist youth movement, Jewish fraternities, and other university organizations, as well as Franz Rosenzweig's Frankfurt *Lehrhaus*, reflect the specifically Jewish manifestation of the larger charged context of Weimar.

85. See, for example, Strauss, "German Nihilism," 369. Strauss quotes the passage that extols the dignity of the soldier who has been ennobled by the purifying experience of war. "What kind of minds are those who do not even know this much that no mind *can* be more profound and more knowing than that of *any* soldier who fell anywhere at the Somme or in Flanders? *This* is the standard of which we are in need." Ernst Jünger, *Der Arbeiter: Herrschaft und Gestalt* (Hamburg: Hanseatische Verlaganstalt, 1932), 201; Jünger, *Werke* (1963), 6:221.

86. See *Social Research* 8, no. 4 (November 1941): 513.

87. I am referring to his preface to *Spinoza's Critique of Religion* (written in 1962, published in 1964) and his joint lecture with Jacob Klein at St. John's, "A Giving of Accounts."

88. Strauss, "German Nihilism," 362.

89. Carl Schmitt's "decisionism" was treated in chapters 2 and 3.

90. Strauss, "German Nihilism," 362–63.

91. For a discussion of "noble youths" in Athenian society and thought during the 420s and 430s, see L. B. Carter, *The Quiet Athenian* (Oxford: Clarendon Press, 1986), 52ff. Carter discusses the theme of noble youths in the works of Plato, Thucydides, Xenophon, and Aristophanes, and lists the possible characteristics that are attributed to them during the 420s: rich young men, Spartan sympathies, and the homosexual atmosphere of the gymnasium.

92. All citations to this text refer to its posthumous publication as "Exoteric Teaching," diligently edited by Kenneth Hart Green in *Interpretation* 14, no. 1 (Jan. 1986): 51–59. This is taken from the final version that is in the Leo Strauss Papers, box 9, folder 18; a previous draft is in box 12, folder 2.

93. The three texts Strauss cites are "Leibniz von den ewigen Strafen" (1773), "Des Andreas Wissowatius Einwürfe wider die Dreieingkeit" (1773), and most significant, "Ernst und Falk" (1777 and 1780).

94. Strauss, "Exoteric Teaching," 52.

95. All quotations from "Persecution and the Art of Writing" are taken from its reprinted version that appeared in *Persecution and the Art of Writing* (Chicago: University of Chicago Press, 1952), 22. The original essay appeared in *Social Research* (November 1941), 488–504.

96. Thoughts (or opinions) and actions become a primary interpretive key to Strauss's understanding of several premodern writers. In the collection of essays in *Persecution and the Art of Writing,* see for example, "The Literary Character of the *Guide for the Perplexed,*" 77, n. 112, and 86–87. See Michael S. Kochin, "Morality, Nature, and Esotericism in Leo Strauss's 'Persecution and the Art of Writing,'" *Review of Politics* 64, no. 2 (Spring 2002): 261–83. Also see Steven B. Smith, "Leo Strauss's Platonic Liberalism," *Political Theory* 28, no. 6 (December 2000): 787–809.

97. Following "Scribere est agere," Strauss cites Sir William Blackstone, *Commentaries on the Laws of England,* 15th ed. (London: The Strand, 1809), book IV, chap. 6. The principle in question is explicitly raised on p. 81, while the more general discussion occurs on pp. 74–92.

98. Strauss also refers to Machiavelli's *Discourses,* III, 6 (I Classici del Giglio, 424–26). The chapter bears the title "Of Conspiracies."

99. Georges Van Den Abbeele offers a provocative and critical treatment of Strauss's view. Abbeele compares Descartes's stand against censorship to what he sees as Strauss's blasé attitude toward basic human freedoms. Notwithstanding the intricate dynamics of Straussian "exoteric writing," Abbeele comments on the moral deficiency of such a view: "What is lost in all this . . . is any strong sense of the scandal of censorship, that is, of the outrage it constitutes even as it is constitutive of the subjectivity who feels so wronged by it." Georges Van Den Abbeele, "The Persecution of Writing: Revisiting Strauss and Censorship," *Diacritics* 27, no. 2 (Summer 1997): 15.

100. On Lecky, see Benjamin Evans Lippincott, *Victorian Critics of Democracy: Carlyle, Ruskin, Arnold, Stephen, Maine, Lecky* (London: Oxford University Press; Minneapolis:

University of Minnesota Press, 1938); and the more recent biographical sketches offered by Donald McCartney, *W.E.H. Lecky, Historian and Politician* (Dublin: Lilliput, 1994) and Benedikt Stuchtey, *W.E.H. Lecky (1838–1903): historisches Denken und politisches Urteilen eines anglo-irischen Gelehrten* (Göttingen: Vandenhœck & Ruprecht, 1997).

101. Strauss, "Persecution and the Art of Writing," 23.

102. See Ernst Kris and Hans Speier, *German Radio Propaganda: Report on Home Broadcasts During the War* (London: Oxford University Press, 1944).

103. Strauss plays on the phrase "horse-drawn logic"; "Persecution and the Art of Writing," 23.

104. Ibid., 23.

105. Ibid., 24.

106. For an example of this infrequently employed paradoxical phrase, see "SSTX," 525ff.

107. Strauss employs this metaphor throughout the essays included in *Persecution and the Art of Writing*.

108. Ibid., 30.

109. Ibid., 30 and 36.

110. "Exoteric Teaching," 23.

111. See Strauss, "Literary Character of the *Guide for the Perplexed*," 38–94.

112. "The Law of Reason in the Kuzari," in *Persecution and the Art of Writing*, 108.

113. Ibid., 109.

114. Cf. Strauss's interpretation of Plato's *Republic*, which in part turns on the possibility that Socrates never successfully demonstrated that Thrasymachus was wrong. Thrasymachus of course figures as an ancient precursor to Machiavelli and Nietzsche: that might makes right. See Leo Strauss, *City and Man* (Chicago: Rand McNally, 1964.)

115. The sources Strauss cites for this argument are: Francis Bacon, *Novum Oragnum*, I, 122; Descartes, *Discours de la méthode*, I; Hobbes, *Leviathan*, book I, chaps. 13 and 15, and *Elements of Law*, I, chap. 10, sec. 8; Kant, *Zum ewigen Frieden*, *Zusatz* part 2; Hegel, *Phänomologie des Geistes*, *Vorrede*, ed. George Lasson, 2nd ed. (Leipzig: F. Meiner, 1921, p. 10); and *Rechtsphilosophie*, *Vorrede* (ed. Edvard Gans, 3rd ed., p. 13).

116. Leo Strauss, "On a New Interpretation of Plato's Political Philosophy," 360.

117. Strauss to Löwith, January 10, 1946, "CCM," 107.

118. Strauss added the following note here: "But we live precisely today in the extremely unfavorable situation: the situation between Alexander the Great and the Italian city-states of the thirteenth to fifteenth centuries was considerably favorable."

119. Horace, *Epistulae*, I, x, 24. Strauss quotes the Latin in the original letter. "Naturam furca expelles, tamen usque recurret." See Strauss's later deployment of this quote in the concluding part of *Natural Right and History*: "The modern contention that man can 'change the world' or 'push back nature' is not unreasonable. One can even safely go much beyond it and say that man can expel nature with a hayfork. One ceases to be reasonable only if one forgets what the philosophic poet adds, *tamen usque recurret*." *Natural Right and History* (Chicago: University of Chicago Press, 1968), 201–2. Cf Nietzsche's use of the quote in *Beyond Good and Evil*, sec. 264.

120. Strauss to Löwith, January 10, 1946, "CCM," 107–8.

121. Strauss to Löwith, August 20, 1946, "CCM," 113. Strauss's well-known political Platonism accompanies references to Aristotle's discussion in the *Politics* of the ideal po-

litical order. And Strauss's conviction that the "natural differences among men" are among the most important truths to acknowledge persists through his mature writings. See, for example, his comment in *Socrates and Aristophanes* (New York: Basic Books, 1966; reprinted, Chicago: University of Chicago Press, 1996), 49.

122. Nietzsche, *The Gay Science,* sec. 14.

123. Nietzsche, *Beyond Good and Evil: Prelude to a Philosophy of the Future,* trans. with an introduction and commentary by R. J. Hollingdale. (New York: Penguin Books, 1987 [1972]). Part III, "The Religious Nature," aphorism 30, p. 43:

> Our highest insights must—and should!—sound like follies and in some cases like crimes when without permission they come to the ears of those who are not predisposed and predestined for them. The exoteric and the esoteric as philosophers formerly distinguished them, among the Indians as among the Greeks, Persians, and Moslems, in short wherever one believed in an order of rank and *not* in equality and equal rights—differ from one another not so much in that the exoteric stands outside, and sees, evaluates, measures, judges from the outside, not the inside: what is more essential is that it sees things from below—but the esoteric sees them *from above!* There are heights of the soul from which even tragedy ceases to be tragic; and, taking all the woe of the world together, who could venture to assert that the sight of it would *have* to seduce and compel us to pity and thus to a doubling of that woe? . . . What serves the higher type of man as food or refreshment must to a very different and inferior type be almost poison. The virtues of the common man would perhaps indicate vice and weakness in a philosopher; it may be possible that if a lofty type of man degenerated and perished, he would only thus acquire qualities on whose account it would prove necessary in the lower world into which he had sunk henceforth to venerate him as a saint. There are books which possess an apposite value for soul and health depending on whether the lower soul, the lower vitality, or the higher and more powerful avails itself of them: in the former case they are dangerous, disintegrative books, which produces dissolution, in the latter they are herald calls challenging the most courageous to *their* courage. Books for everybody are always malodorous books: the smell of pretty people clings to them. Where the people eats and drinks, even where it worships, there is usually a stink. One should not go into churches if one wants to breathe *pure* air.—

124. Strauss, "On a New Interpretation of Plato's Political Philosophy," 361.

125. See, for example, Leo Strauss, review of Karl Löwith's *Von Hegel bis Nietzsche, Social Research* 3 (1941): 514.

126. Strauss, "On a New Interpretation of Plato's Political Philosophy," 357.

127. Strauss took a cue from Paul Kraus in focusing on a nonmystical lineage of philosophical esotericism. See Kraus's analysis of Farabi in his "Plotin chez les Arabes," *Bulletin de l'Institut d'Egypte* 23 (1940–41): 269ff. See Strauss, "The Law of Reason in the *Kuzari,*" 111 n. 46. Cf. Shadia Drury, *Leo Strauss and the American Right* (New York: St. Martin's, 1997), 57–58. Drury claims that the rabbinical and the mystical constitute the "two main currents in the history of Judaism." In so doing, she excludes the philosophic as a main current. Drury relies on David Bakan's *Sigmund Freud and the Jewish Mystical Tradition* (Toronto, Ontario: D. Van Nostrand, 1958) and Gershom Scholem's

seminal works on Jewish mysticism when she posits the tension between the normative and antinomian elements of the rabbinic and mystical currents. She takes Maimonides at his word that he has no intention of violating the rabbinic prohibition against disclosing truths about the account of the beginning and the account of the chariot. Drury states: "Strauss suggests that Maimonides was the first mystic. But how can he be a mystic and an atheist who thinks that he is a god among men and the real lawgiver? The idea seems obscenely narcissistic, but typical of Straussian self-congratulation"; *Leo Strauss and the American Right*, 55–56. For a view that articulates Maimonides's philosophic appropriation of mystical concepts, see Sarah Klein-Braslavy, "King Solomon and Metaphysical Esotericism According to Maimonides," in *Maimonidean Studies* (New York, Yeshiva University Press, 1990), 1:57–86.

128. For examples, James A. Diamond, "'Trial' as Esoteric Preface in Maimonides's *Guide of the Perplexed:* A Case Study in the Interplay of Text and Prooftext," *Journal of Jewish Thought and Philosophy* 7, no. 1 (1997): 1–30. For a treatment of Maimonides's exegetical strategies in his legal works, see Moshe Greenberg, "The Use of Scripture in Classical Medieval Judaism, Prooftexts in Maimonides's *Code*," in *The Return to Scripture in Judaism and Christianity*, ed. P. Ochs (New York: Paulist Press, 1993), 197–232.

129. Strauss refers to Maimonides's "exoteric teaching" in "Der Ort der Vorsehungslehre nach der Ansicht Maimunis" (1937), in *GS*, 2:180, 186–87.

130. Strauss, "Exoteric Teaching," 51–59.

131. *PL*, 68.

132. Strauss, review of Moses Hyamson's edition and translation of *The Mishneh Torah* (1937) appearing in the *Review of Religion* (May 1939).

133. Ibid., 453. Strauss cites *Guide* II, 35; I, introd., compared with *Yesode Latorah* iv, 13.

134. *Sefer hamada* is the first and most philosophic book of the *Mishneh Torah.*

135. Strauss, review of Hyamson, ed., *The Mishneh Torah*, 453–54; transliteration altered.

136. *GS*, 3:549–50.

137. On Freud's motivations for writing *Moses and Monotheism* at a time of crisis, see Peter Schäfer, *Der Triumph der reinen Geistigkeit: Sigmund Freuds Der Mann Moses und die monotheistische Religion* (Berlin: Philo, 2003); Yosef Hayim Yerushalmi, *Freud's Moses: Judaism Terminable and Interminable* (New Haven: Yale University Press, 1991).

138. See section 3 of Strauss, "Literary Character of the *Guide for the Perplexed*" (46f.) on this issue.

139. Ibid., 49.

140. Ibid., 52. Next to "middle course," Strauss adds a footnote to the *Guide*, III, introduction.

141. Ibid., 55.

142. Ibid., 55–56.

143. See, for example, *PG*, 13–14 n. 2; *PL*, 112 n. 2.

144. In a 1944 lecture, "How to Study Medieval Philosophy" (which will be treated below), Strauss described the historicist as "the hostile brother" of the progressivist. One of the mistaken assumptions of progressivism is the belief in the superiority of modern thought to the past. He contrasts the progressivist view to the historicist: "Whereas the progressivist believes that the present is superior to the past, the historicist believes that

all periods are equally 'immediate to God.'" The historicist does not want to judge the past, by assessing the contribution of each period e.g., but to understand and to relate how things have actually been, *wie es eigentlich gewesen ist,* and in particular how the thought of the past has been. The historicist has the intention to understand the thought of the past exactly as it understood itself. But he is constitutionally unable to live up to his intention. For he knows, or rather he assumes, that, generally speaking and other things being equal, the thought of all epochs is equally true, because every philosophy is essentially the expression of the spirit of time" (324).

145. "How to Study Medieval Philosophy," *Interpretation* 23, no. 3 (1996): 322.

146. Strauss probably has Martin Buber in mind as a counterexample.

147. Strauss to Scholem, November 22, 1960; *GS,* 3:741–42.

148. Baer had begun the project in Germany and continued his labors following his immigration to Palestine. In 1936 he completed the German version of *A History of the Jews in Christian Spain,* which he sent to Julius Guttmann. Because of the difficult publishing conditions in Germany, however, Baer redrafted the monograph into Hebrew, *Toldot ha-Yehudim bi-Sefarad ha-Notsrit,* first published in 1945. For a more detailed analysis of the genesis of Baer's work, see David Myers, *Re-Inventing the Jewish Past: European Jewish Intellectuals and the Zionist Return to History* (New York: Oxford University Press, 1995), 109–28.

149. Baer's description of a liberal and assimilated class of Jewish courtiers who did not concern themselves with their fellow Jews reflects Baer's negative understanding of the German-Jewish *Bildungsbürgertum.* A typical description of this group: "Having succumbed—in thought—to convictions so completely antithetical to the faith and traditions of their people, they did not hesitate to trample upon the vital interests of their co-religionists"; *A History of the Jews in Christian Spain,* 1:242.

150. Gershom Scholem, *Major Trends in Jewish Mysticism* (Jerusalem: Schocken, 1941), 7–8.

151. Ibid.

152. For Scholem's earlier position, see Scholem's letter of July 20, 1935, to Chaim Nachman Bialik. The letter was later published in *Ha-Poel Ha-Tzair,* December 12, 1967 (18–19). For a historical account of the letters exchanged between Bialik and Scholem, see David Myers, "From Zion Will Go Forth Torah" (Ph.D. diss., Columbia University, 1991), 304–8.

153. Graetz, for example, argued that Moses de Leon successfully deceived people into believing that the Zohar was attributed to the second-century rabbi Shimon bar Yohai. Heinrich Graetz, *History of the Jews,* ed. and in part trans. Bella Löwy (Philadelphia: Jewish Publication Society, 1894), 3:11–12.

154. Scholem, *Major Trends,* 204.

155. David Biale, "The Demonic in History: Gershom Scholem and the Revision of Jewish Historiography" (Ph.D. diss., University of California, Los Angeles, 1977), 199.

156. See Strauss's letter to Scholem, dated November 21, 1962, where Strauss pushes Scholem on certain continuities between medieval mysticism and philosophy, and especially on the use of pseudepigraphy. "Did not Abulafia say somewhere that the mystics start where the philosophers leave off, which would seem to imply that they cannot start if the philosophers have not laid the foundation?" Strauss presses Scholem to countenance the possibility that Maimonides's "uneasiness" regarding certain questionable teach-

ings and/or texts may in fact point to his own "awareness" that he is innovating. "Does not all pseudepigraphy also presuppose such an awareness?" *GS*, 3:746–47.

157. Scholem, *Major Trends*, 21.

158. Ibid., 205.

159. Strauss quotes this passage from *Major Trends in Jewish Mysticism* in "How to Study Medieval Philosophy," 326.

160. Ibid., 324.

161. Ibid., 325.

162. Ibid.

163. Ibid, 327. Maimonides uses this phrase in his famous parable of the palace in the *Guide*, III, 51 (vol. 2, sec. 51, p. 619 of the Shlomo Pines translation, University of Chicago Press, 1963): "Know, my son, that as long as you are engaged in studying the mathematical sciences and the art of logic, you are one of those who walk around the house searching for its gate, as [the sages], *may their memory be blessed*, have said resorting to a parable: *Ben Zoma is still outside*. If, however, you have understood the natural things, you have entered the habitation and are walking in the antechambers. If, however, you have achieved perfection in the natural things and have understood divine science, you have entered in the ruler's place *into the inner court* and are with him in one habitation. This is the rank of the men of science; they, however, are of different grades of perfection." Cf. on the same page, two paragraphs preceding: "Those who have come up to the habitation and walk around it are the jurists who believe true opinions on the basis of traditional authority and study the law concerning the practices of divine service, but do not engage in speculation concerning the fundamental principles of religion and make no inquiry whatever regarding the rectification of belief." The original source is the *Babylonian Talmud, Hagigah*, 15a.

164. Leo Strauss, *Natural Right and History* (Chicago: University of Chicago Press, 1950), 1.


## Conclusion: Looking Back on Weimar and the Politics of Exile (pp. 118–130)

1. I discovered these notes folded up in an unmarked and unlisted envelope in the National Library of the Hebrew University in Jerusalem in the spring of 1997. Allan Arkush subsequently suggested to me that the notes were most likely related to the memorial ceremony held at the Van Leer Institute in Jerusalem one year after Strauss's death. Based on subsequent conversations with a number of people who were in attendance or who subsequently heard about the ceremony, it seems likely that Scholem's address was based on these notes.

2. See Scholem's account in *The Correspondence of Walter Benjamin and Gershom Scholem, 1932–1940*, trans. Gary Smith and André Lefevere (Cambridge, Mass.: Harvard University Press, 1989), 24.

3. R. Alcalay, *The Complete Hebrew-English Dictionary*, new enlarged ed. (Tel Aviv: Chemed Books / Yehidoth Ahronoth, 1996), 1673, renders the verb *naftal* as "meander." We get a little closer in a second version, *naftulim*, defined as "struggle, wrestlings, contest." In the Hebrew Bible, the word appears in Genesis 30:8 in the name of Naphtali: "And Rachel said: 'Naphtali (*A fateful contest I waged*) with my sister, yes, and I have prevailed.'"

So she named him Naphtali." Substituting "mighty wrestlings" for "a fateful contest" would seem more appropriate here. One editor translates the term in question as "struggle of God": see *Tanakh: A New Translation of the Holy Scriptures According to the Traditional Hebrew Text* (Philadelphia: Jewish Publication Society, 1985), 46, note b. Another form, "Niftalin" (tortuous, perverse, crooked, crafty; struggling, wrestling) gives us the same clues and difficulties. The characteristics of something twisted with which one wrestles and grapples are combined in the famous image of the existential "coil" that appears in *Hamlet*: "To sleep, perchance to dream, ay, there's the rub; For in that sleep of death what dreams may come / When we have *shuffled off this mortal coil* / Must give us pause— there's the respect / That makes calamity of so long life" (act 3, scene 1, lines 65–67; my emphasis). It is only fitting that there is no use of *naftul* in any of the Hebrew translations to *Hamlet* that I have checked. Nevertheless, Shakespeare does bring us closer to Scholem's sense. I thank Katherine Fleming for pointing out this passage to me.

4. Leo Strauss, *Spinoza's Critique of Religion* (New York: Schocken Books, 1965), trans. E. M. Sinclair. Translated from *Die Religionskritik Spinozas als Grundlage seiner Bibelwissenschaft Untersuchungen zu Spinozas Theologisch-Politischem Traktat* (Berlin: Akademie-Verlag, 1930). Note that the version cited contains the original fifty-four paragraphs rather than the shortened forty-two–paragraph posthumous edition. I have no knowledge of why this change occurs.

5. The phenomenon of the modern Jewish intellectual in this context is most adeptly described by Paul Mendes-Flohr as denoting "a cognitive insider who . . . articulates in terms of his society's high culture and cognitive traditions axionormative dissent" and is distinguished by his/her acquisition and devotion to *Bildung*, yet remains defined as an eternal outsider. See Paul Mendes-Flohr, "The Study of the Jewish Intellectual: A Methodological Prolegomena," reprinted in his *Divided Passions: Jewish Intellectuals and the Experience of Modernity* (Detroit: Wayne State University Press, 1991), 37. Also see Michael Löwy, "Jewish Messianism and Libertarian Utopia in Central Europe (1900–1933)," *New German Critique* 20 (1980): 105–15. Löwy argues that early twentieth-century central European radical Jewish intellectuals constitute a sociologically distinct group. While I do have some reservations, Strauss might well fit in this grouping. Strauss was indeed radical, albeit not on the left. While he held strong anti-messianic views, he was a utopian in a certain sense: he believed that Plato's political ideal is the true political order. I shall explore this aspect of Strauss's political beliefs later in this chapter.

6. Preface, 1.

7. Strauss's classic formulation of his "re-discovery" of esoteric writing can be found in "Persecution and the Art of Writing," first published in *Social Research* (November 1941): 488–504; reprinted in *Persecution and the Art of Writing*, new ed. (Chicago: University of Chicago Press, 1980), 25: "Persecution, then, gives rise to a peculiar technique of writing, and therewith to a peculiar type of literature, in which the truth about all crucial things is presented exclusively between the lines. That literature is addressed, not to all readers, but to trustworthy and intelligent readers only. It has all the advantages of private communication without having its greatest disadvantage—that it reaches only the writer's acquaintances. It has all the advantages of public communication without having its greatest disadvantage—capital punishment for the author." With specific reference to Maimonides and his writings on the ideal Jewish Law, see a lecture published in 1937 entitled "On Abravanel's Philosophical Tendency and Political Teach-

ing," in *Isaac Abravanel,* ed. J. B. Trend and H. Loewe (Cambridge: Cambridge University Press, 1937), 99–100. For a view that explicitly rejects the notion that Strauss himself utilized the techniques of esoteric writing, see Joseph Cropsey's article on Leo Strauss in *The International Encyclopedia for the Social Sciences:* "He employed and taught what came to be called 'careful reading,' but he did not use or impart a 'method,' for by the nature of the case there cannot be one; since reticent writing that could be made explicit through the application of rules would be a mere cipher and the interpretation of philosophic texts would be a form of cryptography"; *International Encyclopedia for the Social Sciences,* appendix vol. (1976), 750.

8. Strauss explicitly compares the roles of biblical prophets with Plato and Socrates in "Jerusalem and Athens," the first Frank Cohen Public Lecture in Judaic Affairs, New York, City College, 1967.

9. Leo Strauss, "Why We Remain Jews: Can Faith and History Still Speak to Us?" Lecture at the Hillel Foundation, Chicago, 1962. Recently published in *Leo Strauss: Political Philosopher and Jewish Thinker,* ed. Kenneth L. Deutsch and Walter Nicgorski (Lanham, Md.: Rowman and Littlefield Publishers, 1994); henceforth cited as "JPCM."

10. Throughout the rest of the essay I shall refer to these two main texts simply as the Preface and the Lecture.

11. Note that Strauss had argued four decades earlier that the "essential" condition of the *galut* secured the Jewish people "a maximum possibility for existence by means of a minimum normality." Strauss, "Zionism in Max Nordau" (translation of "Zionismus bei Max Nordau"), in *The Jew: Essays from Martin Buber's Journal* Der Jude, *1916–1928,* ed. Arthur A. Cohen, trans. Joachim Neugroschel (Tuscaloosa: University of Alabama Press), 124.

12. *Hannah Arendt–Karl Jaspers Correspondence, 1926–1969,* ed. Lotte Kohler and Hans Saner, trans. Robert Kimber and Rita Kimber (New York: Harcourt Brace Jovanovich, 1992), letter 156 (May 14, 1954), 241.

13. Ibid., letter 158 (July 24, 1954), 244; further friction with Strauss is related to "The Eichmann Affair," see ibid., letter 343 (November 24, 1963), 534. See also the plausible, but unsubstantiated account of Strauss's unsuccessful attempt at courting Arendt: Strauss received "a curt rejection" from her at the Prussian State Library. "When she criticized his conservative views and dismissed his suit, he became bitterly angry." The bitterness apparently lasted for decades and intensified when they both taught at the University of Chicago in the 1960s. "Strauss was haunted by the rather cruel way in which Hannah Arendt judged his assessment of National Socialism: she had pointed out the irony of the fact that a political party advocating views Strauss appreciated could have no place for a Jew like him." Elizabth Young-Bruehl, *Hannah Arendt: For Love of the World* (New Haven: Yale University Press, 1982), 98.

14. Kohler and Saner, *Hannah Arendt–Karl Jaspers Correspondence,* letter 159 (August 29, 1954), 247.

15. A view that corroberates a shift in Strauss's adherence to Orthodox beliefs is found in Jacob Klein, "Memorials to Leo Strauss," *St. John's Review* 25, no. 4 (January 1974): 2. Klein says that Strauss was once an Orthodox Jew, but he "later changed his religious orientation radically, tying the question of god or of gods to his political reasoning, without letting his own life be dependent on any divinity or on any religious rites."

16. *The Correspondence of Walter Benjamin and Gershom Scholem,* letter 72, 155–58.

17. Preface, 1.

18. May 29, 1962 letter to Kojève, in *On Tyranny,* rev. and enlarged ed., ed. Victor Gourevitch and Michael S. Roth (New York: Free Press, 1991), 309.

19. Gershom Scholem, November 28, 1962, letter to Strauss. Quoted in Kenneth Hart Green, *Jew and Philosopher: The Return to Maimonides in the Jewish Thought of Leo Strauss* (Albany: SUNY Press, 1993); 62 n. 7.

20. Strauss, December 6, 1962, letter to Scholem, ibid.

21. Strauss, May 29, 1962, letter to Kojève in *On Tyranny,* 309; my emphasis.

22. See Strauss's letter to Scholem dated December 15, 1963, typed on University of Chicago letterhead (corrections on manuscript), Gershom Scholem Archive no. 15991 at the National Library in Jerusalem: "But let me say a few words about your *sitra achra,* your admiration for Buber. I have not overlooked the qualifications but it is still too much for me. I always loathed him and I still loathe him. I always sensed the absence of the genuine. . . . The utmost I might be willing to grant is that he is a first-rate perfumer [*sic*]. His absolute indifference to historical truth is perhaps the clearest symptom of his lack of intellectual honesty which shows itself in his uncontrollable drive for acclaim and his showmanship. If I am not altogether mistaken he is a good example of what my teachers called 'priestcraft' for they meant of course that this kind of deceiver is also deceived." *Sitra achra* (literally, other side) in kabbalistic texts refers to the devil. Strauss implies that Scholem's restrained criticisms of Buber issues from Scholem's hidden affection and/or appreciation for him.

23. The original Schocken edition of *Spinoza's Critique of Religion* included both an impressive and helpful appendix to comparative sources Strauss relied on as well as an English translation of his critique of Schmitt. The review of Schmitt has unfortunately been omitted in the 1997 republication by the University of Chicago Press.

24. "WWRJ," 5. This and all subsequent references to "WWRJ" (unless otherwise noted) refer to its manuscript form.

25. "WWRJ," 6–7.

26. See the Preface, 6; and "WWRJ," 7. Strauss later analyzes in more depth, but in a different tone, the split psyche of the liberal citizen's public and private identities. The alienation of the private identity from a public identity is the inevitable realization of political emancipation in the liberal state. See Karl Marx, "On the Jewish Question," in *The Marx-Engels Reader,* 2nd ed., ed. Robert C Tucker (New York: Norton, 1978): "The *decomposition* of man into Jew *and* citizen, Protestant *and* citizen, religious man *and* citizen, is not a deception *against* the political system nor yet an evasion of political emancipation. It is *political emancipation itself, the political* mode of emancipation from religion" (35–36). Strauss does not employ this critique of the schizophrenic liberal against political liberalism as a solution to the Jewish problem explicitly here; later, however, he implicitly picks it up when limiting his focus to German liberal Jewish philosophers (such as Hermann Cohen) who idealize the Jewish tradition to meet the standards of Reason.

27. *SCR,* 3.

28. There is a parallel tension between universalist and particularist impulses in Judaism; ibid., 12–15.

29. Ibid., 3.

30. Ibid.

31. Ibid., 4. It is interesting to note that in the body of the text—especially in light of the recent explosion of historical curiosity in the Heidegger affair—although Heidegger originally spoke of "the inner truth and greatness of National Socialism" in the 1935 Rectoral address at Frieburg, Strauss offers the 1953 date of publication of *Einführung in die Metaphysik* as the proper citation of this utterence because this book consists of a course of lectures given in 1935 that as stated in its preface, had had all "errors . . . removed." Strauss adds in this footnote: "Cf. also the allusion on 36 to a recent 'cleansing' of the German universities." For a more detailed account of the impact and significance of the speech and an account of Heidegger's motivations for lending support to the Nazis, see also, "An Introduction to Heideggerian Existentialism," in Leo Strauss, *The Rebirth of Classical Political Rationalism: An Introduction to the Thought of Leo Strauss: Essays and Lectures,* selected and introd. Thomas L. Pangle (Chicago: University of Chicago Press, 1989), 30–31, 41–42.

32. Strauss, "Comments on *Der Begriff des Politischen* by Carl Schmitt" in *SCR,* 331–51. See specifically his analysis of "pacifist internationalism," 340–43.

33. "WWRJ," 9.

34. *SCR,* 6–7.

35. "WWRJ," 11.

36. *SCR,* 7; my emphasis.

37. Ibid., 4–5.

38. Benedict de Spinoza, *A Theologico-Political Treatise,* trans. R. H. M. Elwes (New York: Dover Publications, 1951), chap. 3: "Of the Vocation of the Hebrews," 56.

39. Preface, 6.

40. Ibid.; my emphasis.

41. Ibid., 16.

42. Ibid., 6.

43. Strauss makes reference to Maimonides, *Mishneh Torah,* H. teshubah VI, 3. Here, he is subtly anticipating his apparent call for a return or "teshuvah" on the model of medieval Jewish philosophy; Preface, 8.

44. Ibid., 7.

45. Ibid.

46. Ibid.; see, for example, p. 30.

47. Ibid., 31.

48. Ibid., 31.

49. "WWRJ," 23–24. Friedrich Nietzsche, Aphorism 205, "Of the People of Israel," in *Daybreak: Thoughts On The Prejudices of Morality,* trans. R. J. Hollingdale, with an introduction by Michael Tanner (New York: Cambridge University Press, 1982), 124–25.

50. "WWRJ," 25.

51. Ibid., 26.

52. Ibid., 27 (my emphasis).

53. Ibid., 28.

54. Ibid., 28–29.

55. The literary scholar Harold Bloom opened his foreword to Yosef H. Yerushalmi's masterpiece *Zakhor: Jewish History and Jewish Memory* by referencing Strauss's Preface. Bloom described Strauss as "a philosopher and Hebraic sage" who "was moved to write his own intellectual elegy for German Jewry." While Bloom's portrayal of Strauss as a

"Hebraic sage" denotes a piety that would have struck Strauss himself as absurdly reverential, Bloom did realize that Strauss's Preface—and particularly his analysis of the Jewish condition of exile—provided profound insight into the dialectics of modern Jewish history and memory. *Zakhor: Jewish History and Jewish Memory,* reissue ed. (Seattle: University of Washington Press, 2005), xiii.

# Index

Abravanel, Don Yitzhak, 66, 79
Academic Assistance Council (AAC), 86
Accommodation to imperfect societies:
and "bashful writing," 92; and historicism, 111; by medieval philosophers,
74–79, 108; and multilevel writing, 55,
76–77, 79, 108, 160n82, 162n107; and
Strauss's career, 79–80, 116–17, 130
Acculturation, 6–7, 52. *See also* Assimilation
Akademie für die Wissenschaft des Judentums, 29, 33–34, 35, 40, 151n142
Albo, Joseph, 33
Alienation: and adoption of atheism, 35; of
Catholics from German liberalism, 36, 57,
63, 141–42n31; of intellectuals from culture, 13, 18, 127; of Jews, 6–7, 9–12, 30,
34–35; of modern humans, 84–85; of
philosophers, 6, 85; Spinoza's, 51, 52; value
for Strauss, 7–8, 19. *See also* Exile *(galut)*
America, 4–5, 7, 79–80, 82
Anarchy and individual use of reason, 66
Ancient philosophers: Aristotle, 36–37,
104–5, 107; vs. modern, 69; and multilevel writing, 92–94, 99; Socrates, 93, 98;
Strauss's return to, 61, 63; truth and
wisdom in, 106; Xenophon, 92–94,
168n60. *See also* Plato
Antisemitism: European reach beyond
Germany, 157n28; German-Jewish
response to, 61–62; at *National Review,*
130; and Nazism, 61–62, 123, 154n8;
and realism for Jews, 43; and Schmitt's
shunning of Strauss, 57, 65–66; and
Stalin, 124–25; in Strauss's childhood
home, 9–12; and Strauss's skepticism on
freedom, 84; and Weimar period, 17;
and Zionism, 42–43

Apologetic thinking, 41–42
Arab philosophers. *See* Islamic philosophers,
medieval
*Der Arbeiter* (Jünger), 97
Arendt, Hannah, 120–21, 177n13
Aristocratic model as best regime, 91, 105
Aristotle, 36–37, 104–5, 107
Aschheim, Stephen, 84
Assimilation: and *galut* consciousness, 19;
impossibility of, 125; as intermediary
step to dominance, 128; and Jewish
identity, 6–7; as response to persecu-
tion, 122–23; Strauss's rejection of,
25, 84; and will to normality, 48, 49;
vs. Zionism, 32–33
Association Universelle pour les Exilés
Allemands, 86
Atheism: and biblical scholarship, 27; and
Enlightenment rationalism, 70, 121;
and Jewish identity, 48; of Maimonides,
109; Nazism as based on, 62; Strauss's,
35, 73–74, 105, 120–21
Authoritarian principles of rulership,
60–61, 63, 91, 105
*Autoemancipation* (Pinsker), 125

Baer, Fritz (Yitzhak), 33, 40, 87, 112–13
Bambach, Charles, 38
Bamberger, Fritz, 40
Barker, Ernest, 74
Baron, Salo, 79, 81
Barth, Karl, 26
"Bashful writing," 92
Behemoth, 65
*Being and Time* (Heidegger), 38, 39
Belief, Jacobi's concept of, 25
Benjamin, Walter, 18–19, 87–88, 141n30

Bernsohn, Marie (Miriam) (wife), 58, 82, 90
*Beyond Good and Evil* (Nietzsche), 105, 172n123
Biale, David, 6, 114
Biblical exegesis: and atheism, 27; Enlightenment rejection of biblical morality, 70; by Spinoza, 40–41, 49, 51; and theocracy as bulwark against secular state, 26; and Torah, 76, 77, 108
"Biblical History and Science" (Strauss), 26
"*Bildung* and No End" (Rosenzweig), 30
*Bildungsbürgertum* model of Weimar Jew, 84
Bivalent texts, 77. *See also* Multilevel writing
Blackstone, William, 100
Blau-Weiss youth movement, 31, 146n91
Bloch, Marc, 87, 166n30
Böckel, Otto, 11–12
*Book of Roots* (Albo), 33
Bourgeois ideal, 18–19, 59, 60
Breuer, Isaac, 48
Britain, Strauss in, 58, 68, 81
Buber, Martin, 28, 178n22
Bush, George W., 2, 133n2

Cambridge University, 74
Capitalism and ideal of civilization, 59, 60
Cassirer, Ernst, 16, 21–22, 25, 27–28, 37, 39–40, 87
Catholics, alienation from German liberalism, 36, 57, 63, 141–42n31
Cave allegory, 71, 85
Charismatic-leader-with-inner-circle model, 98
Chicago, University of, 5
Chosen people, Jews as, 121, 129
Christianity: Catholic alienation from German liberalism, 36, 57, 63, 141–42n31; and Hobbes, 64–65, 66
Christian Scholasticism, 79
Civil disobedience, 66
Coded writings. *See* Multilevel writing
Cohen, Hermann, 12, 14–15, 20–21, 25, 27, 40–41, 49
"Cohen's Analysis of Spinoza's Bible Science" (Strauss), 20–21, 49
Columbia University, 79–80, 81–83, 86–92, 94, 95, 101
*Commentaries on the Laws of England* (Blackstone), 100

"Comments on Carl Schmitt's *Concept of the Political*" (Strauss), 20, 45–47
Communism: dangers for intellectuals, 83; German fears of, 96; lack of safe haven for Jews in, 124; multilevel writing under, 78; Strauss as anti-Communist, 1; Trotskyism vs. Stalinism, 124–25
*Concept of the Political* (Schmitt), 20, 44–47
Conservativism, 1–2, 3, 15, 17, 34–35. *See also* Radical-conservatism
Corporate collective focus of premodern societies, 32
Costa, Uriel da, 52
"Crawling back to the cross" metaphor, 62–63
Crisis thinking, 17, 20
Crossman, R. H. S., 91
Cultural vs. political Zionism, 13, 28, 43, 62, 126
Culture. *See* German culture; Political society

Davos debates, Cassirer vs. Heidegger, 37, 39–40
*Decline of the West* (Spengler), 18
De Lagarde, Paul, 11, 12
Descartes, René, 50, 100
*Deskription*, Husserl's, 24, 142n39
*Destruktion*, Heidegger's, 38
*Discourse on Method* (Descartes), 100
Discrimination and liberal societies, 122
Dissimilation. *See* Alienation
Dissimulation. *See* Multilevel writing
Drury, Shadia, 2, 173n127
Dubnow, Simon, 27

Ebbinghaus, Julius, 21
"Ecclesia militans" (Strauss), 48
École libre des hautes études, 89–90
École pratique des hautes études, 58
Economic ethics and modernity, 59
Education, Strauss's dedication to, 13, 29–30, 34, 90–91, 98, 105
Egalitarianism, liberal, 63, 104
*Einwirklichung*, Strauss's concept of, 32
Elites, intellectual: authoritarian principles of rulership, 60–61, 63, 91, 105; as best qualified for prophecy role, 119; on human nature, 46, 48, 74, 98, 104–5; multilevel writing by, 92–94; Strauss's

German Jewry (*continued*)
of, 30, 52; Strauss's analysis of worldviews, 18, 19–20; and Strauss's character,
84–85; unapologetic approach to, 42
"German Nihilism" (Strauss), 95, 96–98
Gersonides (Rabbi Levi ben Gershon), 68
*Gesammelte Schriften* (Strauss), 3
Glatzer, Nahum, 109
God: extrasubjective knowledge of, 142n39;
immediate experience of, 22–25; irra-
tionality of, 22, 23; as necessary to suc-
cess of Judaism, 129; religion as path
to truth of, 23; as separate from nature,
26; separation from, 25, 113, 120,
141–42n31. *See also* Religion
Gordon, Peter, 30
Graduate Faculty of Philosophy and Politi-
cal Science, 88–89, 90. *See also* New
School for Social Research
Graetz, Heinrich, 113
Great Britain, Strauss in, 58, 68, 81
Greek philosophers. *See* Ancient philosophers
Green, Kenneth Hart, 2
*The Guide of the Perplexed* (Maimonides),
33, 41–42, 77, 109–10
Gunnell, John, 4
Guttmann, Julius: appointment of Strauss,
40; differences with Strauss, 67; emigration of, 74, 87; and Jewish adoption
of Greek ideas, 115; and medieval phi-
losophy, 68; revision of Strauss's work,
33–34, 147n100; Strauss's critique of,
69
Gymnasium Philippinum (Marburg), 12–13

Halevi, Yehuda, 103
Hamburg, University of, 21
Hartmann, Nicolai, 15–16
Hebrew University of Jerusalem, 73–74, 86
Heidegger, Martin: *Destruktion*, 38,
150n126; joining of Nazi party, 56, 57; at
Marburg, 14; and nihilism critique, 97;
philosophy of, 25, 35–40; and Strauss, 20,
21, 25, 44, 143n58, 150n132, 154–55n9
Heine, Henrich, 122, 128–29
Hermeneutic strategy, 3, 20–21, 39, 55, 73,
79. *See also* Multilevel writing
Herzl, Theodor, 41, 43, 125

Hessen, 9–12
Hierarchy of human intellects: and aristocratic model as best regime, 91, 105;
liberalism's neglect of, 101, 104–5; and
multilevel writing, 73, 77, 79, 106–7;
Nietzsche on, 172n122; philosopher
and society, 92–94, 106–7; Strauss's elitism, 79, 171n120
Hirsch, Samson Raphael, 10, 135–36n11
Historian vs. philosopher, 102, 110–11, 116
Historical progress, liberal commitment to:
German questioning of, 18; vs. historicism, 173n143; and modern scientific
progress, 69; Strauss's critique of, 17,
70–71, 111
Historicism, relativistic: liberal faith in,
123; vs. progressivism, 173n143; Strauss's
critique of, 69, 71, 94, 95, 110–11
*History of the Jews in Christian Spain* (Baer),
112–13
Hitler, Adolf, 97, 124–25
Hobbes, Thomas, 45–47, 50, 57–60, 63–67,
155n18
Hochschule Lehranstalt für die Wissenschaft
des Judentums, 33
Holocaust, Strauss's personal losses, 82,
136–37n23, 160n79
Horizon of interpreter, 39, 47, 56
Humanism, 1, 12–13, 15, 70, 144n70
Human nature: elites on, 74, 98, 104–5; fear
of violent death as primary motivator,
60; liberalism's blindness to, 46, 48;
pessimistic view of, 26, 27, 43, 45–46,
60, 129. *See also* Hierarchy of human
intellects
Husserl, Edmund, 21, 23–24, 38–39, 142n39

Idealism: futility of, 105, 120, 122–23,
126–27; German, 18, 21–28, 23, 40,
41–44, 52–53; liberal, 18–19, 45–46, 59,
60; limitations of scientific model, 23
*Ideology and Utopia* (Mannheim), 18,
138–39n4
Illiberal societies, 81, 101. *See also* Authoritarian principles of rulership; Tyranni-
cal/totalitarian regimes
Imagination and ability to speak to masses,
74, 79
Imperfection of societies, 84–85, 103–7,

Rationalism: and fall of Weimar, 123; Hobbes's contribution, 155n18; Kant on reason and knowledge, 142n34; limitations of ethical authority, 23, 66; medieval, 33, 69; and politics, 67; and revelation, 25, 40–41, 71–73, 107; self-destruction of, 127. *See also* Enlightenment rationalism; Modern rationalism

Rauschning, Hermann, 96

Read, Conyers, 75

Realism: vs. idealism, 18, 41–44, 52–53, 59–60; and imperfection of societies, 84–85, 103–7, 126–27; and Jewish role in society, 19, 42–43, 45, 54, 55–56; Strauss's appeal for, 18, 45–47; and Strauss's argument style, 20. *See also* Imperfection of societies

Reason, liberal destruction of, 59, 67. *See also* Rationalism

*Redlichkeit,* 18

Reform Judaism, 10–11, 135–36n11

Refugee experience, 2, 7, 81–82, 86–88

Reimarus, Hermann Samuel, 65

Reinhardt, Karl, 16

Relativism, historical. *See* Historicism, relativistic

Religion: Catholic alienation from German liberalism, 36, 57, 63, 141–42n31; developmental levels, 113; Epicurean critique of, 52–53; and Hobbes, 63–65, 66; Maimonides's accommodation to, 108; obedience and insight, 23, 142n35; vs. philosophy, 3; and rationalism, 19–20, 25, 40–41, 49–50, 68, 69–70, 71–73, 107, 121; return to prescientific experience, 22–25; secular vs. religious tyranny, 108; Strauss on Cassirer, 25; theologico-political predicament, 5, 63–64, 105–6, 118, 121; and theology, 24, 45, 49–50; truth as beyond, 1. *See also* Biblical exegesis; Judaism; Revelation, divine

*Religion of Reason Out of the Sources in Judaism* (Cohen), 14–15

*Die Religionskritik Spinozas als Grundlage seiner Bibelwissenschaft* (Strauss), 33–35, 49, 65, 118–21

Religious Zionism, 126

Rescue organizations for Jewish refugees, 86–87

Research Project on Totalitarian Communication, 101

Return movement, 28–29. *See also* Zionism

Revelation, divine: and Jewish identity, 70, 121; and philosophy, 62, 71–73, 105; political function of, 75; rationalist interpretation of, 25, 40–41, 71–73, 107; vs. scientific rationalism, 22–23, 26; Spinoza's task of liberation from, 49; Zionism's difficulties with, 126. *See also* God; Law, revealed

*The Revolution of Nihilism: The Warning to the West* (Rauschning), 96

Riezler, Kurt, 37

Rockefeller Foundation, 47, 57, 86, 89

Rosenzweig, Franz: on apologetic thinking, 41–42; and divided loyalty issue, 61; on exile and return, 28–31; and Heidegger, 35–36, 39, 40; humanism of, 144n70; on Jewish education, 29–30, 34; on medieval vs. modern philosophers, 115; and Strauss, 26, 143n58

Rural Jewish culture in Germany, 10–11, 13

Russian pogroms, Strauss's response to, 12

Salomon, Albert, 94

Schmitt, Carl: Catholic origins of conservatism, 36; and nihilism critique, 97; as political theologian, 134n8; on politics, 44–47; and Strauss, 3, 56–57, 65–66, 154n8; Strauss's critique of, 20, 124

Scholasticism, 79

Scholem, Gershom: emigration of, 87; Holocaust losses for, 160n79; knowledge of Orthodox practice, 13; and mysticism, 33, 78, 111–12, 113–14, 162–63n108, 174n155; and Strauss, 40, 73–74, 118

Scholem, Werner, 160n79

Scientific rationalism: and historical progress, 69; limitations of, 70; vs. religious experience, 22–23, 26; Strauss's critique of, 22–25; and value-free science, 24, 35, 67–68

"Scribere est agere," 100

Secularization, 48, 64. *See also* Rationalism

*Sefer hamada,* 108. *See also* Maimonides

Seligman, Edwin R. A., 88

Separation from God, 25, 113, 120, 141–42n31

Sephardic mysticism, 112
Simon, Ernst, 31
Socialism, 45–46, 59, 60
*Social Research,* 90
Social science, Strauss's critique of, 95
Sociology of knowledge, 95
Socrates, 93, 98
Socratic writing, 102
Sovereignty, nature of, 44–45, 65, 66
Soviet Communism, 78, 83, 124–25
Spanish Jewry, 33, 122
Sparta, 92–94, 168n60
Speier, Hans, 90, 101, 168n47
Spengler, Oswald, 18
Spinoza, Baruch (Benedictus): vs. Hobbes, 155n18; on possibility of Jewish state, 126; Strauss's analysis of, 20–21, 26, 35, 40–41, 49–53; and Strauss's conservative shift, 33
*Spinoza's Critique of Religion* (Strauss), 33–35, 49, 65, 118–21
"The Spirit of Sparta; or, A Taste of Xenophon" (Strauss), 92–94
Stalinism vs. Trotskyism, 124–25
*The Star of Redemption* (Rosenzweig), 29, 31
State: vs. family in biblical law, 26; as focus of modern politics, 59; Hobbesian, 65–66, 66; interwar disappointment with modern, 58–59; need for theocratic distrust of, 26, 27; and political vs. cultural Zionism, 30; religion as secondary to, 64; Zionist factionalism on function of, 31–32
State of nature, Hobbes vs. Strauss, 46–47, 59–60
Stereotyping of Jews in Germany, 11
Strauss, Bettina (sister), 82
Strauss, David (uncle), 12
Strauss, Hugo (father), 12, 82
Strauss, Jenny David (mother), 12
Strauss, Johanna (Hanna) (stepmother), 82, 136–37n23
Strauss, Leo: accommodation of U.S. society, 116–17; ancestry of, 137n24; antisemitism concerns, 12; birth of, 9; career progression, 29, 33–34, 35, 40, 47, 74–75, 81, 151n142, 159n59; character of, 120–21; childhood and youth, 9–14; and Cohen, 14–15; communal leadership of,

34; dedication to education, 13, 29–30, 34, 90–91, 98, 105; early influences, 118; education of, 12–13, 15–16, 34–35, 140n17; in European exile, 54–55; family losses to Holocaust, 82; financial anxieties of exile, 58, 74, 82, 90; and Heidegger, 20, 21, 25, 44, 143n58, 150n132, 155n9; as Jew, 156n26; legacy of, 1–8, 118–30; marriage of, 20; overview of life phases, 7; psychological sketch, 84–85; Schmitt's shunning of, 56–57, 65–66, 154–55n8; self-description, 118–19; teaching style/abilities, 75, 98; WWI service, 14, 15. *See also* European exile; New York period; Weimar period
Strauss, Marie (Miriam) Bernsohn (wife), 58, 82, 90
Strauss, Meyer (grandfather), 12
Straussianism, 1–2, 4–5, 82, 133n2
Systematic vs. apologetic thinking, 41–42

Talmudic exegesis *(pilpul),* 20
Tanguay, Daniel, 4
Tawney, R. H., 74
Teaching style/abilities, Strauss's, 75, 98
"The Testament of Spinoza" (Strauss), 50
Text and context. *See* Multilevel writing
Theocracy as political system, 26
Theologico-political predicament, 5, 63–64, 105–6, 118, 121
*Theologico-Political Treatise* (Spinoza), 40, 49
Theology, 24, 45, 49–50. *See also* Biblical exegesis
*Thus Spoke Zarathustra* (Nietzsche), 63
Toleration, ideology of, 22, 45
Torah, 76, 77, 108. *See also* Biblical exegesis
Totalitarian regimes. *See* Tyrannical/totalitarian regimes
Tradition, Heidegger's critique of, 38
Transcendence, Strauss on, 25, 26
Treitschke, Heinrich von, 11
Trotskyism vs. Stalinism, 124–25
*Truth and Method* (Gadamer), 49
Truth and wisdom: in ancient sources, 106; Enlightenment rationalism's limitations, 19–20; human reason as only source of, 70; and multilevel writing, 101; in premodern philosophy, 6, 106, 116;

return to Platonic quest, 20; Strauss' concern for, 53; and Strauss's Jewish grounding, 4; as transcendent of religion and nation, 1

Tyrannical/totalitarian regimes: multilevel writing in, 5–6, 78, 83, 93, 94; philosopher's precarious role in, 76, 81, 83; Soviet Communism, 78, 83, 124–25; suppression of speech/writing, 100, 101

United States, 4–5, 7, 79–80, 82
Universal concerns, 7, 48
Universal education, 105
University in Exile, 86–92, 88–89
University of Chicago, 5
University of Freiburg, 21
University of Hamburg, 21
University of Marburg, 9, 14–16, 140n17

Value-free science, critique of, 24, 35, 67–68
Van den Abbeele, Georges, 170n99
Van den Bruck, Möller, 97
Violent death, fear of, as basic human motivation, 60
Virgil, 61

*Wahrnehmung,* Jacobi's, 23
Warburg Institute, 87
*War in Our Time* (Johnson), 90
Weber, Max, 37
*Weekly Standard,* 2
Weimar period: betrayal of liberal ideal in, 122–23; Cohen, 15, 40–41, 49; émigré scholars' analysis of, 91–92, 96–98; evolution of Strauss's style, 17–21; focus of study in, 33–34; formative nature of, 3, 118–19; Heidegger critique, 35–40; realism vs. idealism in, 18, 21–28, 41–44; 52–53; Rosenzweig, 28–31, 35; Schmitt, 44–47; Spinoza, 40–41, 49–53; and

Strauss's conservative roots, 34–35, 36, 84; and Zionism, 31–33, 47–49
Weltsch, Robert, 61
Western philosophical tradition, Strauss's education in, 15–16. *See also* Ancient philosophers; Kantian philosophy; Rationalism
"Why We Remain Jews" (Strauss), 119–29
Wild, John, 91
Will over reason, 59, 67
Will to normality and Zionism, 48, 49
*Will to Power* (Nietzsche), 63
Wisdom and truth. *See* Truth and wisdom
World War I, 14, 15
Writing between the lines, art of. *See* Multilevel writing
Writing style, Strauss's, 20–21. *See also* Multilevel writing

Xenophon, 92–94, 168n60

*Yerushalaim veatunah* (Luz), 4

Zank, Michael, 4, 41
Zionism: antisemitism as catalyst for, 42–43; and Epicurean goals, 53; and exile, 19, 41, 47–48, 126; and Jewish national consciousness, 34; Klein on, 62; and opposition to Enlightenment, 41; political vs. cultural, 13, 28, 43, 62, 126; Rosenzweig on, 30–31, 146n91; and Strauss, 7, 18, 19, 71; Strauss's analysis of, 13, 31–33, 47–49, 125–26
"Zionism and Antisemitism" (Strauss), 42
"The Zionism of Max Nordau" (Strauss), 43–44
*Zohar,* 113
"Zur auseinandersetzung mid der europäischen Wissenschaft" (Strauss), 25
*Zweistromland* (Rosenzweig), 28